Social Integration of Migrant Workers and Other Ethnic Minorities

A Documentation of Current Research

Other Publications of the Vienna Centre

AMANN, A.
Open Care for the Elderly in Seven European Countries

BERTING, J., MILLS, S. C. & WINTERSBERGER, H.
The Socio-Economic Impact of Microelectronics

CAO-PINNA, V. & SHATALIN, S.
Consumption Patterns in Eastern and Western Europe

DURAND-DROUHIN, J-L. & SZWENGRUB, L-M.
Rural Community Studies in Europe, Volumes 1 & 2

FORSLIN, J., SARAPATA, A. & WHITEHILL, A.
Automation and Industrial Workers Volume I, Parts I & 2 and Volume 2

GABROVSKA, S., BISKUP, M. & BOSSILKOVA, A.
European Guide to Social Science Information and Documentation Services
(Euroguide)

MIHAILESCU, I. & MENDRAS, H.
Theory and Methodology in Rural Studies

NIESSEN, M. & PESCHAR, J.
International Comparative Research: Problems of Theory, Methodology
and Organisation in Eastern and Western Europe

PENOUIL, M. & PETRELLA, R.
The Location of Growing Industries in Europe

SZALAI, A. & PETRELLA, R.
Cross-National Comparative Survey Research: Theory and Practice

NOTICE TO READERS

Dear Reader
If your library is not already a standing/continuation order customer to the above series,
may we recommend that you place a standing/continuation order to receive all new
volumes immediately upon publication. Should you find that these volumes no
longer serve your needs, your order may be cancelled at any time without notice.

ROBERT MAXWELL
Publisher at Pergamon Press

Social Integration of Migrant Workers and Other Ethnic Minorities

A Documentation of Current Research

Edited by

MATTHIAS HERFURTH

and

HUBERTA HOGEWEG-DE HAART

with an Introduction by Michel Oriol

Compiled at the Informationszentrum Sozialwissenschaften, Bonn by Annemarie Nase, Oswald Schöberl and Erika Schwefel

PERGAMON PRESS

OXFORD · NEW YORK · TORONTO · SYDNEY · PARIS · FRANKFURT

U.K.   Pergamon Press Ltd., Headington Hill Hall,
                              Oxford OX3 0BW, England

U.S.A.   Pergamon Press Inc., Maxwell House, Fairview Park,
                              Elmsford, New York 10523, U.S.A.

CANADA   Pergamon Press Canada Ltd., Suite 104,
                              150 Consumers Rd., Willowdale, Ontario M2J 1P9, Canada

AUSTRALIA   Pergamon Press (Aust.) Pty. Ltd., P.O. Box 544,
                              Potts Point, N.S.W. 2011, Australia

FRANCE   Pergamon Press SARL, 24 rue des Ecoles,
                              75240 Paris, Cedex 05, France

FEDERAL REPUBLIC   Pergamon Press GmbH, 6242 Kronberg-Taunus,
OF GERMANY   Hammerweg 6, Federal Republic of Germany

First edition 1982

Library of Congress Cataloging in Publication Data

Main entry under title:
Social integration of migrant workers and other ethnic
minorities.
Includes indexes.
1. Alien labor—Research—Europe. 2. Minorities—
Research—Europe. 3. Social integration—Research.
I. Herfurth, Matthias. II. Hogeweg-de Haart, H. P.
HD8378.5.A2S63 1982   305.8′007204   81-23495
AACR2

British Library Cataloguing in Publication Data

Social integration of migrant workers and other
ethnic minorities: a documentation of current
research.
1. Social integration 2. Minorities—Europe
I. Herfurth, Matthias II. Hogeweg-de Haart,
Huberta III. European Coordination Centre for
Research and Documentation in Social Sciences
IV. European Cooperation in Social Science
Information and Documentation
305.8′04   HN380.M/
ISBN 0-08-028957-6

*In order to make this volume available as economically and
as rapidly as possible the authors' typescripts have been
reproduced in their original forms. This method unfortunately has its typographical limitations but it is hoped that
they in no way distract the reader.*

This book is published on behalf of the European Cooperation in Social Science Information and Documentation
(ECSSID) programme which is coordinated by the
European Coordination Centre for Research and Documentation in Social Sciences (the Vienna Centre)

Printed in Great Britain by A. Wheaton & Co. Ltd., Exeter

Preface

At the first ECSSID conference, held in June 1977 in Moscow, three
international working groups were formed to promote cooperation between social science information and documentation centres in Europe.
Working group II is to deal with information and documentation on on-
going research in the social sciences, especially with the aim of ensuring the exchange of information between national institutions collecting such data.

As a first step, the working group explored the methods of documentation of on-going research applied in the participating countries:
the aims of registration, type and number of disciplines included,
the instruments used to collect and disseminate the information and
the use made of the research data collected. As a second step, a
set of common data elements to be included in the registration of on-
going research was agreed upon in order to harmonize collection and
publication of the data from the participating national information
and documentation services. Thirdly, a topical subject for a pilot
project was chosen: Social integration of ethnic minorities, including foreign workers. The results of these activities are presented
to the European social science community in this volume of ECSSID
Working Group II's Series on research in progress.

The working group's members agreed that they will continue to
publish specialized registers on European research in progress on
well-defined subjects that are likely to stimulate professional interest
not only of researchers dealing with the subject fields concerned but
also of administrative and political circles having to solve pertinent
problems. The subjects to be chosen should neither be too broad nor
too restricted, cover a topical European problem, preferably of interdisciplinary nature within the social sciences and should avoid
overlap with similar activities.

We hope that this first attempt of information exchange about research in progress will prove that national social sciences information and documentation services are able to cooperate on the international level, and that those concerned with the subject will obtain
useful information from the volume.

H.P. Hogeweg-de Haart   M. Herfurth

Contents

Contributors of Input

The following centres contributed descriptions of projects from
their country to the volume. Most of them were able to take data
from their holdings, but others started a special survey for
collecting the data. In all cases the centres had to transform
the data for the questionnaire which the ECSSID Working Group 2
had agreed upon. This included in all cases except one the translation of texts. We thank all the contributing centres and their
staff for their readiness to elaborate the recorded research data.
Without this international co-operation the compilation of the
publication would not have been possible.

Austria

Sozialwissenschaftliche Dokumentation
der Kammer für Arbeiter und Angestellte
Bettina Schmeikal
Prinz-Eugen-Straße 20
A-1041 Vienna

Belgium

Belgian Archives for the Social Sciences
Philippe Laurent
UCL Batiment J. Leclerq
Place Montesquieu 1 Bte 18
B-1348 Louvain-la-Neuve

Denmark

Danish Research Administration
Hans Møller Andersen
Holmens Kanal 7
DK-1060 Copenhagen K

Federal Republic of Germany

Informationszentrum Sozialwissenschaften
Wilfried von Lossow
Lennéstraße 30
D-5300 Bonn 1

France

Centre National de la Recherche Scientifique
Centre de Documentation Sciences Humaines
Véronique Campion-Vincent
54, boulevard Raspail
F-75206 Paris Cedex 06

Greece

EKKE
National Centre of Social Research
Vassilis Filias
1, Sophocleous
GR-Athens 122

Netherlands

SWIDOC
Sociaal-Wetenschappelijk Informatie-
en Dokumentatiecentrum
H.P.Hogeweg-de Haart
Herengracht 410
NL-1017 BX Amsterdam

Norway

Institute of Comparative Politics
University of Bergen
Kirsti Thesen Saelen
Christiesgt. 15
N-5014 Bergen-U

United Kingdom

The British Library
Bibliographic Services Division
Trevor J. Johnson
2 Sheraton Street
GB-London W1V 4BH

USSR

Institute of Ethnography
of the USSR Academy of Sciences
Jury Arutjunjan
Ul Dm. Uljanova 19
USSR-Moscow 117036

Coordinator in the EUROPEAN COORDINATION CENTRE FOR RESEARCH AND
DOCUMENTATION IN SOCIAL SCIENCES for ECSSID Working Group 2
Manfred Biskup
Grünangergasse 2,P.O. Box 974
A-1011 Vienna, Austria

Author of the Introduction
Michel Oriol,IDERIC Institut d'Etudes et de Recherches
Interethniques et Interculturelles
34,rue Verdi
F-06000 Nice,France

Introduction

The development of research on social integration of ethnic minorities is of recent date in Europe. This is a major reason why an inventory of on-going projects is very useful. Unlike America, Europe has no tradition of scientific exchange and theoretical debate about this topic. In such a situation, the risk has been to import American paradigms without actually appreciating the validity of their transposition to another continent and to substitute a multiplicity of bilateral projects carried out in cooperation with American institutions and researchers instead of building up an efficient network of communication and scientific initiative which would be genuinely European.

There are several reasons for this lack of development. Clearly enough the spreading of authoritarian states all over Europe between the two world wars forbade any application of the newly conceived methods and theories of social sciences to minority problems, lest they jeopardised the nationalist mystics and the Machiavellian manipulation of racism. But even in democratic Western states studies concerning the integration of minority groups were scanty. When integration concerned foreign workers - which was the case in Belgium, France, Switzerland - it looked like an almost silent process. One might venture to say that, however painful and demanding it was, there was no public expression about it, because it was not a matter of importance for electoral platforms. Moreover, the migrants, deprived of political rights, had no spokesmen to voice their needs. Eventually, the melting pot worked more efficiently than in America in spite of this lack of public debate for complex reasons which cannot be covered in this short introduction, the compensation of the low rate of birth by naturalisations not being the least one of these.

At the same time, quite a few "regional" minority problems were strongly voiced. But this loud publicity was too tightly linked with political propaganda to give any chance to scientific discussions. Breton, Flemish or Corsican specificities were merely used as weapons against enemy states by Nazi or Fascist propagandas.

After the Second World War, it became possible to study both types of
population having integration problems, migrants and "regional" ethnic groups. But it was a long time before it was possible to look at
both groups in the same theoretical and methodological framework.

Two very different traditions had to converge beforehand. The first,
which was at the same time more oriented towards basic research, was
developed in Britain in the 50's when authors like Kenneth Little and
Michael Banton began to apply anthropological methods to the study of
various "minority groups". The main reason why Africans, Asians or
West Indians were labelled in such a way instead of "migrant workers
and their families" was merely political: they could enjoy political
rights as citizens of the Commonwealth. Whereas this denomination
made continental scholars unaware of the similarity of these groups
with people coming from Southern Europe and Northern Africa, it
brought the question of integration into sharp criticism of ethnocen-
tric views. From the very beginning, British anthropologists under-
lined the fact that integration had to be conceived of as a reciprocal
adjustment. The role of prejudice and discrimination was then scru-
tinised as factors explaining the inability of foreigners to cope
with the new environment. Thus, a long time before Roy Jenkins proposed his celebrated definition of integration (not "a flattening
process of assimilation, but... equal opportunity accompanied by cultural diversity in an atmosphere of mutual tolerance"), British anthropology had proposed a very sound starting point which had remained
unfortunately neglected for too long by other scientific currents.

Ethnocentrism was precisely the main drawback of continental research
on migrant workers and their families between 1950 and 1970. Several incorrect basic assumptions contributed to this defect. The
first was the very general belief that migrants were not supposed to
stay. Patterns of adjustment among migrants were conceived of as a kind
of capacity of fast modernisation along lines which were not basically different from the evolutionism inspiring "modernisation theories" in the Third World. Another factor which led to very poor theoretisation of the migrants' situation was the conviction that, during
their short period of stay, it was necessary to provide social as-
sistance, educational facilities, acceptable lodgings as quickly as
possible.

Then, basic concern for understanding the broad historical changes
initiated by such massive arrival of foreigners were disregarded and
a lot of studies were carried out, aiming at fast pragmatic solutions
and succeeding only in a disorderly collection of data and in repeat-
ed failures in the course of actions. It should be added that continental countries were not very open to raising questions inspired by
pluralism: some of them, such as Sweden or even the FRG had a limited
historical experience of social and cultural heterogeneity; others,
like France or Belgium, were still steeped in assimilationist ideolo-
gies linked with their former colonial domination.

After the 1973 crisis, it became obvious that a large proportion of
migrants living in Western Europe were to settle permanently. The decisions taken for stopping the flow of immigration were not influen-
tial by themselves. Long before they were taken, the process of per-
manent settlement became deeply rooted but they brought about the
opportunity of having a better look at the real situation. The expression: "minority group" began to be applied to migrant communities.

Such was the case in Sweden and The Netherlands which created special commissions for dealing with policy problems concerning "minorities". In France, the outburst of the ideological upheaval in May 1968 led to the definition of the same political platforms for regional minorities and for migrant workers as expressed in the celebrated slogan: "Live and work in the home country".

This is not to say that the task of defining concepts and methods which could account for the eventual comparability of regional minorities and migrant communities is over. We are only proposing a cue for helping to consult the repertory in a dynamic perspective. The "fiches" it contains are very different and at first do not allow appreciation of something like a well unified scientific field. Therefore, we shall use the systematic comparison of Britain with the continent, of basic research with applied studies in order to evaluate and possibly predict the capacity of European research to face the challenge of pluralism. We shall begin with a tentative definition of the research fields concerned, then deal with the institutional framework of research. After an assessment of the scientific contributions of diverse disciplines, we shall compare "minority studies" and "migrant studies", ending with an attempt to evaluate the chances of "identity theories" to become an efficient tool of unification of the scientific debates.

I. Definition of research fields

It is possible to divide studies of integration into two parts: the first comprises research questioning processes of "integration", and, therefore, the meaning of the notion itself; the second deals with more or less empirical approaches of integration into the various sectors of society: school, town, hospital, factory, mass-media, etc. The first batch is obviously more theory-oriented than the second.

Contrary to what could be expected a few years ago and to the wishes expressed in our foreword, there is still a gap between both orientations, and a disproportion in volume.

Except in Britain and a few other countries, theoretical studies of integration remain scanty. But, surprisingly enough, Britain itself seems to drop its own anthropological tradition by discussing American conceptualisation, especially in the field of urban segregation. This gives little chance for eventual comparisons across the Channel which seems to remain an intellectual barrier between the Anglo-Saxon scientific world and Continental Europe. One exception is provided, as we shall see below, by studies inspired on both sides by concepts of ethnicity and identity.

An interesting phenomenon which is being developed on the continent is the multiplication, in almost every country, of studies of integration carried out in historical perspective. But they remain very specific: they deal with the old national emigration (generally from Europe to North or South America), with regional nationalism, or with quite traditional minority groups: Jews, Gypsies, or even nomads. In the FRG, there is a sharp contrast between a deep historical concern for such groups and the ways of dealing with present migrant communities, either by factorial analysis indifferent to historical depth or by applied studies.

Such studies dealing with integration at the various levels of
schooling, in different urban environments, in various sectors of
economy or society are very heterogeneous in their scope, methods,
disciplinary orientations, operational aims. It seems that there is
a sort of historical lag: they are conceived of as if the sense of
urgency which, for right or for wrong, prevailed till 1973, has been
still inspiring the questions of the day. One might suppose that it
is at least partially due to the inadequacy of the institutional
supports of research.

II. Institutional organisation and orientation of research

It is pretty obvious that the main reason why there is such an over-
whelming orientation towards practical issues is the pressure of
funding agencies. Local or national administrations provide resources only for trying to improve the definition of short-term
policies. Hence the multiplication of evaluations of diverse by-
products of minority policies: effects of schooling, of various
methods of language acquisition, of urban planning, of conceptions
of social lodgings, ...

One cannot help questioning such an amount of so-called "practical
projects". Such studies have been steadily carried out for twenty
years without visible effects on public opinion or political deci-
sion-making. In scientific terms, comparison is the only valid
means of assessing results. Very local short-sighted inquiries cannot shed any kind of light on social processes.

Comparative studies are far too few and generally financed by foun-
dations. Such projects, developed in Belgium, France - in cooperation with Portugal - , FRG, could hopefully lead to promising out-
comes, especially from a prospective point of view. In Belgium and
France, comparisons are carried out between groups in the country
of origin and in the country of residence. In the FRG, the process
of integration of several migrant communities is measured by the
same criteria.

One may wonder whether the cost of such comparisons is the main
obstacle to their development. It is more probable that, in most
cases, a too tight institutional control prevents the use or the
setting up of international or even simply interregional networks
which could allow quite relevant scientific cooperation without
demanding extraordinary resources. Two positive examples may be provided by the European Science Foundation and its comparative international study of the second generation, and by the French CNRS
which, within the national territory, helps to build up a cooper-
ative group (GRECO 13, which is now developing several interdisciplinary projects).

But even in those positive cases, the scientific networks are far
behind the level of international organisation of minorities and migrants themselves. Such relevant research fields as the transnation-
al networks of religious, political or educational associations,
which link migrant communities across the borders, are still to be
studied. (Only Britain shows some kind of interest for associative
behaviour, but looks at it from a psychological view-point).

Without being conducted in comparative terms, a few projects concern
foreign countries; they are generally carried out by University departments. We can mention Austrian projects about a Japanese minority
group, and Danish projects dealing with the question of ethnicity in
Africa, giving examples of concern about very distant fields. These
projects seem to be defined very much like research responding to the
needs of development studies, or within the usual framework of anthropology departments.Another case is provided by one British research
project dealing with migrants in Marseilles and a German one dealing
with regional minorities in France.Whereas we may support the will
to broaden the geographical area covered, we cannot help being somewhat surprised by the fact that these projects are not widely known
and a fortiori followed by the French scientific community.

A good example of the close relation between policy orientations and
the selection of research topics is given by countries of emigration.
Only two of them appear in this inventory, Greece and Turkey, with
only one project each. Both projects deal with repatriation, a topic
which is ignored by receiving countries (at least according to the
list of answers that they provided).

III. Disciplinary specificities

In a previous report, we concluded that relations between disciplines
in the field under scrutiny are not necessarily any better than relations between countries.

We have, indeed, to emphasise that interdisciplinary projects are
very few. The concern for meeting practical needs could have, however,
contributed to discard the specific approaches. But we may guess that
the lack of a theoretical framework is the principal factor which
accounts for this spread of projects over separate disciplinary
fields. Moreover, each discipline allows precise, but very limited
application: such is the relationship between social psychology and
vocational or social training, between linguistics and pedagogy of
foreign language, between sociological surveys and urban planning.
Educational science is still more obviously developed according to
this pattern.

These four disciplines, with the addition of history, cover most of
the projects listed in the inventory. There is very little space for
anthropology, contrary to our expectations, except in combination
with social psychology for studying "life styles" of Turkish migrants
(Belgium, FRG). Political science is involved, but without a care for
theoretisation. Its contribution is limited to policies only. One exception is the study of the role of international relations on minority problems (Austria). Developmental psychology contributes at times
to interpretations of the development of ethnicity, or the role of
the family in integration. As pointed out above, ethnicity and identity are indeed the only comprehensive concepts allowing for interdisciplinary exchanges and cooperations.

Social psychology is mainly represented by studies about prejudices,
intercultural attitudes, as in theory-oriented projects (Belgium, The
Netherlands),and deviance, counselling as in more practical projects
(France, FRG).

Language arouses a very general interest. A few researchers try to give an interpretation of the role of language in the development of social or ethnic identity. But most studies are centred on language acquisition, with a strong emphasis on pedagogy. The absence of research about the status and maintenance of the language of the country of origin among migrant communities seems to us quite significant.

Sociology is mainly represented by surveys and by urban studies. Very few projects are oriented towards questioning the sociological theories of integration. These can be found principally in Britain. The FRG seems most interested in statistical sampling. But this specific interest does not necessarily correspond to basically scientific concern, and seems rather to cover the needs of evaluation of policies.

Educational sciences are also mainly represented in the FRG. They are almost confined to the task of evaluating pilot studies or local policies.

History is, of course, independent of such concerns. Its contribution, focusing generally on regional minority problems or old migration processes, is quite apart from other disciplines. This separation seems regrettable since it is really difficult to develop prospective views without good retrospective analyses. One exception worth mentioning is an Austrian project aiming at better understanding the general conditions of language conflicts in Austria-Hungary before 1918. It will be interesting to check how such projects could bear on present and forthcoming situations in Europe.

IV. "Minorities" studies and "migrant" studies

Contrary to the wishes expressed in our foreword, the convergence between projects devoted to regional or traditional minority groups do not converge strongly with projects dealing with migrants.

In broad terms, we can characterise one side by studies of domination, prejudice and discrimination, and the other by studies of integration, conceived of as an adjustment to a foreign environment. This general orientation is a matter of concern. It seems the consequence of underlying basic assumptions which imply, on the one hand, that regional minorities must get the recognition of a legitimacy deeply rooted in history, whereas, on the other hand, the only legitimate alternative for migrant workers and their families is to make the best use of social facilities for being accepted in the country of residence.

If our statement is right, the criticism that we formulated above against ethnocentrism still holds true. There are, fortunately, a few projects concerning discrimination processes in labour and housing markets (in Britain, France, and the FRG). But the number is not sufficient to alter the apparently dominant paradigm.

This may account for failures in the coverage of specific topics. For instance, whereas political studies of regional minorities are fully documented, the political life of migrant communities is only considered in terms of participation in the dominant society. Integration into rural areas and agricultural labour is ignored, probably because it does not raise obvious policy problems. Whenever migrant women are studied, it is with the aim of helping them to overcome cultural obstacles to their adjustment to urban and "modern" life.

V. Towards a theoretical debate ?

These drawbacks cannot be overcome without endeavours for raising basic questions and thereby ensuring a firm ground for interdisciplinary exchange and international cooperation.

Marxist proposals could have contributed to bridge the present gap between research on economic integration, on the one hand, about political integration, on the other hand. Some British projects seem oriented in such a direction. But approaches inspired by "classical Marxism" are still lacking conceptual resources for tackling cultural questions. It is not only, according to us, an ideological bias which explains the limitation of references in this inventory to relations between minority groups and working class associations or consciousness. It only reflects a lack of relation in actual daily life, especially of migrants.

The development of references to collective identity was mainly inspired by the desire to deepen the analysis of the links between objective social conditions and subjective feelings or "world views". In most countries, this concept, or notions akin to it, is used as a guideline for undertaking some projects, either about migrants or about regional minorities. In some cases, they put more emphasis on history, in others on psychology, but on the whole they seem to give a chance to dialectical conceptions bringing together environmental processes, on the one hand, and subjective aspects of self-definition, on the other hand. Some studies concerning the "second generation" seem especially relevant for improving such a theoretical framework. They could enable social scientists to face basic prospective questions more directly: will migrant communities be progressively transformed into some kind of minority groups? Will Europe move towards cultural and political pluralism, or will it repeat the previous options between assimilation and exclusion? Is America a good model for forecasting this future? What is the intensity and the scope of conflicts to be expected along these views?

It must be admitted that we are still very far from being able to cope with these interrogations in scientific terms. Above all, we need some clarification about the use of identity theories which may be confusing either by lack of definition - what is the precise distinction between ethnicity and identity? - or by development of merely ideological uses.

Moreover, we need a clearer conception of Europe as a present field of cultural conflicts and changes. It is generally presented in terms of political agencies, as the product of formally institutionalised decisions favouring its unity or not. Europe as a place where peoples and groups interact informally - in positive or negative terms - is not well known. However, the international circulation of persons and goods is now a dominant phenomenon. It is, for instance, more and more significant that, contrary to most "modernisation" theories, these intense currents of economic and cultural exchange did not suppress groups' diversity, but contributed to renewed or newly voiced assertions of specific "identity" or "ethnicity". One can expect that the comparative project to be launched at the beginning of 1982 by the European Science Foundation will permit some progress to be made in the treatment of such issues.

But one kind of study is especially lacking although it is relevant
for strengthening these orientations:namely the contribution of scientists belonging to minority groups or migrant communities. Some
universities, especially in Austria and in France (Rennes in Britanny),are trying to voice the claim of local minorities in the field of
research, which is not necessarily contrary to the needs of objectiv-
ity. But it does not seem that scholars belonging to migrant communities play an important role in projects listed below. We shall, therefore, conclude by advocating an increase in their number and audience.
Such scholars could be the best experts in understanding and promoting
cultural pluralism within the scientific community.

Michel ORIOL

Directions for Users

Contents:

The documentation on hand contains descriptions of social science research projects which were either being dealt with or had been completed in the years 1978, 1979 and 1980. The actual duration of the projects can go beyond this point of time (e.g. Start: Feb. 1976, End: Oct. 1982).

Systematics:

The research projects are arranged according to the division of contents (cf. "Contents": 1. to 2.3.). Within the individual items of the division the projects are sorted out alphabetically according to countries, within the countries themselves according to the seat of the research institution.

Language:

All descriptions of the research projects are English translations. The names of the research institutions are given in the original language; an English translation is added in brackets. "Publications" and "Unpublished Papers" and partly "Type of research" and "Sources of Funds" were also retained in the original language. A reference to the "Working language" can be found in the individual descriptions of the projects.

Contents of the Description of a Research Project:

The description of a research project contains maximally the following categories:

NO.   Current number of documentation

TITLE   Title or working title of project

INSTITUTION   Name and address of one or several research
               institutions

RESEARCHER   Names of workers on the project; if a project
                    leader was mentioned his name was entered at the
                    first place and underlined

CONTACT   Name and, if possible, telephone number and/or
                    address of a person that may be contacted

DISCIPLINE   Reference to the scientific discipline to which
AND SUBFIELD   the research project belongs

ABSTRACT   Short description of the research project

GEOGR.AREA   Geographical area which the research project
                    refers to

PROCEDURE   Details about the procedure for collecting data
                    on the size of the sample and on the universe of
                    empirical projects

LANGUAGE   Language in which the results of the projects
                    are made accessible

DURATION   Duration of the research project

TYPE OF   Information on the kind of the project, particu-
RESEARCH   larly on its academic status

FUNDS   Reference to the financing institutions and/or
                    persons

PUBLICATIONS   Bibliographical references to publications which
                    resulted from the project

UNPUBLISHED   Reference to working papers concerning the
PAPERS   research project

If the information given in the questionnaire (cf. p...) was in-
complete the categories concerned have been left out in this book.

Name Index:

Here the leaders of and the workers on the research projects are
listed. The numbers following the names refer to the current number
of the research projects that have been documented. It is possible
that because of non-uniform details in the questionnaires some
persons are listed several times (e.g. with and without their first
names).

Subject Index:

The titles and contents of the research projects were made accessible by the controlled distribution of key-words. When looking for
projects dealing with particular topics it is recommended to consult related, more general or more specific key-words as well as
the division of contents (table of contents).

The figures following the key-words refer to the relevant current numbers of the research projects documented in this book.

Institution Index:

Here the research institutions are listed alphabetically according to countries as well as within the countries themselves.
The figures following the institutions refer to the relevant current numbers of the research projects documented in this book.

Further Information:

Further information on the individual research projects can be obtained from the research institutions or from the persons listed in the category "CONTACT".
If you wish to obtain further information on sociological informa-tion services in individual countries, please apply to the institutions which helped to prepare this documentation (cf.: "Con-tributors of Input" p. IX).

Register of Projects

Migrant Workers: Description and Analysis

The Situation of the Migrant
Specific Problems of the Migrants

CULTURAL IDENTITY, ASSIMILATION

<u>NO. 001</u>   Acculturation and Ethnicity among Sicilian Immigrant
          Workers in Brussels, Ghent (Belgium) and Sicily.

INSTITUTION: Katholieke Universiteit Leuven, Centrum voor Sociale
          en Culturele Antropologie (Catholic University of Lou-
          vain, Centre of Social and Cultural Anthropology)
          Tiensestraat 102
          B-3000 Leuven
          Belgium
          Tel.No.: 016/233941

RESEARCHER: Leman, Johan

CONTACT: Leman, Johan
          Centrum voor Watzynszorg v.z.m.
          Delvastraat 35
          B-1020 Brussels
          Belgium
          Tel.No.: 02/4289900

DISCIPLINE   Anthropology, Ethnology
AND SUBFIELD:

ABSTRACT: Historical approach; case studies; cultural code of
          Sicily; first generation implantation models; second
          generation model; symbolization: Graphic expression,
          language, motivation, disease.

GEOGR: AREA: Belgium (Ghent, Brussels)/Morocco/Italy (Sicily)

PROCEDURE: Personal interview;
          Questionnaire;
          Participant observation;
          Test.

LANGUAGE: Dutch

DURATION: Oct. 1975 - Dec. 1980

TYPE OF
RESEARCH: Doctorate

FUNDS: Internal Sources

* * *

NO. 002   Cross-cultural Differences in Socialization: A Comparison between Turks in Turkey, Turkish Migrants in Belgium and Belgian Adolescents. With Special Reference
to Their Motivational Content and Future Time Perspective.

INSTITUTION: Katholieke Universiteit Leuven, Fakulteit der Psycho-
logie en Pedagogische Wetenschappen (Catholic Univer-
sity of Louvain, Department of Psychology)
Tiensestraat 102
B-3000 Leuven
Belgium
Tel.No.: 016/233941

RESEARCHER: Gailly, Antoine F.

DISCIPLINE
AND SUBFIELD: Anthropology (Social and Cultural Anthropology/Psycho-
logical Anthropology), Ethnology
Education and Training
Psychology (Cross-cultural Psychology)

ABSTRACT: Our research deals with motivation (the behavioral pre-
ferential orientation towards goal objects) and future
time perspective (the temporal space created by the
cognitive elaboration of needs into plans and projects)
as important behavioral determinants. From our literature review it seems that groups differ in motivational
contents and in dynamic involvement in the future. In
our opinion these differences are due to different social and cultural backgrounds. We intend to investigate
this relation more closely.

For this purpose we will investigate groups whose social and cultural backgrounds are quite different so
that the expected relation with motivation and future
time perspective becomes clear. This project cannot be
realized within a single culture because the social and
cultural backgrounds are about the same for everyone.
Therefore, a cross-cultural research is more appropriate.
Furthermore, it seems that differences in social and
cultural variables covary with degree of "modernism"
(i.e. the evolution from a traditional towards a tran-
sitional and modern society). This evolution consists
not only of a change in value orientations but also of
a change in socialization practices (imposed on younger
members of the society) according to these new value
orientations. These changes are important since future
time perspective is essentially a cognitive-dynamic

space and since values are the basis for making plans
and projects. Therefore, we hypothesize that parents
differing in degree of modernism and in value orientations have children who show differences in motivational content and in future time perspective because of
differences in socialization practices.

There are two reasons why we chose to do research in
Turkey. First, so far as modernism is concerned Turkey is
still in development. Therefore, Belgian and Turkish
youth will differ in future time perspective and motivational contents since their parents differ in degree
of modernism and in value orientations. Second, in Belgium there are a lot of Turkish immigrants who are con-
fronted with our modern society. With respect to modernism and value orientations the immigrants are in an
intermediate situation between Belgian and Turkish
people. By extending our research to Turkish immigrants
in Belgium we will be able to show the relation between
social and cultural variables and motivation and time
perspective more clearly.
Our results have to show the nature of the social and
cultural variables determining differences in motivation and future time perspective. Also the processes
accounting for these differences will become apparent.
Once these variables isolated one can explain differences in motivational content by means of social and
cultural variables. Moreover, one can act upon motivational contents and extension of the future time perspective in order to influence the motivation for actual behavior. For previous research has shown that motivation for actual behavior can be intensified by cre-
ating a certain future time perspective.

GEOGR.AREA: Turkey (Istanbul and Black Sea Area)/Belgium (Brussels,
              Ghent and Limburg)

PROCEDURE: Personal interview (Villages in Turkey/Turkish migrants
              in Brussels);
              Questionnaire(160 Belgian adolescents - higher and
              lower socio-economic class -/400 Turkish migrants in
              Belgium - Ghent and Limburg -/220 Turkish adolescents
              in Istanbul - higher and lower socio-economic class);
              Participant observation (Villages in Turkey/Turkish
              migrants in Brussels);
              Test: Thematic Apperception/ Motivational Induction
              Method (220 Adolescents in Istanbul - higher and lower
              socio-economic class -/50 Villagers/400 Turkish adoles-
              cents in Ghent and Limburg/160 Belgian adolescents).

LANGUAGE: Dutch/English

DURATION: Jan. 1976 - Dec. 1982

TYPE OF   Researcher's project/Doctoraatsproefschrift
RESEARCH:

FUNDS: Internal sources
                    External sources: Ministerie van Nationale Opvoeding
                    en Nederlandse Cultuur/ Nationaal Fonds voor Weten-
                    schappelijk Onderzoek

PUBLICATIONS: Gailly, A.; Hermans, P.; Leman, J.: Mediterrane dorps-
                    kulturen. Deel I: Strukturen, symbolen en instituties.
                    Kultuurleven, 1980, 47, 9, 820-840.
                    Gailly, A.; Hermans, P.; Leman, J.: Mediterrane dorps-
                    kulturen. Deel II: De Socialisatie in de Mediterrane
                    dorpen en de gevolgen in de immigratie. Kultuurleven,
                    1980, 47, 10, XXX-XXX.
                    Gailly, A.: De familie en socialisatie binnen een dorp
                    in Turkije. Lezing gehouden tijdens de studiendagen
                    omtrent "Cultuurverschillen en Ethnische Identiteit"
                    POCG, Hasselt, maart 1980.
                    Gailly, A.: Het schoolsysteem in Turkije. Lezing ge-
                    houden tijdens de studiedagen omtrent "Migrantenkinde-
                    ren in het Onderwijs", POG, Hasselt, november 1980.

UNPUBLISHED   Gailly, A.: Verschuivingen in motieven en toekomstper-
PAPERS: spectief van motivationele gerichtheden door accultura-
                    tieprocessen. Fak. Psych. & Pedag. Wet., intern werk-
                    rapport, mei 1977.
                    Gailly, A.: Socioculturele determinanten van motivatio-
                    nele inhouden en extensie van het toekomstperspectief.
                    Een onderzoek bij Turken, Turkse immigranten en Vla-
                    mingen. Fak. der Psych. en Pedag. Wet., intern werk-
                    rapport, december 1978.
                    Gailly, A.: Ethnografie van een dorp in Turkije. Pre-
                    publikatie manuscript, 1980.

                              * * *

NO. 003   A Psychological Study of the Situation of Turkish Women
                    in Denmark.

INSTITUTION: University of Copenhagen
                    Institute of Clinical Psychology
                    Njalsgade 90
                    DK-2300 København S
                    Denmark

RESEARCHER: Mirdal, Gretty M./Duran, Fatma

DISCIPLINE   Psychology (Clinical Social Psychology)
AND SUBFIELD: Women's Studies

ABSTRACT: The main aim of the study is to formulate a clinical
                    psychological theory applicable to migrant women of
                    Islamic origin who are now living in Denmark. This work
                    shall be based on intensive interviews with 120 Turkish
                    women, that is on the information obtained regarding
                    their present living conditions, psychological state
                    and socio-economic problems as well as on general know-

ledge of their cultural, religious and historic background.

The more immediate and practical goals of the project
can be summarized as follows: 1) to provide a coherent
description of the psychological stresses that Turkish
migrant women are exposed to and of their coping me-
chanisms, 2) to analyse the variables that effect these
women's psychological adjustment to their new environment (for example ethnic background, age, education,
number of children, housing situation, employment situation, social relations with countrymen/Danes, family
relations, economic situation, future plans, and the
like).

GEOGR.AREA: Denmark

PROCEDURE: Personal interview (120 Turkish women)

DURATION: Dec. 1979 - Dec. 1981

FUNDS: External sources: Private funds

* * *

NO. 004   Changing in the Chilean Family Model in the Exile Sit-
               uation in Denmark. A Pilot Study.

INSTITUTION: University of Copenhagen,
               Institute of Criminology
               Sankt Peder Straede 19
               DK-1453 København K
               Denmark

RESEARCHER: Friedman, Loreley

DISCIPLINE   Sociology (Family Sociology)
AND SUBFIELD:

ABSTRACT: Being a political refugee creates a specific framework
               for restructuring the family pattern as well as
               personal life. The study is concentrated on the family
               pattern of Chilean refugees in Denmark.

GEOGR.AREA: Denmark

DURATION: June 1978 - Oct. 1980

TYPE OF   Sponsored research
RESEARCH:

FUNDS: External sources: The Danish Social Science Research
               Council

* * *

NO. 005   The Role of the Parent-Child Relationship in Migration.
                 A West Indian Case Study.

INSTITUTION: University of Copenhagen
                 Institute of Ethnology and Anthropology
                 Frederiksholms Kanal 4
                 DK-1220 København K
                 Denmark

RESEARCHER: Olwig, Karen Fog

DISCIPLINE   Anthropology, Ethnology
AND SUBFIELD: Sociology (Family Sociology)

ABSTRACT: The project examines migration from an area that has
                 been characterized by a subsistence economy to an area
                 that has become dominated by a wage economy with par-
                 ticular reference to elucidating the role of the par-
                 ent-child relationship in migration. The research is
                 based on a case study of the migration which takes
                 place from the British West Indian island of Nevis to
                 the former Danish West Indian island of St. John, which
                 is now one of the American Virgin Islands. The rela-
                 tionship between the emigrants and their home island
                 is viewed as consisting of a system of rights and obli-
                 gations that bind emigrants and relatives on the home
                 island together in a relationship of mutual dependence.
                 It is hypothesized that the parent-child tie provides
                 a mechanism whereby Nevisian youths are enabled to seek
                 work in the wage economy outside their home island at
                 the same time as it creates a moral bond that ties the
                 migrants to their home island, thus hindering them
                 from being fully integrated into the society of the mi-
                 gration destination.

GEOGR.AREA: West Indies (St. John, Nevis, Virgin Islands)

DURATION: Oct. 1979 - Oct. 1982

                              * * *

NO. 006   The Immigration of Polish Rural Workers and the Integ-
                 ration / Assimilation of the Immigrants in the Danish
                 Society.

INSTITUTION: Dansk Folkemuseum
                 Brede
                 DK-2800 Lungby
                 Denmark

DISCIPLINE   Anthropology, Ethnology
AND SUBFIELD: Sociology
                 Social History

ABSTRACT: In the period 1893-1929 Danish agriculture imported al-
               most every summer workers from Poland, especially for
               work at sugar beet growing farms. Some of the workers -
               approximately 3-4,000 stayed - most of them because of
               World War I. The study deals with this immigration in
               two generations and comprises archive studies,the inter-
               viewing of 700 old immigrants and an enquete answered
               by 1,250 of their children.

               The historical background of the emigration - and of
               its final conclusion - is explained and a picture is
               drawn of the fate of the immigrants and their children
               in the Danish society: degree of assimilation, rela-
               tions to the Danish population, the trade unions and
               to the Catholic Church. Immigrants' association,
               schools and press as well as the groups' position dur-
               ing World War II is described. Finally, it is discussed
               if this caused the formation of an ethnic minority
               group.

GEOGR.AREA: Denmark

PROCEDURE: Personal interview (700 old Polish immigrants);
               Questionnaire (1,250 children of Polish immigrants);
               Document analysis.

DURATION: Dec. 1965 - Dec. 1980

TYPE OF   Sponsored research
RESEARCH:

FUNDS: External sources: The Danish Social Science Research
               Council

                              * * *

NO. 007   Evolution of Cultural Identity of Adolescents and Young
               Adults Belonging to the Second Generation of Immi-
               grants.

INSTITUTION: Université de Nice
               Institut d'études et de recherches interethniques et
               interculturelles - IDERIC - (University of Nice, Inter-
               cultural and Interethnic Research and Studies Insti-
               tute)
               34, rue Verdi
               F-06000 Nice
               France
               Tel.No.: 93/870175

RESEARCHER: Oriol, Michel / Hily, Marie-Antoinette

CONTACT: Hily, Marie-Antoinette
                  IDERIC
                  34, rue Verdie
                  F-06000 Nice
                  Tel.No.:93/870175

DISCIPLINE   Anthropology, Ethnology
AND SUBFIELD: Linguistics
                  Psychology (Social Psychology)
                  Sociology
                  History

ABSTRACT: Comparison in Europe of the evolution of cultural iden-
                  tity of the second generation of immigrants (young
                  adults and adolescents). The use of an interdiscipli-
                  nary methodology will help to situate the observations
                  amongst great historical processes. The project con-
                  cerns especially two groups :
                  . of moslem origin   . of southern European origin

                  This fundamental research intends to provide a contri-
                  bution to the general theory of national and cultural
                  affiliation.

GEOGR.AREA: France (Paris, Toulouse, Provence-Côte d'Azur)/ Portu-
                  gal (rural and urban zones)/ Algeria (rural and urban
                  zones)

PROCEDURE: Personal interview;
                  Questionnaire;
                  Participant observation;
                  Non-participant observation;
                  Document analysis;
                  Qualitative content analysis;
                  Quantitative content analysis;
                  Anthropological methods.

LANGUAGE: English/French

DURATION: Oct. 1980 - Mar. 1982

TYPE OF   Sponsored research
RESEARCH:

FUNDS: External sources:
                  European Science Foundation
                  1, quai Lezai Marnésia
                  F-67000 Srasbourg
                  France
                  Tel.No.: 88/353063

PUBLICATIONS: Oriol, M.: Bilan des études sur les aspects culturels
                  et humains des migrations internationales en Europe
                  occidentale (1918-1979). Fondation européenne de la
                  science, Strasbourg, décembre 1980.

* * *

NO. 008   Adaptation of Migrant Populations. Medical Anthropolo-
                gy of Prevention.
_____

INSTITUTION: Centre de recherche et d'études des dysfonctions de
                l'adaptation - CREDA (Centre of Research and Study of
                the Malfunctions of Adaptation)
                45, rue des Saints Pères
                F-75270 Paris Cédex 06
                France
                Tel.No.: 1/2603720

                Laboratoire d'anthropologie écologique des populations
                contemporaines et préhistoriques (Laboratory of Ecolo-
                gical Anthropology of Contemporary and Prehistoric
                Populations)
                45, rue des Saints Pères
                F-75270 Paris Cédex 06
                France
                Tel.No.: 1/2603720

RESEARCHER: Raveau, François/ Coudin, Geneviève/ Duchanel,
                Dominique/ Galap, Jean/ Lecoutre, Jean-Pierre/ Lirus
                Galap, Lynne/ Velay, Germaine

CONTACT: Raveau, François
                CREDA
                45, rue des Saints Pères
                F-75270 Paris Cédex 06
                France
                Tel.No.: 1/2603720

DISCIPLINE   Anthropology (Medical Anthropology), Ethnology
AND SUBFIELD:

ABSTRACT: Multidisciplinary studies of man and environment cen-
                tered upon the role of adaptation in genesis of arteri-
                al hypertension, cancer, diabetis, mental illness.
                Hypothesis: role of bioclimatic and socio-cultural en-
                vironment upon the expression of illnesses.
                Approaches: environmental studies complement clinical
                and biogenetic inventories of mixed populations in
                France, West Indies, Macao, Morocco.
                Typologies of adaptability are established with the
                help of previous research results upon West Indian mi-
                grants.

GEOGR.AREA: France/ West Indies/ China (Macao)/ North Africa
                (Morocco)

PROCEDURE: Personal interview (100);
                Expert interview (10);
                Participant observation (100);
                Document analysis (40 newspapers);
                Qualitative content analysis (40 newspapers);
                Quantitative content analysis (40 newspapers);
                Test (100).

LANGUAGE: French

DURATION: Nov. 1980 - Nov. 1983

TYPE OF   Sponsored research/ Institution project
RESEARCH:

FUNDS: External sources: Délégation générale à la recherche
                 scientifique et technique (DGRST)/ Institut national
                 de la santé et de la recherche médicale (INSERM)

PUBLICATIONS: Raveau, F.; Galap, J.; Lirus, J.; Lecoutre, J.P.:
                 Approche psycho-anthropologique de l'adaptation des mi-
                 grants antillais, in: Cahiers Anthropologiques 1976, n°
                 3, 71-107.
                 Raveau, F.; Galap, J.; Lirus, J.; Lecoutre J.P.: Phéno-
                 type et adaptation, in: Ethnologie française 1977, n° 3,
                 255-276.
                 Lirus, J.: Identité antillaise. Contribution à la con-
                 naissance psychologique anthropologique des Guadeloupé-
                 ens et des Martiniquais, Paris, Editions caribéennes,
                 1979, 270 p.

                            * * *

NO. 009   Cultural Communities and National Identities.

INSTITUTION: Université de Haute Bretagne - Rennes II, Centre
                 d'études des minorités (University of Rennes II, Minor-
                 ities Studies Centre)
                 6, avenue Gaston Berger
                 F-35043 Rennes Cédex
                 France
                 Tel.No.: 99/592033

RESEARCHER: Galissot, René/ Simon-Barouh, Ida/ Bourdet, Yvon/
                 Couper, Kristin/ Cuche, Denys/ Marienstras, Elise/
                 Marienstras, Richard/ Weill, Claudie

CONTACT: Galissot, René
                 1, rue Pierre Brossolette
                 F-92400 Courbevoie
                 France
                 Tel.No.: 1/3331071

DISCIPLINE   Anthropology (Social Anthropology), Ethnology
AND SUBFIELD: Education and Training
                 Sociology
                 History

ABSTRACT: Study of community relations and of cultural ties in im-
                 migrant groups: their relations to the national society,
                 their own identification, their cultural differentia-
                 tion or their assimilation. Application to the colonial
                 immigrations in the United Kingdom (from Commonwealth,
                 from Ireland, from Europe) and to France (foreigners in
                 Britany, especially refugees from south-east Asia, ac-
                 culturation and non-acculturation in daily life).

GEOGR.AREA: France (Britany)/ United Kingdom

PROCEDURE: Personal interview;
                 Participant observation;
                 Document analysis;
                 Qualitative content analysis.

LANGUAGE: French

TYPE OF   Institution project
RESEARCH:

FUNDS: Internal sources

PUBLICATIONS: Bourdet, Y.: Fonction économique et rôle politique des
              migrants, in: Ethnologie française, tome VIII, fasc. 3,
              1977.
              Simon-Barouh, I.: La population enfantine d'origine in-
              dochinoise à Noyant d'Allier, Université de Paris V,
              1978, 445 p.
              Weill, C.: Le débat sur les migrations ouvrières dans
              la IIe internationale,in: Pluriel,n°13,1978, pp. 55-73.
              Galissot, R.: Histoire des migrations de la classe
              ouvrière, UNESCO, Paris, avril 1980.

                          * * *

NO. 010   Adolescence Crisis, Social Identity and Deviant Behav-
                 ior amongst Young Immigrants Belonging to the Second
                 Generation.

INSTITUTION: Centre de formation et de recherche de l'éducation sur-
                 veillée (Centre of Research and Formation on Correction-
                 al Education)
                 4, rue de Garches
                 F-92420 Vaucresson
                 France
                 Tel.No.: 1/9701833

                 Centre d'études sociologiques, Equipe de recherches sur
                 les migrations internationales (Centre of Sociological
                 Studies, Research Team on International Migrations)
                 82, rue Cardinet
                 F-75017 Paris
                 France
                 Tel.No.: 1/2670760

RESEARCHER: Malewska-Peyre, Hanna/ Taboada Leonetti, Isabelle/
                 Zaleska, M.

CONTACT: Malewska-Peyre, Hanna
                 CEFRES
                 4, rue de Garches
                 F-92420 Vaucresson
                 France
                 Tel.No.: 1/7419109

DISCIPLINE   Psychology (Social psychology)
AND SUBFIELD: Sociology

ABSTRACT: Comparative study from different samples: Immigrants
                 (of several nationalities) and French adolescents stay-
                 ing in corrective institutions and adolescents that
                 have never appeared in court. The delinquence of adoles-
                 cents is considered as a product of society.

GEOGR.AREA: France

PROCEDURE: Test

LANGUAGE: French

DURATION: 1979 - June 1981

TYPE OF   Sponsored research/ Institution project
RESEARCH:

FUNDS: Internal sources

PUBLICATIONS: Malewska, H.; Zaleska, M.: Problèmes d'identité, con-
                 flits de valeur et déviance chez les enfants des tra-
                 vailleurs immigrés maghrébins et portugais, in: Identi-
                 té collective et changements sociaux, Editions Privat,
                 Toulouse 1980.

                           * * *

NO. 011   Integration Obstacles Which are Specific to Certain Na-
                 tionalities, Socialization and Integration Potential of
                 Greek, Yugoslav, and Turkish Population Groups.

INSTITUTION: Institut für Zukunftsforschung GmbH (Institute for Fu-
                 ture Research)
                 Giesebrechtstrasse 15
                 D-1000 Berlin 12
                 Germany, Federal Republic
                 Tel.No.: 030/8801222

RESEARCHER: Schröter, Ralf/ Welzel, Ute

CONTACT: Schröter, Ralf
                 Tel.No.: 030/8801222

DISCIPLINE   Political Sciences (Immigration Policy)
AND SUBFIELD: Sociology

ABSTRACT: The starting point was the consideration that integra-
                 tion measures have to take into account the different
                 integration potentials and handicaps of foreigners
                 which depend on the specific national and, furthermore,
                 regional characteristics. To this extent, this report
                 serves as a basis for further investigations aiming at
                 the development of integration measures in the field of
                 alien policy.

GEOGR.AREA: Germany, Federal Republic (Berlin-West)/ Native coun-
                 tries

PROCEDURE: Personal interview (30 foreign workers and their fami-
                  lies);
                  Expert interview (about 25 competent institutions and
                  individuals);
                  Qualitative content analysis (literature);
                  Quantitative content analysis (statistics).

LANGUAGE: German

DURATION: Jan. 1979 - June 1979

TYPE OF   Commissioned research
RESEARCH:

FUNDS: External sources: Der Regierende Bürgermeister, Senats-
                  kanzlei, Planungsleitstelle, Berlin

PUBLICATIONS: Planned for 1981

                              * * *

NO. 012   Future Aspirations and the Adaptive Behavior of the
                  Second Generation of Foreign Migrant Workers.

INSTITUTION: Technische Universität Berlin, Institut für Soziologie
                  (Technical University Berlin, Institute of Sociology)
                  Dovestrasse 1
                  D-1000 Berlin 10
                  Germany, Federal Republic
                  Tel.No.: 030/3145291

RESEARCHER: Wilpert, Czarina

DISCIPLINE   Psychology (Social Psychology)
AND SUBFIELD: Sociology (Social Mobility)

ABSTRACT: This study attempts to identify the most important fac-
                  tors which influence the adaptation of the children of
                  foreign workers in the Federal Republic. It focuses on
                  the aspirations and expectations of the second genera-
                  tion and relates these to their attitudes about work,
                  education, school, and parental expectations. It is
                  based on an empirical study of a sample of Turkish and
                  Yugoslav children and a German control group in Berlin
                  schools. The results indicate high future aspirations
                  and low perception of opportunity in Germany. Various
                  potential modes of adaptation are discussed.

GEOGR.AREA: Germany, Federal Republic (Berlin-West)

PROCEDURE: Personal interview (290 foreign children of the 5th,
                  6th, and 8th class from integrated and foreigners'
                  classes, Turkish, Yugoslav, and German children).

LANGUAGE: German

DURATION: Nov. 1975 (start). The project is completed.

TYPE OF   Sponsored research/ Dissertation
RESEARCH:

FUNDS: External sources: Wissenschaftszentrum Berlin GmbH,
                   Berlin

PUBLICATIONS: Wilpert, Czarina: Die Zukunft der Zweiten Generation -
                   Erwartungen und Verhaltensmöglichkeiten ausländischer
                   Kinder, Königstein/Ts., Verlag Anton Hain, 1980.

* * *

NO. 013   Alternative Futures: The Perception of Opportunity and
                   the Adaptive Behavior of Migrant Families and Youths in
                   Berlin.

INSTITUTION: Technische Universität Berlin, Institut für Soziologie
                   (Technical University Berlin, Institute of Sociology)
                   Dovestrasse 1
                   D-1000 Berlin 10
                   Germany, Federal Republic
                   Tel.No.: 030/3145291

RESEARCHER: Wilpert, Czarina

DISCIPLINE   Psychology (Social Psychology)
AND SUBFIELD: Sociology

ABSTRACT: In this project the behavioral development of second
                   and third generation migrants is placed in the context
                   of their perception of opportunity at home and in Ger-
                   many as well as their subcultural situation and fami-
                   ly resources. In addition the study explores the role
                   of ethnic/social identity in terms of the social and
                   cultural marginality at home and in the recipient
                   country. Both, retrospective and prospective analyses,
                   are being carried out including archive analysis, in-
                   depth case studies, and standardized interviews of
                   Turkish and Yugoslav families and youths.

GEOGR.AREA: Germany, Federal Republic (Berlin)

PROCEDURE: Personal interview (400 Turkish and Yugoslav juveniles/
                   400 Turkish and Yugoslav parents);
                   Document analysis (100);
                   Secondary data analysis (290 Turkish, Yugoslav, and
                   German children).

LANGUAGE: German

DURATION: Oct. 1979 - Oct. 1981

TYPE OF   Sponsored Research
RESEARCH:

FUNDS: External sources: Stiftung Volkswagenwerk

PUBLICATIONS: Planned

UNPUBLISHED   Yes
PAPERS:

                          * * *

NO. 014   The Stranger and His Everyday World - A Study of Tur-
                  kish Migrant Workers.

INSTITUTION: Universität Bielefeld, Fakultät für Soziologie (Univer-
                  sity of Bielefeld, Faculty of Sociology)
                  Universitätsstrasse 25
                  D-4800 Bielefeld 1
                  Germany, Federal Republic

RESEARCHER: Maurenbrecher, Thomas

CONTACT: Maurenbrecher, Thomas
                  Am Wittenbrink 7
                  D-4800 Bielefeld
                  Germany, Federal Republic
                  Tel.No.: 0521/440196

DISCIPLINE   Psychology (Social Psychology)
AND SUBFIELD: Sociology

ABSTRACT: Analysis and description of some aspects of the every-
                  day life of Turkish migrant workers and their families,
                  e.g. illness, working life, authorities, presumably
                  school, too.
                  All actions of Turkish migrant workers are those of
                  strangers and underlie the following conditions:
                  1. temporal acculturation, 2. limited knowledge, 3.
                  reduced capacity to act (little or no knowledge of the
                  language spoken in the host country), 4. heteronomous
                  conditions of the system.

GEOGR.AREA: Germany, Federal Republic (Cologne, Bielefeld)/Turkey

PROCEDURE: Personal interview;
                  Group discussion;
                  Expert interview;
                  Participant observation;
                  Non-participant observation.

LANGUAGE: German

DURATION: Oct. 1976 - Mar. 1981

TYPE OF   Dissertation
RESEARCH:

FUNDS: Internal sources
                  External sources: Deutscher Akademischer Austausch-
                  dienst - DAAD -, Bonn

PUBLICATIONS: Planned

UNPUBLISHED   Maurenbrecher, Thomas: Der Fremde und seine Alltags-
PAPERS: welt - Eine Studie über türkische Gastarbeiter.

                              * * *

NO. 015   Assimilation Problems Experienced by Foreign Women -
                  Explication of the Sex Variable According to the Theory
                  of Action.

INSTITUTION: Universität Bochum, Zentrales Sozialwissenschaftliches
                  Seminar Prof. Dr. Korte (University of Bochum, Central
                  Social Science Seminar)
                  Universitätsstrasse 150
                  D-4630 Bochum
                  Germany, Federal Republic

RESEARCHER: Esser, Elke

CONTACT: Esser, Elke
                  Tel.No.: 0234/7005413

DISCIPLINE   Sociology
AND SUBFIELD: Women's Studies

ABSTRACT: Illustration of the attitude toward integration shown
                  by foreign women (housewives and employed women). Sex
                  differences regarding the willingness to be integrated;
                  identify variables that hold up or help integration.
                  Explication of the main variable sex as a conglomera-
                  tion of different personal and environment-related
                  background variables.

GEOGR.AREA: Germany, Federal Republic

PROCEDURE: Secondary data analysis (1800 German and foreign resi-
                  dents)

LANGUAGE: German

DURATION: June 1979 - Jan. 1981

TYPE OF   Dissertation
RESEARCH:

FUNDS: Internal sources

                              * * *

NO. 016   Children of Migrant Workers in Germany.

INSTITUTION: Universität Bonn, Pädagogische Fakultät, Forschungs-
                projekt: Gastarbeiterkinder (University of Bonn, Facul-
                ty of Education, Research Project: Children of Migrant
                Workers)
                Römerstrasse 164
                D-5300 Bonn 1
                Germany, Federal Republic
                Tel.No.: 0228/550275

RESEARCHER: Sayler, Wilhelmine

DISCIPLINE   Education and Training
AND SUBFIELD: Psychology
                Sociology

ABSTRACT: Analysis of drawings and comments made by children re-
                garding the problem area "integration". A survey will
                be made of the following: 1. Disposition of foreign
                and German children and their parents to be integrated.
                2. Desire for mutual and regular contacts. 3. Motives
                for mutual contacts. 4. Ideas and expectations concern-
                ing joint contacts (e.g. counsellors, topics of conver-
                sation, help with homework, etc.). 5. Existing contacts
                and possibilities for contact.

GEOGR.AREA: Germany, Federal Republic (Cologne, Bonn, Rhein-Sieg
                Kreis)

PROCEDURE: Personal interview (8 German and foreign parents in
                Bonn);
                Group discussion (19 German and foreign parents in
                Bonn);
                Questionnaire (562 German and foreign 6-10 year-old
                children in Bonn, Cologne and the Rhein-Sieg district/
                639 German and foreign parents of these children in
                Bonn, Cologne and the Rhein-Sieg district);
                Projective (124 German and foreign children from Bonn,
                Cologne, Rhein-Sieg district).

LANGUAGE: German

DURATION: June 1978 - Feb. 1980

TYPE OF   Institution project
RESEARCH:

FUNDS: Internal sources

PUBLICATIONS: Sayler, Wilhelmine M.: Gastarbeiterkinder in Deutsch-
                land, Bonn 1980.

* * *

NO. 017   Assimilation and Integration of Migrant Workers

INSTITUTION: Universität Duisburg, Gesamthochschule, Fachbereich 1,
                 Fach Soziologie (University of Duisburg, Department of
                 Sociology)
                 Lotharstrasse 63
                 D-4100 Duisburg
                 Germany, Federal Republic

RESEARCHER: Esser, H. / Hill, P.B. / Kurosch, Ingo / Trube, A.

CONTACT: Esser, H.
                 Tel.No.: 0203/305532

DISCIPLINE   Sociology
AND SUBFIELD:

ABSTRACT: Development of an overall concept for the integration
                 and assimilation of migrant workers by non-experimental
                 causal analyses.

GEOGR.AREA: Germany, Federal Republic / Countries of origin (Greece,
                 Italy, Yugoslavia, Spain, Turkey)

PROCEDURE: Personal interview (1513 migrant workers from five
                 European countries and comparable group of German wor-
                 kers);
                 Secondary data analysis (1513 migrant workers from five
                 European countries and comparable group of German wor-
                 kers).

LANGUAGE: German

DURATION: Mar. 1980 - Feb. 1982

TYPE OF   Sponsored research
RESEARCH:

FUNDS: External sources: Stiftung Volkswagenwerk, Hannover

PUBLICATIONS: Planned

                           * * *

No. 018   Comparative Study of the Acculturation Process of Amer-
                 icans of German and Irish Descent.

INSTITUTION: Universität Hamburg, Historisches Seminar (University
                 of Hamburg, Department of History)
                 Von-Melle-Park 6
                 D-2000 Hamburg 13
                 Germany, Federal Republic
                 Tel.No.: 040/821850

RESEARCHER: Doerries, Reinhard R.

DISCIPLINE   Social History
AND SUBFIELD:

ABSTRACT: A comparative approach has been chosen in order to
                    study the social process of acculturation of two so-
                    called minorities and of the American 'dominant cul-
                    ture' or majority society. Hypothesis of mutual socio-
                    cultural change. The practical relevance of this study
                    consists obviously in the so-called 'guest worker'
                    problem of Western Europe.

GEOGR.AREA: USA

PROCEDURE: Personal interview (in some cases in the USA);
                    Expert interview (many in the USA);
                    Questionnaire (minority institutions and organizations);
                    Document analysis (US archives);
                    Qualitative content analysis (US archives);
                    Quantitative content analysis (US archives);
                    Secondary data analysis.

LANGUAGE: German/ English

DURATION: Oct. 1973 - Apr. 1981

TYPE OF   Sponsored research/ Researcher's project/ Habilitation
RESEARCH:

FUNDS: Internal sources
                    External sources: American Council of Learned Socie-
                    ties, New York

PUBLICATIONS: Doerries, Reinhard, R.: The Americanizing of the Ger-
                    man Immigrant: A Chapter from U.S. Social History, in:
                    Amerikastudien/ American Studies, Jahrg. 22, 1977.
                    Doerris, Reinhard, R.: Zwischen Kirche und Staat:
                    Peter Paul Cahensly und die deutschen Katholiken in
                    den USA, in: Festschrift für Fritz Epstein, Wiesbaden
                    1978.
                    Doerris, Reinhard R.: Church and Faith on the Great
                    Plains Frontier: Acculturation Problems of German
                    Americans, in: Amerikastudien/ American Studies, Jahrg.
                    24, 1979.

UNPUBLISHED   Reports and Lectures for American Scientific Associa-
PAPERS: tions.

                              * * *

NO. 019   Integration of Refugees from Indochina.

INSTITUTION: Infratest Sozialforschung GmbH
                    Landsberger Strasse 338
                    D-8000 München 21
                    Germany, Federal Republic

RESEARCHER: Jungjohann, Knut/ Ronge, Volker

CONTACT: Jungjohann, Knut
                  Tel.No.: 089/5600416

DISCIPLINE   Sociology
AND SUBFIELD:

ABSTRACT: Study examining the conditions of enculturation in
                  Vietnam, as well as of acculturation and the effects of
                  integration in the Federal Republic of Germany.

GEOGR.AREA: Germany, Federal Republic

PROCEDURE: Personal interview (312/904 Vietnamese heads of family/
                  members of family);
                  Group discussion (20 German sponsor groups);
                  Questionnaire (20 social workers - persons who help to
                  integrate);
                  Qualitative content analysis (Evaluation of American
                  studies on integration).

LANGUAGE: German

DURATION: Mar. 1980 - Oct. 1980

TYPE OF   Commissioned research
RESEARCH:

FUNDS: External sources: Diakonisches Werk der Evangelischen
                  Kirche in Deutschland, Stuttgart

PUBLICATIONS: Planned

UNPUBLISHED   Jungjohann, Knut; Ronge, Volker: Integration der Indo-
PAPERS: china-Flüchtlinge. Erste Ergebnisse einer Untersuchung
                  über die Integration der Flüchtlinge aus Südostasien in
                  der Bundesrepublik Deutschland, Diakonisches Werk der
                  EKD-Infratest Sozialforschung, November 1980.

                            * * *

NO. 020   Second Generation Poles Born in England. Question of
                  Ethnic Identity.

INSTITUTION: University of Surrey
                  GB-Guildford, Surrey
                  United Kingdom

                  "Veritas" Foundation
                  4/8 Praed Mews
                  GB-London W2
                  United Kingdom

RESEARCHER: Tropp, Asher/ Zebrowska, Anna

CONTACT: Zebrowska, Anna
                c/o "Veritas" Foundation
                4/8 Praed Mews
                GB-London W2
                United Kingdom

DISCIPLINE   Psychology
AND SUBFIELD: Sociology

ABSTRACT: The purpose of the research is to seek the answer to a
                question "Who am I?" in an ethnic/national sense posed
                to second generation Poles born in England. The re-
                spondents' selfperceived and selfexpressed identities
                and their opinions and attitudes towards Polish and
                English matters - are the focal point of the investiga-
                tion. The investigation is concerned with selfperceived
                national/ethnic identity and its correlates such as:
                preference for maritial(sic) partner, friendship pat-
                terns, group and community involvement, observance of
                cultural patterns and emotional responses to Polish or
                English matters. The empirical material is gathered by
                employing indepth interviewing complemented by Rep.
                Grid/Kelly's Personal Construct theory . The empirical
                data is being analysed presently, so it is rather dif-
                ficult to make any comments on preliminary results.

GEOGR.AREA: United Kingdom (Slough-London, Oldham Lancs, Manches-
                ter)

PROCEDURE: Personal interview (100 estimation - 28.000);
                Questionnaire (100 estimation - 28.000);
                Participant observation (100);
                Qualitative content analysis;
                Quantitative content analysis.

LANGUAGE: English

DURATION: Dec. 1978 - 1981

TYPE OF   Sponsored research/ Ph. D
RESEARCH:

FUNDS: External sources: by grant

                            * * *

NO. 021   Linguistic Problems of Children of Migrant Workers.

INSTITUTION: Rijksuniversiteit Gent (University of Ghent)
                Blandijnberg 2
                B-9000 Gent, Oost-Vlaanderen (East Flanders)
                Belgium
                Tel.No.: 91/257571, ext. 4589

RESEARCHER: Rosseel, Eddy

DISCIPLINE   Education and Training
AND SUBFIELD: Linguistics (Socio/Psycho Linguistics)

ABSTRACT: The aim of the study is to formulate proposals for the
                education schooling of children of migrants, especial-
                ly for the acquisition of two languages: the mother
                tongue and the language of the host country (French).
                Problems studied: the socio-cultural situation of mi-
                grants and their families; a socio-linguistic and psy-
                cho-linguistic approach of bilinguism migrant children
                are confronted with (semi-lingualism, double semi-lin-
                gualism, migrant pidgin, etc...); study of cross-cul-
                tural problems, cultural shock; study of theory and
                practice of bilingual-bicultural education; survey of
                institutional problems and pilot experiment in the
                schooling of migrant children; teacher training and in-
                service re-training.

GEOGR.AREA: Western Europe (particularly France and Belgium)

PROCEDURE: Personal interview;
                Document analysis.

LANGUAGE: French

DURATION: 1974 - 1981

TYPE OF   Doctorat (Ph.D.)
RESEARCH:

FUNDS: Internal sources

PUBLICATIONS: De Greve, M.; Rosseel, E. (Eds.): Problèmes linguis-
                 tiques des enfants de travailleurs migrants. Actes du
                 10e colloque de l'AIMAV, avec la collaboration de la
                 Commission des Communautés européennes, 1977.
                 Rosseel, E.: Le dépassement de l'anomie.
                 Rosseel, E.: Réflexion sur le bilinguisme des enfants
                 migrants en Europe Occidentale. Rijksuniversiteit Gent,
                 Documentatiecentrum Romaanse Filologie, 1979/1.
                 Rosseel, E.: L'éducation des enfants de travailleurs
                 migrants en Europe Occidentale. (Bibliographie sélec-
                 tive). Québec, CIRB (Centre intern. de recherche sur le
                 bilinguisme), 1980, (Publication B-92).

                              * * *

NO. 022   Linguistic Problems of Migrants and Their Children.

INSTITUTION: Faculté des sciences psycho-pédagogiques, Département
                 de linguistique (Faculty of Psychological Sciences,
                 Department of linguistics)
                 22, place du Parc
                 B-7000 Mons
                 Belgium
                 Tel.No.: 065/336373

                 Ecole d'alphabétisation de Jemappes (Alphabetization
                 School of Jemappes)

RESEARCHER: Vriendt, Marie J. de/ Arryd, Omer

CONTACT: Arryd, Omer
                 60, rue Grande
                 B-7310 Jemappes II
                 Belgium
                 Tel.No.: 065/882897

DISCIPLINE   Education and Training
AND SUBFIELD: Linguistics
                 Psychology
                 Sociology

ABSTRACT: Training of people working with migrants and migrants'
                 children. Pedagogical guidance. Compilation of scienti-
                 fic material.

GEOGR.AREA: Belgium (Province of Hairaut)

PROCEDURE: Participant observation;
                 Non-participant observation;
                 Document analysis.

LANGUAGE: French

TYPE OF
RESEARCH: Researcher's project

UNPUBLISHED   Some Syllabus for Benevolent Teachers of French   as a
PAPERS: Second Language.

                          * * *

NO. 023   Communication Behavior Patterns of Migrant Populations.

INSTITUTION: Université de Grenoble III, Centre de didactique des
                   langues (University of Grenoble III, Languages Teaching
                   Centre)
                   BP 25 X Centre de tri
                   F-38040 Grenoble Cédex
                   France

RESEARCHER: Dabene, Louise/ Taleb Ibrahimi, Khaoula/ Miranda,
                   Antonio

CONTACT: Dabene, Louise
                   Université de Grenoble III
                   BP 25 X Centre de tri
                   F-38040 Grenoble Cédex
                   France

DISCIPLINE   Anthropology, Ethnology
AND SUBFIELD: Education and Training
                   Linguistics (Socio linguistics)
                   Sociology (Language Sociology)

ABSTRACT: Study of linguistic behavior amongst the migrant popu-
                   lations of the Grenoble region. Three communities are
                   studied:
                   - 1 - Arab speaking (mostly Algerian)
                   - 2 - Portuguese speaking
                   - 3 - Spanish speaking

                   Aims of the study:
                     I - Analysis of communication situations that con-
                         front the immigrant populations. Respective use
                         and influence of the two codes: vernacular and
                         foreign languages in communication situations:
                         - of daily occurences (family and community life)
                         - of exceptional occurences (feasts, hospitaliza-
                           tion)
                    II - Observation of communicative behavior patterns
                         within those situations, in the original communi-
                         ty and in the foreign community
                   III - Elaboration of a methodology in teaching migrants'
                         languages and cultures to the French speaking
                         adults.

GEOGR.AREA: France (Grenoble region)/ Spain/ Tunisia/ Portugal

PROCEDURE: Personal interview;
                  Questionnaire;
                  Participant observation;
                  Qualitative analysis.

LANGUAGE: French

DURATION: Oct. 1977 - Oct. 1982

TYPE OF   Sponsored research/ Institution project/ Doctorat
RESEARCH: d'état et de 3° cycle

FUNDS: External sources

PUBLICATIONS: Dabenne, L.; Billiez, J.; Vaglia, N.; Boumaza-Vallverdu,
                  Y.: De l'analyse de la demande à l'élaboration méthodo-
                  logique, in: Etude de linguistique appliquée, n° 29,
                  janvier-mars 1978.
                  Dabenne, L.; Miranda, A.: La formation aux langues de
                  migration, in: Revue formation de France, n° 28,
                  septembre 1979.

                              * * *

NO. 024   Language and Language Training for Ethnic Minorities in
                  the Federal Republic of Germany.

INSTITUTION: Universität Essen, Gesamthochschule, Forschungsgruppe
                  ALFA - Ausbildung von Lehrern für Ausländerkinder -
                  (University of Essen, Group ALFA - Training of Teachers
                  for Children of Migrant Workers)
                  Universitätsstrasse 2
                  D-4300 Essen 1
                  Germany, Federal Republic
                  Tel.No.: 02166/40585

RESEARCHER: Boos-Nuenning, Ursula

DISCIPLINE   Education and Training
AND SUBFIELD:

ABSTRACT: Survey of school regulations and school conditions ex-
                  perienced by children of migrant workers.

GEOGR.AREA: Germany, Federal Republic (Bavaria, Berlin, North-Rhine
                  Westphalia)

PROCEDURE: Document analysis

LANGUAGE: German

DURATION: Mar. 1979 - Dec. 1979

TYPE OF   Commissioned research
RESEARCH:

FUNDS: Internal sources
                  External sources: Organisation für Wirtschaftliche
                  Zusammenarbeit und Entwicklung - OECD -, Paris

PUBLICATIONS: Planned

UNPUBLISHED   Boos-Nuenning, U.: Sprache und Sprachunterricht für
PAPERS: ethnische Minderheiten in der Bundesrepublik Deutsch-
                  land, Paris 1979.

                              * * *

NO. 025   Language Attitudes and the Acquisition of Dutch by Mi-
                  grant Workers.

INSTITUTION: Universiteit van Amsterdam, Instituut voor Algemene
                  Taalwetenschap (University of Amsterdam, Institute of
                  General Linguistics)
                  P.O.Box 19188
                  NL-1000 GD Amsterdam (Noord-Holland)
                  The Netherlands
                  Tel.No.: 020/5252864

RESEARCHER: Muysken, Pieter

CONTACT: Muysken, Pieter
                  Spuistraat 210
                  Amsterdam
                  The Netherlands
                  Tel.No.: 020/5252864

DISCIPLINE   Linguistics (Sociolinguistics)
AND SUBFIELD:

ABSTRACT: Competence and level of acquisition in Dutch, related
                  to language attitudes and social position.

GEOGR.AREA: The Netherlands

PROCEDURE: Personal interview;
                  Experiment.

LANGUAGE: Dutch

DURATION: Sept. 1978 (start)

TYPE OF   Institution project
RESEARCH:

FUNDS: Internal sources

                              * * *

NO. 026   Dutch spoken by Turkish and Moroccan Migrant Workers.

INSTITUTION: Rijksuniversiteit Leiden, Vakgroep Algemene Taalweten-
                schap (University of Leyden, Department of General Lin-
                guistics)
                Stationsplein 10
                NL-2312 AK Leiden (Zuid-Holland)
                The Netherlands
                Tel.No.: 071/148333 (4019)

RESEARCHER: Vries, Jan W. de

DISCIPLINE   Linguistics (Sociolinguistics)
AND SUBFIELD:

GEOGR.AREA: The Netherlands

PROCEDURE: Personal interview;
                Questionnaire;
                Participant observation;
                Non-participant observation.

LANGUAGE: Dutch

DURATION: 1976 - 1981

TYPE OF   Institution project
RESEARCH:

FUNDS: Internal sources

PUBLICATIONS: Vries, Jan W. de: Het Nederlands van Buitenlandse werk-
                nemers (Dutch spoken by foreign workers), juli 1978
                (interim-report).

                            * * *

NO. 027   Dutch Used by Migrant Workers in the Netherlands.

INSTITUTION: Rijksuniversiteit Leiden, afd. Algemene Taalwetenschap
                (University of Leyden, Department of General Linguis-
                tics)
                Stationsplein 12
                NL-2312 AK Leiden (Zuid-Holland)
                The Netherlands
                Tel.No.: 071/148333 (4019)

RESEARCHER: Vries, Jan W. de

DISCIPLINE   Sociology
AND SUBFIELD:

GEOGR.AREA: The Netherlands

PROCEDURE: Personal interview;
                Participant observation.

LANGUAGE: Dutch

DURATION: 1978 - 1981

TYPE OF   Institution project
RESEARCH:

FUNDS: Internal sources

PUBLICATIONS: Vries, Jan W. de: Taalgebruik buitenlandse arbeiders
              (Language use of migrant workers).

* * *

NO. 028   The Acquisition of Dutch by Turkish and Moroccan
                 Children.

INSTITUTION: Rijksuniversiteit Utrecht, Instituut voor Ontwikkelings-
                 psychologie (University of Utrecht, Institute of De-
                 velopmental Psychology)
                 Bijlhouwerstraat 6
                 NL-Utrecht
                 The Netherlands
                 Tel.No.: 030/331123

RESEARCHER: Appel, René

DISCIPLINE   Linguistics (Sociolinguistics)
AND SUBFIELD:

ABSTRACT: Following hypothesis will be tested: "Turkish children
                 learn Dutch in an easier and faster way than Moroccan
                 children."

GEOGR.AREA: The Netherlands

PROCEDURE: Personal interview

LANGUAGE: Dutch

DURATION: Sept. 1977 - Dec. 1980

TYPE OF   Institution project
RESEARCH:

FUNDS: Internal sources

* * *

EDUCATION

NO. 029   Immigration Policy in Austria. Resultant School and
          Labour Market Situation for Yugoslavs and Turks.

INSTITUTION: Europäisches Zentrum für Ausbildung und Forschung auf
               dem Gebiet der sozialen Wohlfahrt (European Centre for
               Social Welfare Training and Research)
               Berggasse 17
               A-1090 Wien
               Austria
               Tel.No.: 0222/314505

RESEARCHER: Matuschek, Helga

CONTACT: Matuschek, Helga
               Institute for Sociology
               Neutorgasse 12
               A-1010 Wien
               Austria
               Tel.No.: 0222/632878

DISCIPLINE   Education and Training (Elementary Schools)
AND SUBFIELD: Law (Employment of Foreign Workers)
               Sociology (Migration, Education, Labour)

ABSTRACT: Research aims: Determine what consequences an unde-
               fined immigration policy will have on the school and
               labour market for Yugoslavs and Turks. Results: The
               lack of clear instructions regarding the stay of for-
               eign workers in Austria leads to shortcomings in the
               educational systems, e.g.
               - the number and quality of German language courses
               - adequate help for school and cultural problems ex-
                 perienced by foreign pupils
               - adequate teacher training courses
               - adequate teaching material
               Therefore, school achievements of pupils from Yugosla-
               via and Turkey are below the average of Austrian wor-
               kers' children. Low success in school and pertinent

regulations (Ausländerbeschäftigungsgesetz) which have
controlled the entry of foreigners into the labour market since 1976 preclude a foreign youth from learning
a profession. But also a division of the apprenticeship market is evident. Since the 'Ausländerbeschäftigungsgesetz' has come into effect, a foreign youth can
only learn occupations which are not regarded as high
in the prestige scale, e.g. bricklayer, painter, etc.

GEOGR. AREA: Austria (especially Vienna and Lower Austria)

PROCEDURE: Group discussion (2);
                  Expert interview (15);
                  Document analysis (12 laws);
                  Secondary data analysis (1218 indentures - total from
                  1975 - February 1979).

LANGUAGE: German

DURATION: July 1978 - Nov. 1980

TYPE OF   Sponsored research
RESEARCH:

FUNDS: External sources: Österreichische Nationalbank, Wien

PUBLICATIONS: Zur Schul- und Berufssituation der jugoslawischen und
                  türkischen Jugendlichen in Wien und Niederösterreich
                  (im Druck), Publikationsreihe des Europäischen Zentrums
                  Wien.
                  Réflexions sur la situation des formations scolaire et
                  professionnelle des jeunes Yougoslaves et Turcs en
                  Autriche (Beitrag f. d. Internationale Katholische
                  Kommission für Wanderungsfragen Strassburg 1979).
                  Schulpolitische Förderungsmassnahmen für jugoslawische
                  und türkische Kinder in Österreich. Einige Probleme und
                  Folgen. (Beitrag f. d. Bildungswissenschaftliche Tagung
                  des Europarates Dillingen, Bayern 1980).
                  Die Chancenlosigkeit der Migrantenkinder in der schuli-
                  schen und beruflichen Bildung, in: Start und Aufstieg,
                  Wien 1981.

UNPUBLISHED   Problems of Social Measure for Guest Workers in Austria
PAPERS: (Paper präsentiert am 9. Weltkongress für Soziologie
                  Uppsala 1978. Interim report, Wien 1980).

* * *

NO. 030   Social and School Integration of Migrant Workers'
                 Children.

INSTITUTION: Université Libre de Bruxelles, Seminaire Sociologie de
                 l'Education Prof. Raimundo Dinello (Free University of
                 Brussels, Seminar of Sociology of Education)
                 50, av. Franklin Roosevelt
                 B-1050 Bruxelles C.P. 186
                 Belgium
                 Tel.No.: 6490030 (ext. 3559)

                 Fondation Julie Renson
                 c/o Mme Francine Hulet
                 12, rue Forestière
                 B-1050 Bruxelles
                 Belgium
                 Tel.No.: 02/6495665

RESEARCHER: Dinello, Raimundo

CONTACT: Dinello, Raimundo
                 69, chemin du champ de l'Eglise
                 B-1640 Rhode St. Genèse
                 Belgium
                 Tel.No.: 02/3587035

DISCIPLINE   Anthropology, Ethnology
AND SUBFIELD: Education and Training
                 Psychology
                 Sociology

ABSTRACT: The immigrant population increasingly tends to estab-
                 lish itself in the host country. But the fundamental
                 problem of social integration has remained unsolved.
                 Schooling and socialization processes are determinants
                 for achieving social integration without losing the
                 culture of their home country. Hence the necessity to
                 study the phenomenon of social integration and trans-
                 culturation that determine the future of migrant popu-
                 lations.

GEOGR.AREA: Belgium

PROCEDURE: Personal interview;
                 Group discussion;
                 Expert interview;
                 Questionnaire;
                 Participant observation;
                 Qualitative content analysis;
                 Quantitative content analysis;
                 Test.

LANGUAGE: French

DURATION: Jan. 1978 - Dec. 1982

TYPE OF   Researcher's project
RESEARCH:

FUNDS: Internal sources
                External sources

PUBLICATIONS: Dialogue des Cultures, in: Cahier JEB du Ministère de
                la Culture, N° 4 de 1978: Galerie Ravenstein 78 -
                Bruxelles 2000
                Les Adolescents Migrants, in: Cahier JEB du Ministère
                de la Culture, 1980: Galerie Ravenstein 78 - Bruxelles
                1000.

                          * * *

NO. 031   Immigrant Children's Educational Situation in Denmark.

INSTITUTION: Danmarks Laererhøjskole
                Emdrupvej 101
                DK-2400 København NV
                Denmark

RESEARCHER: Pedersen, Birgitte / Skutnabb-Kangas, Tove

DISCIPLINE   Anthropology (Social Anthropology), Ethnology
AND SUBFIELD: Education and Training

ABSTRACT: The aim of the project is to describe and evaluate the
                present situation as regards immigrant children's edu-
                cational situation, and furthermore,to form a scientific
                and practical basis for future planning and decision-
                making.

                Knowledge on immigrant children's educational situation
                will be collected. Possible lacks in this knowledge -
                theoretical as well as basic information - will be
                pointed out.
                Information will be collected from all local author-
                ities by use of questionnaires
                Different educational systems are to be evaluated and
                proposals for further research in this specific area
                will be made.

GEOGR.AREA: Denmark

PROCEDURE: Questionnaire (Local Authorities)

DURATION: Mar. 1980 - Aug. 1981

                          * * *

NO. 032   School Attendance of Migrant Workers' Children.
_____

INSTITUTION: Université de Nice, Institut d'études et de recherches
                 interethniques et interculturelles - IDERIC (Universi-
                 ty of Nice, Intercultural and Interethnic Research and
                 Studies Institute)
                 34, rue Verdi
                 F-06000 Nice
                 France
                 Tel.No.: 93/870175

RESEARCHER: Zirotti, Jean-Pierre/ Novi, Michel

CONTACT: Zirotti, Jean-Pierre
                 IDERIC
                 34, rue Verdi
                 F-06000 Nice
                 France
                 Tel.No.: 93/870175

DISCIPLINE   Education and Training
AND SUBFIELD: Sociology

ABSTRACT: The analysis of the conditions and consequences of
                 schooling amongst migrant workers' children is conduct-
                 ed referring to three hypotheses:
                 - school failure results from the negation of cultural
                   specificity
                 - a discriminatory selection and orientation process
                   appears that tends to integrate those children in an
                   unqualified work force
                 - the very conditions of school attendance are an ob-
                   stacle to the social integration of many of those
                   children who are marginalized by the alienation of
                   their cultural identity.
                 The first results verify the first two hypotheses.

GEOGR.AREA: France (Alpes maritimes)

PROCEDURE: Personal interview;
                 Non-participant observation;
                 Document analysis;
                 Qualitative content analysis;
                 Quantitative content analysis.

LANGUAGE: French

DURATION: Jan. 1976 - Sept. 1981

TYPE OF   Commissioned research
RESEARCH:

FUNDS: External sources

PUBLICATIONS: Zirotti, J.-P.: Le jugement professoral: un système de
                 classement qui ne fait pas de différence, in: Langage
                 et société, n° 14, décembre 1980, Maison des Sciences
                 de l'homme, Paris.

Zirotti, J.-P.; Novi, M.: La scolarisation des enfants
de travailleurs immigrés, tome 1: évaluation, sélection
et orientation scolaire, Université de Nice, IDERIC,
1979, 192 p.

* * *

NO. 033   Children of Migrants in France: Their Educational Level

INSTITUTION: Institut national d'études démographiques - INED
               (National Institute of Demographic Studies)
               27, rue du Commandeur
               F-75013 Paris
               France
               Tel.No.: 1/3201345

RESEARCHER: Girard, Alain/ Bastide, Henri

CONTACT: Bastide, Henri
               27, rue du Commandeur
               F-75013 Paris
               France
               Tel.No.: 1/3201345

DISCIPLINE   Education and Training
AND SUBFIELD: Sociology (Educational Sociology)

ABSTRACT: Study of the schooling of children of migrants in the
               26 school regions of France at all levels of primary
               and secondary education.

               . Their knowledge level
               . Their problems with educational teams
               . Comparison with French school population

GEOGR.AREA: France

PROCEDURE: Questionnaire (10,000 Primary Schools/ 10,000 Secondary
               Schools)

LANGUAGE: French

DURATION: May 1978 - Dec. 1981

TYPE OF   Institution project
RESEARCH:

FUNDS: Internal sources

PUBLICATIONS: Enquêtes nationales sur le niveau intellectuel des en-
               fants d'immigrés d'âge scolaire, in: Cahiers de Tra-
               vaux et Documentation de l'INED. 1969, n° 54; 1973, n°
               64; 1978, n° 82.

* * *

NO. 034   Teaching of the Children of Migrant Workers.

INSTITUTION: Ecole normale supérieure de Saint Cloud, Centre de re-
               cherche et d'étude pour la diffusion du français
               (Research and Study Centre for Diffusion of French)
               11, avenue Pozzo di Borgo
               F-92211 Saint Cloud
               France
               Tel.No.: 1/6026301

RESEARCHER: Boulot, Serge/ Delrieu, Jacqueline/ Fradet, Danièle,

CONTACT: Boulot, Serge
               Apt. 409
               16 A, rue Archereau
               F-75019 Paris
               France
               Tel.No.: 1/2015016

DISCIPLINE   Education and Training
AND SUBFIELD:

ABSTRACT: Language learning amongst foreign adolescents in
               schools.
               Insertion of foreign adolescents in different sur-
               roundings (school, society, profession).
               Helping the children of migrant workers to a better in-
               sertion in the French school system.
               Language acquisition of children speaking no French
               (or little) in relation to mathematical and "awaken-
               ing" activities.
               Orientation of foreign children after one year in "non
               French speaking" form.
               Evaluation of the training sessions in eight "Centres
               of information and training for teachers concerned with
               the schooling of foreign children".

GEOGR.AREA: France (region of Paris: Puteaux, Pantin, Saint-Ouen,
               Noisy le Grand, Evry, Vitry, Villejuif, Aubervilliers;
               Douai, Marseille, Lyon, Grenoble, Metz).

PROCEDURE: Personal interview;
               Group discussion;
               Questionnaire (110 teachers/ 1698 students);
               Participant observation;
               Qualitative content analysis.

LANGUAGE: French

TYPE OF   Commissioned research
RESEARCH:

FUNDS: External sources: Council of Europe / Ministry of Edu-
                cation

PUBLICATIONS: Boulot, S.; Fradet, D.; Clevy: Langue et culture d'ori-
                gine des enfants étrangers, in: Migrants formation, nu-
                méro spécial, mars 1980.

                              * * *

NO. 035   Children of Immigrants: Their Cultural Identity and
                Their Schooling Problems.

INSTITUTION: Université de Toulouse le Mirail - Toulouse II, Centre
                de recherches sociologiques (University of Toulouse II,
                Sociological Research Centre)
                109 bis, rue Vauquelin
                F-31081 Toulouse Cédex
                France
                Tel.No.: 61/411105

RESEARCHER: Serra-Santana, Ema

CONTACT: Luca, Yvette
                Institut des sciences sociales - CRS
                109 bis, rue Vauquelin
                F-31081 Toulouse Cédex
                France
                Tel.No.: 61/411105

DISCIPLINE   Anthropology (Social Anthropology), Ethnology
AND SUBFIELD: Demography
                Education and Training
                Sociology (Educational Sociology)

ABSTRACT: Situated in the field of sociology of international mi-
                grations, this project is a study of the consequences
                of immigration upon the schooling of the immigrants'
                children.
                Approach: Immigration, basis of the destruction of cul-
                tural identity entails
                1) problems of social insertion for the parents
                2) disappearance of the cultural support necessary to
                   children for their schooling.
                Do those schooling problems come from immigration it-
                self or from the low level of instruction of the par-
                ents who, once in the foreign countries, lose most of
                their own culture?

GEOGR.AREA: France (Toulouse)

PROCEDURE: Personal interview (100 pupils - ten years old - end of
                vocational training - end of secondary school/ 60
                teachers, parents and children);
                Questionnaire;
                Qualitative content analysis.

LANGUAGE: French

DURATION: Aug. 1980 - Aug. 1982

TYPE OF   Commissioned research/ Institution project/ Resear-
RESEARCH: cher's project

PUBLICATIONS: Serra-Santana, E.: Les immigrés dans la ville, analyse
                 d' un espace écologique à Toulouse, in: Revue géogra-
                 phique des Pyrénées et du Sud-ouest, tome 51, fascicule
                 2, avril 1980, pp. 137-151.

* * *

NO. 036   Educational Situation of Foreign Adolescents in the
                 Federal Republic of Germany.

INSTITUTION: Bundesinstitut für Berufsbildung (Federal Institute for
                 Vocational Education)
                 Fehrbelliner Platz 3
                 D-1000 Berlin 31
                 Germany, Federal Republic

RESEARCHER: Schmidt-Hackenberg, Dietrich/ Hecker, Ursula

DISCIPLINE   Education and Training (Vocational Training)
AND SUBFIELD:

ABSTRACT: Analysis of the situation of foreign adolescents on the
                 basis of a representative survey (GEWOS-Survey).
                 Results aimed for: Report on the findings (first pre-
                 sentation of the central points of interest of the pro-
                 ject).
                 Detailed reports according to age-groups; men/women;
                 occupational status (pupils, apprentices, etc.); na-
                 tionalities (especially Turks); regional report; sum-
                 mary (total results).

GEOGR.AREA: Germany, Federal Republic

PROCEDURE: Personal interview (Foreigners born between Oct. 1,
                 1953 and Oct. 1, 1964)

DURATION: Aug. 1980 - Sept. 1981

TYPE OF   Institution project
RESEARCH:

FUNDS: Internal sources

UNPUBLISHED   Expertise on Prerequisites and Conditions of a Repre-
PAPERS: sentative Survey, Final Report GEWOS.

* * *

NO. 037   Integration of Foreign Children in the Field of Pre-
                 School Education.
_____

INSTITUTION: Universität Bonn, Pädagogische Fakultät, Seminar für
                 Soziologie (University of Bonn, Faculty of Education,
                 Department of Sociology)
                 Römerstrasse 164
                 D-5300 Bonn 1
                 Germany, Federal Republic

RESEARCHER: Nauck, Bernhard/ Kleffmann, Doris

CONTACT: Nauck, Bernhard
                 Tel.No. 0228/550365

DISCIPLINE   Education and Training (Pre-School Education / Social
AND SUBFIELD: Pedagogics)
                 Sociology (Sociology of Education)

ABSTRACT: This empirical study examines, by means of case stud-
                 ies, the effect of two different types of pre-school
                 education for foreign children on their social behavior
                 at kindergarten. The results of this study show consid-
                 erable differences in the manners of behaving of German
                 and Turkish children. The study demonstrates the modi-
                 fying influence of educational institutions which are
                 orientated towards monistic concepts of integration on
                 the one hand and those institutions that are orientated
                 towards interactionistic concepts of integration on
                 the other hand.

GEOGR.AREA: Germany, Federal Republic (Rhineland)

PROCEDURE: Non-participant observation (38 - two kindergarten
                 groups in different institutions)

LANGUAGE: German

DURATION: Apr. 1978 - Oct. 1979

TYPE OF   Researcher's project
RESEARCH:

FUNDS: Internal sources

PUBLICATIONS: Nauck, B.; Kleffmann, D.: Integration von Ausländer-
                 kindern im Vorschulbereich, in: H.G. Lehmann (Hrsg.):
                 Die Europäische Integration in der interdisziplinären
                 Lehrerbildung, Bonn 1980, S. 31-59.

UNPUBLISHED   Kleffmann, D.: Integration türkischer Gastarbeiterkin-
PAPERS: der in deutschen Kindergärten. Eine empirische Unter-
                 suchung zum Problem bikultureller Sozialisation, 163 S.

                          * * *

NO. 038   School Situation of Foreign Children.

INSTITUTION: Universität Essen, Gesàmthochschule, Forschungsgruppe
                 ALFA - Ausbildung von Lehrern für Ausländerkinder (Uni-
                 versity of Essen, Group ALFA - Training of Teachers for
                 Children of Migrant Workers)
                 Universitätsstrasse 2
                 D-4300 Essen 1
                 Germany, Federal Republic

RESEARCHER: Boos-Nuenning, Ursula/ Hohmann, Manfred

CONTACT: Boos-Nuenning, Ursula
                 Tel.No.: 02166/40585

DISCIPLINE   Education and Training
AND SUBFIELD: Sociology

ABSTRACT: 1. Social integration of foreign children into German
                    classes
                 2. Occupational prospects of foreign and German pupils
                    of secondary-level compulsory school

GEOGR.AREA: Germany, Federal Republic (North-Rhine Westphalia)

PROCEDURE: Group discussion (1047 and 2500 foreign and German pu-
                 pils in North-Rhine Westphalia)

LANGUAGE: German

DURATION: Jan. 1973 - Dec. 1979

TYPE OF   Commissioned research
RESEARCH:

FUNDS: External sources: Kultusminister des Landes Nordrhein-
                 Westfalen, Düsseldorf/ Bundesminister für Bildung und
                 Wissenschaft, Bonn

                             * * *

NO. 039   Kindergarten Attendance of Foreign Children.

INSTITUTION: Stadt Mannheim, Amt für Stadtentwicklung und Statistik
                 Postfach 2203
                 D-6800 Mannheim 1
                 Germany, Federal Republic

RESEARCHER: Liprecht, Wolfgang/ Abstein, Lidy

CONTACT: Liprecht, Wolfgang
                 Tel.No.: 0621/2933340

DISCIPLINE   Education and Training (Pre-School Education)
AND SUBFIELD: Sociology (Social Stratification/Sociology of Education)

ABSTRACT: Identification and investigation of the motives of for-
                   eigners to send or to refuse to send their children to
                   German kindergartens. Can the differences in the kin-
                   dergarten attendance be attributed to national charac-
                   teristics? To which extent is the class-position rele-
                   vant? From this analysis strategies are to be developed
                   which induce foreign parents to send their children in
                   greater numbers to kindergartens. The fact has to be
                   kept in mind, that bringing German and foreign children
                   of the age from 3 to 6 together offers to the foreign
                   children the best opportunities for integration. Due to
                   the kindergarten attendance foreign children have more
                   chances to learn successfully from the start at primary
                   schools.
                   Results: 1. The main reason for foreigners not to send
                   their children to kindergartens is in most cases the
                   low level of information about what actually happens at
                   kindergartens. 2. The differences in the kindergarten
                   attendance are to a large extent determined by national
                   characteristics.

GEOGR.AREA: Germany, Federal Republic (Mannheim)

PROCEDURE: Personal interview (5 per cent foreigners according to
                   nationality and urban district);
                   Expert interview (representatives of foreigners, social
                   workers, members of welfare bodies).

LANGUAGE: German

DURATION: June 1978 - June 1979

TYPE OF   Institution project
RESEARCH:

FUNDS: Internal sources

UNPUBLISHED   Liprecht, W.: Ausländer zum Kindergartenbesuch ihrer
PAPERS: Kinder, approx. June 1979.

                              * * *

NO. 040   Turkish and Moroccan Migrant Children in The Nether-
                   lands.

INSTITUTION: Raad voor het Jeugdbeleid (Council of Youth Policy)
                   Koningslaan 46
                   NL-1075 AE Amsterdam
                   The Netherlands
                   Tel.No.: 020/768995

RESEARCHER: Pels, Trees

DISCIPLINE   Sociology (Education/Youth)
AND SUBFIELD:

GEOGR.AREA: The Netherlands

PROCEDURE: Personal interview;
                 Document analysis;
                 Secondary data analysis.

LANGUAGE: Dutch

DURATION: 1978 - 1980

TYPE OF   Institution project
RESEARCH:
FUNDS: Internal sources

* * *

NO. 041   Inventory of Second Generation Problems of Migrant Wor-
                 kers.

INSTITUTION: Rijksuniversiteit Leiden, Centrum voor Onderzoek van
                 Maatschappelijke Tegenstellingen (University of Leyden,
                 Centre for the Study of Social Conflicts)
                 Hooigracht 15
                 NL-2312 KM Leiden (Zuid-Holland)
                 The Netherlands
                 Tel.No.: 071/148333 (ext. 6380)

RESEARCHER: Vries, M.H. de

DISCIPLINE   Sociology
AND SUBFIELD:

ABSTRACT: Research on the second generation problems of ethnic
                 minorities in The Netherlands, aggravated by education
                 and labour market.

GEOGR.AREA: The Netherlands

PROCEDURE: Personal interview;
                 Document analysis;
                 Secondary data analysis.

LANGUAGE: Dutch

DURATION: Oct. 1979 - Oct. 1980

TYPE OF   Commissioned research
RESEARCH:

FUNDS: External sources: Government

* * *

NO. 042   Migrant Children in the Dutch School System.

INSTITUTION: Rijksuniversiteit Leiden, Centrum voor Onderzoek van
                 Maatschappelijke Tegenstellingen (University of Leyden,
                 Centre for the Study of Social Conflicts)
                 Hooigracht 15
                 NL-2312 KM Leiden (Zuid-Holland)
                 The Netherlands
                 Tel.No.: 071/148333 (ext. 6380)

RESEARCHER: Berg-Eldering, L. van den

DISCIPLINE   Sociology (Educational Sociology)
AND SUBFIELD:

ABSTRACT: Description of the actual situation in the Dutch educa-
                 tional system.

GEOGR.AREA: The Netherlands

PROCEDURE: Personal interview;
                 Participant observation;
                 Non-participant observation;
                 Document analysis;
                 Secondary data analysis.

LANGUAGE: Dutch

DURATION: 1979 - 1981

TYPE OF   Commissioned research
RESEARCH:

FUNDS: External sources: Ministry of Culture/Social Work

                              * * *

NO. 043   Factors Influencing the Educational Achievement of Ni-
                 gerian Children in the United Kingdom.

INSTITUTION: University of Surrey, Department of Sociology
                 GB-Guildford, Surrey GU2 5 XH
                 United Kingdom
                 Tel.No.: 0483/71281 (ext. 391)

RESEARCHER: Ososanwo, Remi

DISCIPLINE   Sociology (Educational Sociology)
AND SUBFIELD:

ABSTRACT: By close examination of
                 a) the demographic background,
                 b) the social and economic situation of Nigerian adults,
                 c) the Nigerian cultural norms as expressed in Britain,
                 d) the Nigerian attitude to the English society and its
                    institutions,

e) the process of schooling,
I hope it will be possible to identify the factors influencing the educational achievement of Nigerian
children in Britain.

GEOGR.AREA: United Kingdom (London)

LANGUAGE: English

DURATION: Oct. 1980 - Sept. 1983

TYPE OF   Researcher's project
RESEARCH:

FUNDS: Internal sources

* * *

NO. 044   Employees in the Tyrolian Catering Trade.

INSTITUTION: Universität Innsbruck, Institut für Soziologie (University of Innsbruck, Institute of Sociology)
               Sillgasse 8
               A-6020 Innsbruck (Tirol)
               Austria
               Tel.No.: 05222/33601 (ext. 9676)

RESEARCHER: Meleghy, Tamas/ Morel, Julius/ Preglau, Max/
               Tafertshofer, Alois

CONTACT: Preglau, Max
               Institut für Soziologie, Universität Innsbruck
               Sillgasse 8
               A-6020 Innsbruck
               Austria
               Tel.No.: 05222/33601 (ext. 9676)

DISCIPLINE   Sociology (Labour)
AND SUBFIELD:

ABSTRACT: The aim of this research project was to describe in
               detail the working and living conditions of the people
               working in this trade to achieve a basis for argumen-
               tation and decision for the bodies representing the
               interests of these people.
               Main results: The average income is relatively low
               considering the number of working hours. Skilled wor-
               kers (especially male Austrians) hold a relatively
               favourable position both from a subjective and an ob-
               jective point of view. Unskilled workers (female
               Austrians) hold a medium position, unfavourable from
               an objective, favourable from a subjective point of
               view and foreign unskilled workers are in a relative-
               ly unfavourable position both subjectively and objec-
               tively.

GEOGR.AREA: Austria (Tyrol)

PROCEDURE: Personal Interview (670 - 17.000 Employees);
                 Intensive Interview (20 - 630 Employees);
                 Secondary data analysis (Census-Data).

LANGUAGE: German

DURATION: May 1978 - Mar. 1979

TYPE OF   Commissioned research
RESEARCH:

FUNDS: External sources: Kammer für Arbeiter und Angestellte
                 für Tirol

PUBLICATIONS: Meghely; Morel; Preglau; Tafertshofer: Arbeitnehmer im
                 Tiroler Gastgewerbe, Innsbruck 1979. Kammer für Arbei-
                 ter und Angestellte für Tirol.

                              * * *

NO. 045   The Process of Integration into the Labour Market of
                 the Second Generation of Yugoslavs and Turks.

INSTITUTION: Europäisches Zentrum für Ausbildung und Forschung auf
                 dem Gebiet der sozialen Wohlfahrt (European Centre for
                 Social Welfare Training and Research)
                 Berggasse 17
                 A-1090 Wien
                 Austria
                 Tel.No.: 0222/314505

RESEARCHER: Matuschek, Helga

CONTACT: Matuschek, Helga
                 Institute of Sociology
                 Neutorgasse 12
                 A-1010 Wien
                 Austria
                 Tel.No.: 0222/632878

DISCIPLINE   Education and Training (Professional Training)
AND SUBFIELD: Law (Labour Market/ Alien Law)
                 Sociology (Labour/ Education/ Migration)

ABSTRACT: Aim: Analysis of the decisive factors in the process of
                 integration into the labour market of Yugoslavs and
                 Turks.
                 Hypothesis: The age of foreign children upon their im-
                 migration to Austria, their degree of assimilation, fa-
                 mily situation, school success and especially the
                 Austrian legal system have an influence on the process
                 of integration into the labour market.

GEOGR.AREA: Austria (Vienna and Lower Austria)

PROCEDURE: Personal interview (160 of 855 Apprentices)

LANGUAGE: German

DURATION: Sept. 1979 - July 1981

TYPE OF   Sponsored research
RESEARCH:

FUNDS: External sources: Österreichische Nationalbank, Wien

                          * * *

NO. 046   Job Prospect of Second Generation Immigrants.

INSTITUTION: Centre de recherches économiques, sociologiques et de
                  gestion (Management, Economical and Sociological Re-
                  search Centre)
                  1, rue François Baes
                  F-59046 Lille Cédex
                  France
                  Tel.No.: 20/571853

RESEARCHER: Abou Sada, Georges/ Tricart, Jean-Paul

CONTACT: Abou Sada, Georges
                  1, rue François Baes
                  F-59046 Lille Cédex
                  France
                  Tel.No.: 20/571853

DISCIPLINE   Sociology
AND SUBFIELD:

ABSTRACT: Longitudinal study; updating of the survey conducted in
                  1976 upon a sample of young second generation immi-
                  grants of North African and Portuguese origin in the
                  (northern region).Study of the job prospects of these
                  youngsters, their modes of social insertion, their be-
                  havior on labour market comparison with parents and
                  elders.

GEOGR.AREA: France (northern region)

PROCEDURE: Questionnaire

LANGUAGE: French

DURATION: 1980 - Feb. 1981

TYPE OF   Institution project
RESEARCH:

FUNDS: Internal sources

PUBLICATIONS: Abou-Sada, G.; Tricart, J.P.: La condition de la deuxi-
                ème génération d'immigrés, in: Revue Française des
                affaires sociales, n° 2, 1978.

                                * * *

NO. 047   Sociological Expertise Regarding the Living and Working
                Conditions of Foreign Workers Employed by the Ruhrkohle
                AG (RAG)

INSTITUTION: Universität Bochum, Zentrales Sozialwissenschaftliches
                Seminar Prof. Dr. Korte (University of Bochum, Central
                Social Science Seminar)
                Universitätsstrasse 150
                D-4630 Bochum
                Germany, Federal Republic

RESEARCHER: Korte, Hermann/ Koch, Claudia/ Schmidt, Karola

CONTACT: Korte, Hermann
                Tel.No.: 0234/7005413

DISCIPLINE   Management
AND SUBFIELD: Sociology (Urban Sociology)

ABSTRACT: 1. Description and analysis of the living conditions of
                   migrant workers in the light of typical housing con-
                   ditions
                2. Development of decision parameters for the for-
                   eigner-related housing and personnel planning

GEOGR.AREA: Germany, Federal Republic (Ruhr district)

PROCEDURE: Secondary data analysis (RAG owned apartments)

LANGUAGE: German

DURATION: June 1980 - Jan. 1981

TYPE OF   Commissioned research
RESEARCH:

FUNDS: External sources: Ruhrkohle AG, Essen

                                * * *

NO. 048   Sample Inquiry on the Situation of Migrant Workers and
                 Members of Family in the Federal Republic of Germany.

INSTITUTION: Friedrich-Ebert-Stiftung, Forschungsinstitut (Research
                 Institute of the Friedrich-Ebert-Stiftung)
                 Godesberger Allee 149
                 D-5300 Bonn 2
                 Germany, Federal Republic

RESEARCHER: Hofmann, Roland/ König, Peter/ Krause, Hans-Jürgen/
                 Mehrländer, Ursula

CONTACT: Mehrländer, Ursula

DISCIPLINE   Sociology
AND SUBFIELD:

ABSTRACT: Information about social, cultural and economic condi-
                 tions of the foreign resident population living in the
                 Federal Republic of Germany is needed for political de-
                 cisions concerning migrant workers. For reasons of com-
                 parability the statements formulated in the inquiry
                 follow the sample inquiries carried out by the Federal
                 Institute of Labour in 1968 and 1972. It includes ques-
                 tions on which data were collected in the 1968 and 1972
                 inquiries. On the other hand the current study has laid
                 new accents because of the changes taken place since
                 1973 in the structure of the foreign resident popula-
                 tion, the migrant workers' longer duration of stay and
                 the present quite different situation on the labour
                 market. This has led to taking into account new and es-
                 pecially interesting problems such as the situation of
                 foreign adolescents when they begin work, the specific
                 problems of jobless migrant workers, the situation of
                 young girls and women not gainfully employed, and in-
                 dications for a gradual integration process. Therefore,
                 the inquiry does not only comprise migrant workers but
                 also foreigners who are not gainfully employed.

GEOGR.AREA: Germany, Federal Republic

PROCEDURE: Personal interview (6500 migrant workers from Turkey,
                 Yugoslavia, Italy, Spain, Greece, Portugal - males and
                 females of 15 years and over -).

LANGUAGE: German

DURATION: Jan. 1980 - Mar. 1981

TYPE OF   Commissioned research
RESEARCH:

FUNDS: External sources: Bundesminister für Arbeit und Sozial-
                 ordnung, Bonn

                              * * *

NO. 049   The Occupational Situation of Turkish Adolescents in
                 the Federal Republic of Germany.

INSTITUTION: Friedrich-Ebert-Stiftung, Forschungsinstitut (Research
                 Institute of the Friedrich-Ebert-Stiftung)
                 Godesberger Allee 149
                 D-5300 Bonn 2
                 Germany, Federal Republic
                 Tel.No.: 0228/8831

RESEARCHER: Mehrländer, Ursula

DISCIPLINE   Education and Training (Vocational Training)
AND SUBFIELD: Sociology (Social Stratification/ Social Mobility)

ABSTRACT: An analysis of the occupational and social situtation
                 shall show whether an understratification of the occu-
                 pational and therewith of the social structure by for-
                 eign adolescents does or does not occur. It is decisive
                 to determine, if the so-called second generation of for-
                 eigners is able to surmount the threshold of being semi-
                 skilled and to take up vocational training and later to
                 advance to senior positions. This implies the question
                 of vertical mobility. Therefore, the question has to be
                 asked, whether the vertical mobility of foreign adoles-
                 cents is already prevented by obstacles e.g. regarding
                 the admittance to schools of advanced education.

GEOGR.AREA: Germany, Federal Republic

PROCEDURE: Personal interview (1,000 young Turks - aged 15-25 -
                 girls and boys - as well as their parents -)

LANGUAGE: German

DURATION: Jan. 1978 - Dec. 1981

TYPE OF   Sponsored research
RESEARCH:

FUNDS: External sources: Stiftung Volkswagenwerk, Hannover

                              * * *

NO. 050   Effects of the Family Communication Structure on Voca-
                 tional Orientation, Exemplified by Turkish Adolescents
                 in the Federal Republic of Germany.

INSTITUTION: Universität Essen, Gesamthochschule, Forschungsgruppe
                 ALFA - Ausbildung von Lehrern für Ausländerkinder (Uni-
                 versity of Essen, Group ALFA - Training of Teachers for
                 Children of Migrant Workers)
                 Universitätsstrasse 2
                 D-4300 Essen 1
                 Germany, Federal Republic
                 Tel.No.: 02101/197343

RESEARCHER: Hohmann, Manfred/ Boos-Nuenning, Ursula/ Neumann,
                Ursula/ Reich, Hans H./ Scheinhardt, Saliha/ Yakut,
                Atilla

DISCIPLINE   Linguistics (Social Linguistics)
AND SUBFIELD: Sociology

ABSTRACT: Investigation on how authority, roles and language
                structure within Turkish migrant families influence
                their children in their choice of occupation, job de-
                cision and attitude at work. From the results
                recommendations will be made and information will be de-
                veloped which may help to improve the vocational orien-
                tation of foreign adolescents.

GEOGR.AREA: Germany, Federal Republic (Duisburg, Mönchengladbach,
                Wuppertal)

PROCEDURE: Personal interview (80 adolescents and their family
                members, peers, teachers);
                Group discussion (18 Turkish families/ 10 labour office
                employees, teachers, Turkish sociologists and lin-
                guists);
                Participant observation (18 Turkish families);
                Document analysis (20-50 texts regarding vocational
                orientation for German and foreign adolescents);
                Qualitative content analysis (20-50 texts regarding vo-
                cational orientation for German and foreign adoles-
                cents).

LANGUAGE: German

DURATION: July 1978 - June 1981

TYPE OF   Sponsored research
RESEARCH:

FUNDS: External sources: Stiftung Volkswagenwerk, Hannover

                          * * *

NO. 051   Protection of Turkish Workers against Dismissal.

INSTITUTION: Max-Planck-Institut für ausländisches und internatio-
                nales Privatrecht, Sozialwissenschaftliche Forschungs-
                gruppe (Max-Planck-Institute for Foreign and Interna-
                tional Civil Law, Social Science Research Group)
                Mittelweg 187
                D-2000 Hamburg 13
                Germany, Federal Republic

RESEARCHER: Berkau, Reinhard

CONTACT: Berkau, Reinhard
                Tel.No.: 040/385896

DISCIPLINE   Law (Alien Law/ Labour Legislation)
AND SUBFIELD: Sociology (Industrial Sociology)

ABSTRACT: In this project data will be collected about dismissal
                 practices experienced by foreign (Turkish) workers as
                 well as the protection of these workers against dis-
                 missal. Special emphasis is placed on a possible rela-
                 tionship between a migrant worker's legal position
                 (Alien Law), the so-called "language barrier", and his
                  attitude towards institutions like work councils,
                 trade unions, guidance bureaus, law courts on the one
                 hand and the employee's protection against dismissal on
                 the other hand. In addition, the specific economic
                 effects of a dismissal will be investigated.

GEOGR.AREA: Germany, Federal Republic (Hamburg)

PROCEDURE: Personal interview (150 Turkish male and female workers
                 dismissed during 1978/1979);
                 Document analysis (75 cases of legal action concerning
                 protection against dismissal at the Labour Court of
                 Hamburg during 1978/1979).

LANGUAGE: German

DURATION: Oct. 1978 - Feb. 1980

TYPE OF   Sponsored research/ Researcher's project
RESEARCH:

FUNDS: External sources: Stiftung Volkswagenwerk, Hannover

                           * * *

NO. 052   Industrial Integration of Foreign Workers.

INSTITUTION: Universität Mannheim, Lehrstuhl und Seminar für allge-
                 meine Betriebswirtschaftslehre, Personalwesen und Ar-
                 beitswissenschaft (University of Mannheim, Insitute for
                 Business Administration, Personnel Management and Er-
                 gonomy)
                 Schloss Ostflügel
                 D-6800 Mannheim
                 Germany, Federal Republic

RESEARCHER: Gille, Gerd/ Link, Rudolf/ Martin, Albert/ Vollmer,
                 Marianne

CONTACT: Gille, Gerd
                 Tel.No.: 0621/2925459

DISCIPLINE   Psychology (Social Psychology)
AND SUBFIELD: Sociology (Industrial Sociology)

ABSTRACT: Questions regarding work behavior and work attitudes.
                 Analysis of the social relationships, especially of

role management, prejudice research, implementation and impact of integration measures. Description of the structural conditions of the employment of foreigners in German industrial enterprises as well as of the determinants of illness, fluctuation, frequency of accidents, qualification etc.

GEOGR.AREA: Germany, Federal Republic

PROCEDURE: Personal interview (German and foreign workers, foremen);
                 Questionnaire (Industrial enterprises in the Federal Republic of Germany).

LANGUAGE: German

DURATION: Aug. 1975 - Dec. 1979

TYPE OF   Sponsored research
RESEARCH:

FUNDS: External sources: Bundesminister für Forschung und Technologie, Bonn

PUBLICATIONS: Gaugler, E.; Weber, W.; Gille, G.; Kachel, H.; Martin, A.; Werner, E.: Ausländer in deutschen Industriebetrieben, Köln 1978.
                 Weber, W.; Gille, G.; Martin, A.; Werner, E.: Theoretische Analyse der betrieblichen Integration ausländischer Arbeitnehmer, Köln 1979.

UNPUBLISHED   Gaugler, E.; Martin, A.; Weber, W.; Werner, E.: Betrieb-
PAPERS: liche Integration von Gastarbeitern, (Pre-Study), Mannheim 1974.

* * *

NO. 053   Choice of Occupation by Pupils of Foreign Nationality.

INSTITUTION: Zentrum für Bildungsforschung, Staatsinstitut für Bildungsforschung und Bildungsplanung (State Institute for Educational Research and Planning)
                 Arabellastrasse 1, VI
                 D-8000 München 81
                 Germany, Federal Republic

RESEARCHER: Nowey, Waldemar

CONTACT: Nowey, Waldemar
                 Tel.No.: 089/92142560

DISCIPLINE   Education and Training
AND SUBFIELD:

ABSTRACT: Choice of occupation made by foreign pupils finishing the second-level compulsory school and German pupils

from a comparable region. Apprenticeship places filled
by second-level compulsory school pupils with school-
leaving examination at the end of school year 1978/79
(qualified leaving certificate, with or without school-
leaving examination from the second-level compulsory
school). Effects of measures taken to alleviate the
lack of apprenticeship places.

GEOGR.AREA: Germany, Federal Republic (Bavaria)

PROCEDURE: Questionnaire (by mail - approx. 6,500 German and for-
                eign children of the 7th, 8th and 9th school year);
                Qualitative content analysis (Analysis of reports/Situa-
                tion analysis - e.g. Federal Institute of Labour -);
                Secondary data analysis (Statistical data provided by
                the Bavarian Statistics Office regarding wishes for vo-
                cational training as of May 10, 1979).

LANGUAGE: German

DURATION: Jan. 1979 - Dec. 1979

TYPE OF   Institution project
RESEARCH:

FUNDS: Internal sources

PUBLICATIONS: Nowey, W.: Zwischen Schule und Beruf. Bildungswege der
                Hauptschüler. München, Ehrenwirth Verlag, 1973.
                Nowey, W.: Berufswahl der einheimischen und ausländi-
                schen Schüler in Bayern. München, IfB, 1979.
                Nowey, W.: Berufswahl und Lehrstellen der ausländischen
                und deutschen Hauptschulabgänger in Bayern. München,
                IfB, 1980.

* * *

NO. 054   Working and Career Possibilities for Immigrant Women.

INSTITUTION: International Peace Research Institute
                Rådhusgata 4
                N-Oslo 1
                Norway

RESEARCHER: Heibers, T.

DISCIPLINE   Sociology
AND SUBFIELD:

ABSTRACT: The aim of this investigation is to express some of the
                terms set by the Norwegian society for active participa-
                tion in the society by immigrant women, and their con-
                tacts in, and reactions to the Norwegian society. The
                investigation concentrates on women in industry and the
                analysis is based on studies on labour market and mobil-
                ity surveys.

Project part of: Innvandrerkvinners møte med Norge
('Migrant Women's Encounter with Norway').

GEOGR.AREA: Norway

LANGUAGE: Norwegian

DURATION: Mar. 1980 - Mar. 1981

FUNDS: External sources: Ministry of Local Government and
               Labour

PUBLICATIONS: Backer, B.; Heibers, T.; Kran, T.: Innvandrerkvinner,
               utlendighet og sosialisering, noen analytiske betrakt-
               ninger, Oslo, 1979, PRIO Publications, S-37/79, 12 p.
               Backer, B.; et al.: Innvandrerkvinners møte med Norge,
               en prosjektbeskrivelge, Oslo, 1979, PRIO Publications,
               S. 27/79, 49 p.
               Heibers, T.; Roli, B.O.: Innvandrerkvinner i Norge,
               ufrie og undertrykte, Oslo, 1980, P-1/80, 9 p.

* * *

NO. 055   Immigrant Women's Situation in Norway.

INSTITUTION: Diakonhjemmet School of Social Work, Research Depart-
               ment
               Borgenvein 3 c
               N-Oslo 3
               Norway

               University of Oslo, Department for Educational Research
               N-Oslo
               Norway

RESEARCHER: Lie, S./ Mikkelsen, A.

DISCIPLINE   Sociology
AND SUBFIELD:

ABSTRACT: Background: Lack of information about foreign women's
               situation in Norway. Aim: Getting information on three
               nationality groups: British, Chilean, and Yugoslavian.
               Main variables: Reasons for immigration, social network,
               work, family situation, questions on social problems
               and social service. Method: Survey.

GEOGR.AREA: Norway

DURATION: Dec. 1979 - Dec. 1981

FUNDS: External sources: Ministry of Consumer Affairs and
               Government Administration

* * *

NO. 056   Black Workers and the Labour Process: The Case of the
                 Foundry Industry.

INSTITUTION: University of Aston in Birmingham, St. Peter's College,
                 Social Science Research Council, Research Unit on Eth-
                 nic Relations
                 College Road, Saltley
                 GB-Birmingham B8 3TE
                 United Kingdom
                 Tel.No.: 021/3270194

RESEARCHER: Duffield, Mark Roderick

CONTACT: Cross, Malcolm
                 Research Chair on Ethnic Relations, St. Peter's College,
                 College Road, Saltley
                 GB-Birmingham B8 3TE
                 United Kingdom
                 Tel.No.: 021/3270194

DISCIPLINE   Anthropology, Ethnology
AND SUBFIELD: Economics
                 Political Sciences
                 Sociology

ABSTRACT: The aim of this research is to locate the historical
                 specificity of post-war immigration in the spread of
                 automated forms of production in Britain and the capi-
                 talization of agriculture in its former colonies: the
                 focus being Asian workers in the West Midland foundry
                 industry from the war years to the present. The re-
                 search, which it is intended to publish as a book, ex-
                 amines the structural effects of the mechanization of
                 the foundry industry on the labour market. From the
                 start mechanized foundries, especially ferrous found-
                 ries, have been dependant on immigrant labour, first
                 European and then Asian. The work also traces the poli-
                 tico-ideological effects of technical innovation on the
                 definition of 'skill', 'training', and so on, and how
                 these changing definitions have been an important
                 source of institutionalized racism and segregation
                 within the foundry labour force.

                 The position of Asian workers in the labour process and
                 the particular form of accumulation that they made pos-
                 sible are cast within a temporal framework character-
                 ized by a long period of boom which gave way to reces-
                 sion at the beginning of the 1970's. The changing ele-
                 ments of this framework are analysed in relation to the
                 distinct forms of shop floor struggle which emerged in
                 each of these periods. That is, the growth of the shop
                 stewards' movement and the demand for better pay and
                 conditions during the 1960's and the set backs and de-
                 moralization of the 1970's following the growing wave
                 of foundry closures and redundancies. Throughout this
                 period the research attempts to show that Asian workers,
                 far from lagging behind their English counterparts,
                 have played an important and often seminal role in the
                 growth of trade unionism.

GEOGR.AREA: United Kingdom (West Midlands, England)

PROCEDURE: Personal interview;
                Group discussion;
                Expert interview;
                Non-participant observation;
                Document analysis;
                Qualitative content analysis;
                Quantitative content analysis;
                Secondary data analysis.

LANGUAGE: English

DURATION: Oct. 1979 - Sept. 1982

TYPE OF   Sponsored research
RESEARCH:

FUNDS: Internal sources

PUBLICATIONS: Planned

UNPUBLISHED   The Theory of Underdevelopment or the Underdevelopment
PAPERS: of Theory: the pertinence of recent debate to the ques-
                tion of post-colonial immigration to Britain.

                            * * *

NO. 057   Ethnic Minorities in the Labour Market.

INSTITUTION: University of Aston in Birmingham, St. Peter's College,
                Social Science Research Council, Research Unit on Eth-
                nic Relations
                College Road, Saltley
                GB-Birmingham B8 3TE
                United Kingdom
                Tel.No.: 021/3270194

RESEARCHER: Jenkins, Richard

DISCIPLINE   Anthropology, Ethnology
AND SUBFIELD:

ABSTRACT: To investigate the place of ethnic minorities in a spe-
                cified local labour market in the West Midlands region,
                both from the point of view of the job-seeker and job-
                search strategies, and the hiring and firing strategies
                of employers and the institutional recruitment proce-
                dures of their enterprises. Particular attention is be-
                ing paid to the manipulation of personal networks in
                the labour market arena. Allied to this is the attempt
                to develop a theoretical model of the labour market as
                process.

GEOGR.AREA: United Kingdom (West Midlands region)

PROCEDURE: Personal interview (200(all)employers in specified
                 area);
                 Expert interview (300 employees of certain specified
                 firms);
                 Participant observation (certain specified firms);
                 Document analysis;
                 Secondary data analysis.

LANGUAGE: English

DURATION: Oct. 1980 - Sept. 1983

TYPE OF   Institution project
RESEARCH:

FUNDS: Internal sources

                              * * *

NO. 058   Intake of Ethnic Minorities into Apprenticeships and
                 Other Areas of Skilled Work in Birmingham.

INSTITUTION: University of Aston in Birmingham, Sociology Department
                 158 Corporation Street
                 GB-Birmingham B4 6TE
                 United Kingdom
                 Tel.No.: 021/3593611 (ext. 6152)

RESEARCHER: Lee, Gloria/ Wrench, K.

CONTACT: Lee, Gloria
                 University of Aston, Dept. of Sociology & Social History
                 158 Corporation Street
                 GB-Birmingham B4 6TE
                 United Kingdom
                 Tel.No.: 021/3593611 (ext. 6152)

DISCIPLINE   Sociology
AND SUBFIELD:

ABSTRACT: To identify areas of disadvantage and discrimination
                 for ethnic minority school leavers seeking jobs offering
                 training for skilled work.
                 3 Phases of research: Postal questionnaire to employers
                 in Birmingham about their need for trainees and their
                 recruitment problems; employment interview programme
                 covering employers, trade unionists, government agen-
                 cies, training boards, careers service, teachers, etc.
                 to ascertain their approach to training and ethnic mi-
                 nority youth school leavers; study of four inner ring
                 schools in Birmingham, studying their aspirations, their
                 success in achieving these aspirations, and their exam-
                 ination record.
                 Findings identify areas of disadvantage and potential
                 indirect discrimination, and aspirations and success
                 rates of school leavers.

GEOGR.AREA: United Kingdom (Birmingham)

PROCEDURE: Personal interview (91 Birmingham employers and other
               officials);
               Questionnaire (192 Birmingham employers);
               Participant observation (Work of Careers Service).

LANGUAGE: English

DURATION: 1978 - Apr. 1981

TYPE OF   Commissioned research
RESEARCH:

FUNDS: External sources: Commission for Racial Equality

PUBLICATIONS: Forthcoming: Summary of Findings. Also Full Report. Due
               for publication - Spring 1981 by Commission for Racial
               Equality.
               Paper for BSA Conference, April 1981: Inequality in the
               skilled labour market, the case of black youth in Birm-
               ingham.

UNPUBLISHED   Report to the Commission for Racial Equality.
PAPERS:

* * *

HOUSING

NO. 059   Urban Insertion amongst Ethnic Minorities as Revealing
          and Structuring the Attitudes and Projects of Integra-
          tion.

INSTITUTION: Université de Nice, Institut d'études et de recherches
                interethniques et interculturelles - IDERIC (University
                of Nice, Intercultural and Interethnic Research and
                Studies Institute)
                34, rue Verdi
                F-06000 Nice
                France
                Tel.No.: 93/870175

RESEARCHER: Borgogno, Victor

DISCIPLINE   Sociology (Urban Sociology)
AND SUBFIELD:

ABSTRACT: The aim is to differentiate the urban insertion patterns
                of migrants (dispersion/regrouping) and to assert the
                influences of those patterns upon the attitudes, pro-
                jects and strategies of integration. These influences
                are reciprocal.

GEOGR.AREA: France (Alpes maritimes, Nice region)

PROCEDURE: Personal interview;
                Group discussion;
                Document analysis;
                Case study.

LANGUAGE: French

DURATION: Jan. 1979 - Dec. 1981

TYPE OF   Researcher's project/ Doctorat de 3° cycle
RESEARCH:

PUBLICATIONS: Borgogno, Victor: L'espace de l'immigration, in: Pluri-
               el, n° 14, 1978.

* * *

NO. 060   Space and Inter-Ethnic Relations. Urban Behavior and
                 Spatial Interactions in Multi-Ethnic Contact Situation.

INSTITUTION: Centre d'études sociologiques, Equipe de recherches sur
                 les migrations internationales (Centre of Sociological
                 Studies, Research Team on International Migrations)
                 82, rue Cardinet
                 F-75017 Paris
                 France
                 Tel.No.: 1/2670760

RESEARCHER: Rudder, Véronique de/ Guillon, Michèle/ Taboada-
                 Leonetti, Isabelle

CONTACT: Rudder, Véronique de
                 9, rue Abel
                 F-75012 Paris
                 France
                 Tel.No.: 1/3075132

DISCIPLINE   Demography
AND SUBFIELD: Sociology

ABSTRACT: Research in multi-ethnic neighbourhoods. Two aims:
                 1) establishment of a spatial typology for the situa-
                    tions of urban contacts
                 2) study of the socio-urban behavior as an expression of
                    collective and national identities and as an index
                    to the inter-ethnic relations. Those relations will
                    be studied through several activities: ways, itiner-
                    aries, markings of space, spatio-temporal occupation
                    of space.

GEOGR.AREA: France

PROCEDURE: Group discussion;
                 Expert interview (Informants);
                 Non-participant observation.

LANGUAGE: French

DURATION: 1980 - 1982

TYPE OF   Sponsored research/ Institution project/ Researcher's
RESEARCH: project

FUNDS: Internal sources

* * *

NO. 061   Analysis of Housing Conditions as Experienced by the
                Foreign Working Population in the Federal Republic of
                Germany with Special Regard to Turkish Workers' House-
                holds in Kreuzberg, Berlin (West).

INSTITUTION: Technische Universität Berlin, Institut für Wohnungsbau
                und Stadtteilplanung (Technical University Berlin, In-
                stitute for Housing Construction and Town Planning)
                Strasse des 17. Juni 135
                D-1000 Berlin 12
                Germany, Federal Republic

RESEARCHER: Arin, Y. Cihan

CONTACT: Arin, Y. Cihan
                Tel.No.: 030/3145359

DISCIPLINE   Sociology (Urban Sociology)
AND SUBFIELD: Town Planning

ABSTRACT: This project deals with the current housing conditions
                of migrant workers in the Federal Republic of Germany
                and in particular in Berlin (West). On the basis of ex-
                isting literature and an empiric study conducted in a
                redevelopment area in Kreuzberg, Berlin (West), it is
                illustrated that this population group is provided with
                insufficient housing (which must be considered in the
                broader context of the bad housing situation of low-in-
                come groups). The specific problems of foreigner se-
                gregation are analysed; the effects of housing
                on concentration and ghetto-formation by the migrant
                population are investigated. Measures concerning the
                living conditions of foreigners (especially those pe-
                culiar to Berlin) are reviewed and an attempt is made
                to determine which actions could help to improve the
                living conditions of foreigners and to what degree such
                measures should be considered in urban redevelopment.

GEOGR.AREA: Germany, Federal Republic (Berlin-West)

PROCEDURE: Personal interview (100 households of approx. 860 Tur-
                kish households in the research area);
                Non-participant observation.

LANGUAGE: German

DURATION: Dec. 1976 - Dec. 1979

TYPE OF   Sponsored research/ Dissertation
RESEARCH:

FUNDS: External sources: Deutscher Akademischer Austausch-
                dienst - DAAD -, Bonn

PUBLICATIONS: Planned

                              * * *

NO. 062   Institutional Determinants of Spatial Segregation and
                 Social Integration of Foreign Workers in Western Euro-
                 pean Industrial Countries.

INSTITUTION: Universität Frankfurt, FB 03, Gesellschaftswissenschaf-
                 ten, Arbeitsgruppe Soziale Infrastruktur (University of
                 Frankfort, Working Group Social Infrastructure)
                 Bockenheimer Landstrasse 142
                 D-6000 Frankfurt
                 Germany, Federal Republic

RESEARCHER: Hoffmann-Nowotny, H.J. (University of Zürich)/ Hondrich,
                 Karl Otto (University of Frankfurt)/ Helmert, Uwe
                 (Frankfurt)/ Schöneberg, Ulrike (Frankfurt)/ Unger,
                 Klaus (Frankfurt)/ et alii (Zürich)

DISCIPLINE   Geography (Social Geography)
AND SUBFIELD: Sociology

ABSTRACT: The general question which this investigation attempts
                 to answer is how type and degree of spatial concen-
                 tration or dispersion of various groups of the popula-
                 tion correlate with the specific institutional regula-
                 tory mechanisms in the economic, political, and cultur-
                 al field which exist in a particular country. This
                 very broad question has been reduced in this study,
                 to the exemplary investigation of the phenomenon
                 of spatially concentrated and socially segregated for-
                 eign workers.

GEOGR.AREA: Germany, Federal Republic (Frankfurt and Lippstadt)/
                 Switzerland (Zürich and Frauenfeld)

PROCEDURE: Personal interview (about 2000 Turkisn, Italian, and
                 Spanish married workers);
                 Expert interview (24 important organizations engaged in
                 immigration policy/ Federal, state, and local authority
                 politicians);
                 Document analysis (Alien Law/ Immigration policy/ Ger-
                 man Trade Union Congress/ German Employers' Associa-
                 tion);
                 Secondary data analysis (data of the official statis-
                 tics concerning the urban district, demography, and the
                 building structure).

LANGUAGE: German

DURATION: May 1977 - Oct. 1979

TYPE OF   Sponsored research
RESEARCH:

FUNDS: External sources: Stiftung Volkswagenwerk / Ford Foun-
                 dation, New York

PUBLICATIONS: Planned in 1981, Campus Publishing House.

UNPUBLISHED   Intermediate report 1978, March 1979, final reports,
PAPERS: February 1980.

                            * * *

NO. 063   Foreign Worker Project.

INSTITUTION: University of Bergen, Department of Social Anthropology
              N-5014 Bergen
              Norway

RESEARCHER: Kramer, J.Y./ Ryall, R.B./ Salvesen, M.M./ Tambs-Lyche,
              H.

DISCIPLINE   Anthropology (Social Anthropology), Ethnology
AND SUBFIELD:

ABSTRACT: A study of the adaptation of four immigrant groups to
              Norwegian society. The cases include: Sikh Punjabi im-
              migrants, Uganda Asian refugees, Pakistani immigrant
              families, and contract workers in oil-based industries.
              One project report on housing, network and households
              among all four groups has been published. The main
              thrust of the work has been in 'mapping out' the sit-
              uation while comparative studies of the four groups
              have also yielded several conclusions, both of a gener-
              al and more practical nature, concerning the Norwegian
              immigrant situation and policies.
              Project comprises subprojects: Pakistani Families in
              Bergen (M.M. Salvesen, 1978-79).

GEOGR.AREA: Norway

LANGUAGE: Norwegian

DURATION: Jan. 1976 - Dec. 1979

FUNDS: External sources: Ministry of Local Government and La-
              bour, Ministry of Health and Social Affairs

PUBLICATIONS: Kramer, J. Y., (et al.) : Hushold, bolig og kontakt-
              mønster blant innvandrerne. Bergen, University of
              Bergen, Department of Social Anthropology, 1979. Occa-
              sional Papers, 15. 130 p.
              Kramer, J. Y., (et al.): Innvandrerne i arbeid og ut-
              danning (prelim. title). Bergen, University of Bergen,
              Department of Social Anthropology, 1980. Occasional
              Papers, 80 p.

Kramer, J. Y. (et al.): Språk og kultur blant innvand-
rerne (prelim. title). Bergen, University of Bergen,
Department of Social Anthropology, 1980. Occasional Pa-
pers, 100 p.
Salvesen, M. M.: Pakistanske familier i Norge. Bergen,
University of Bergen, Department of Social Anthropolo-
gy, 1979. Thesis, 130 p.
Salvesen, M. M.: Den pakistanske innvandrerkvinnen.
Hvem er hun, in: Invandrare och minoriteter, vol. 6,
1979, no. 3, pp. 28-33.

* * *

NO. 064   The Social Situation for Foreign Workers in Oslo -
                  with Emphasis on Work- and Family Situation, the Migra-
                  tion Process and Network.

INSTITUTION: Diakonhjemmet School of Social Work, Research Depart-
                  ment
                  Borgenvein 3 c
                  N-Oslo 3
                  Norway

RESEARCHER: Bø, B.P.

DISCIPLINE   Sociology
AND SUBFIELD:

ABSTRACT: The information on the immigrants' social situation was
                  collected by means of personal interviews with approx.
                  500 foreign workers in Oslo, from Pakistan, India, Mor-
                  occo and Turkey. One main purpose was to describe their
                  housing situation because this was (and still is) the
                  most serious problem for foreign workers in Oslo. A
                  special report on housing was published in 1979. The
                  other main purpose of the interview was to set a pic-
                  ture of the background situation in the foreign wor-
                  kers' home countries as well as information on what
                  kind of jobs they had in Norway, whether their families
                  live in Norway as well, and whether they have social
                  contacts with Norwegians or with countrymen. The effect
                  of the migration process is described as well. The work
                  situation for foreign workers in Norway is the largest
                  single topic in this project.
                  The project comprises subprojects: Part I: Housing sit-
                  uations . Part II: Social conditions.

GEOGR.AREA: Norway

PROCEDURE: Personal interview (500 Foreign workers from Pakistan,
                  India, Morocco, and Turkey in Oslo)

LANGUAGE: Norwegian

DURATION: 1978 - 1980

FUNDS: External sources: Ministry of Health and Social Affairs,
                  Ministry of Local Government and Labour

PUBLICATIONS: Bø, B.P.: Internasjonal arbeidskraftmigrasjon, in:
                  Arbeid og sysselsetting foran 80-âra, ed. by K. Hal-
                  vorsen, Oslo, Pax, 1980, 20 p.
                  Bø, B.P.: Fremmedarbeidernes boligsituasjon i Oslo,
                  Oslo, Universitetsforlaget, 1980, 290 p.
                  Bø, B.P.: Fremmedarbeidernes boligsituasjon i Oslo, in:
                  Sosialt forum/ Sosialt arbeid, 1980, no. 4, pp. 67-69.
                  Bø, B.P.: Arbeidsvandringen til Norge, in: Kirke og
                  Kultur, vol. 85, 1980, no. 5, pp. 283-.
                  Bø, B.P.: Muslimer i Norge, in: Kontrast, vol. 15,
                  1979, no. 6.

                           * * *

NO. 65   Spatial Distribution of Black People in South London
                  (Asian and Negro). Factors Influencing Ethnic Residen-
                  tial Differentiation Particularly Role of Housing and
                  Skin Colour.

INSTITUTION: University of London, King's College, Department of
                  Geography
                  Strand
                  GB-London WC2 2LS
                  United Kingdom
                  Tel.No.: 01/8365454 (ext. 2463)

RESEARCHER: Baboolal, Errol Rudal

DISCIPLINE   Geography (Urban/ Human/ Social)
AND SUBFIELD:

ABSTRACT: The study investigates the spatial distribution of black
                  people in South London on a very small scale (1961 &
                  1971 Enumeration Districts). Particular attention is
                  given to the nature and magnitude of black residential
                  concentration in 1971 (e.g. morphology of black clusters)
                  and to changes in residential distribution between 1961
                  and 1971. An attempt is made to analyse the processes
                  which have brought about the observed distributions -
                  particularly the role of the housing market and skin-
                  colour discrimination. Black population distribution is
                  related to the physical and social condition of the
                  housing stock of South London. Study area findings are
                  related to features observed in other British and Unit-
                  ed States cities. Preliminary results are "in press"
                  (IBG Special Publication Series; Academic Press).

GEOGR.AREA: United Kingdom (South London, all GLC area south of
                  R. Thames)

PROCEDURE: Personal interview (50-200 white and black people in
                  Lambeth and Croydon);
                  Participant observation;
                  Secondary data analysis (1961 & 1971 Census Data South
                  London Enumeration Districts).

LANGUAGE: English

DURATION: 1973 - 1981

TYPE OF   Sponsored research/ Ph.D.
RESEARCH:

FUNDS: External sources: Social Science Research Council

PUBLICATIONS: "In press", IBG Special Publications Series, Academic
                Press.

* * *

NO. 066   Ethnic Segregations, Community Institutions and Retail
                Activity: A Case Study of Croydon 1961-79.

INSTITUTION: University of London, London School of Economics and
                Political Science, Department of Geography
                Houghton Street
                GB-London WC2A 2AE
                United Kingdom
                Tel.No.: 01/4057686

RESEARCHER: Mullins, David

DISCIPLINE   Geography (Social/ Economic)
AND SUBFIELD:

ABSTRACT: An investigation of the nature and extent of residen-
                tial and activity segregation of 'black' ethnic minor-
                ities in the London Borough of Croydon.
                Residential segregation is examined using traditional
                statistical methods of analysis of secondary data
                sources including the Census of Population and Elector-
                al Register. Activity segregation and its relationship
                to residential segregation is explored both by primary
                research methods including field observation; question-
                naire survey and informal interview and by analysis of
                secondary sources. A detailed study of the expansion of
                Asian owned retail business is conducted to test the
                validity of a number of theories of institutional de-
                velopment. A preliminary conclusion is that patterns
                of business expansion in the study area showed a limit-
                ed relationship to patterns of residental segregation
                and that structural theories of minority business de-
                velopment are of greater explanatory power than are
                ecological theories.

GEOGR.AREA: United Kingdom (London Borough of Croydon)

PROCEDURE: Personal interview (population of 100 out of 214 Asian
                retail entrepreneurs in London Borough of Croydon);
                Expert interview (Local community leaders/ Estate
                agents/ Local authority officer);

Questionnaire (40 local community groups);
Participant observation (English language scheme);
Document analysis (Local press);
Qualitative content analysis (Local press);
Secondary data analysis (Census / Electoral Register /
Valuation lists).

LANGUAGE: English

DURATION: Oct. 1976 - Oct. 1981

TYPE OF   Sponsored research/ Ph. D. in Geography
RESEARCH:

FUNDS: External sources: Social Science Research Council Grant
                (1976 - 79)

PUBLICATIONS: Mullins, D.: Asian Retailing in Croydon. Commission for
                Racial Equality journal "New Community", vol. 7, no. 3,
                1979, pp. 403-5.

UNPUBLISHED   Mullins, D.: Problems of Explanation in the Study of
PAPERS: Urban Ethnic Segregation. Presented to Urban Geography
                Study Group of Institute of British Geographers. Con-
                ference at King's College, London, September 1979,
                24 pp.
                Mullins, D.: Race and Retailing: The Asian Owned Retail
                Sector in Croydon. Presented to Annual Conference of
                Institute of British Geographers, Lancaster, January
                1980, 51 pp.

                            * * *

NO. 067   Immigrants. Segregation and Interaction in the UK.

INSTITUTION: University of Oxford, School of Geography
                Mansfield Road
                GB-Oxford OX1 3TB
                United Kingdom
                Tel.No.: 0865/41791

RESEARCHER: Peach, Ceri/ Robinson, Vaughan/ Smith, Susan/ Colpi,
                Terri/ Simmons, Ian

CONTACT: Peach, Ceri
                School of Geography, University of Oxford
                Mansfield Road
                GB-Oxford OX4 4DU
                United Kingdom
                Tel.No.: 0865/41791

DISCIPLINE   Geography (Social)
AND SUBFIELD:

ABSTRACT: The project is a group of individual studies tackling
                related topics. The central theme relates the patterns

and degrees of immigrant residential segregation to
processes of social interaction. The main groups of immigrants concerned are Asians (Robinson, Simmons,
Smith), West Indians (Peach, Smith), Italians (Colpi).

GEOGR.AREA: United Kingdom (all of the studies relate to the UK
generally, but London, Birmingham, Blackburn and Bed-
ford are treated individually)

LANGUAGE: English

DURATION: 1975 - 1985

TYPE OF   Sponsored research/ Researcher's project/ Academic de-
RESEARCH: gree

FUNDS: Internal sources
External sources: Social Science Research Council and
Nuffield Foundation

PUBLICATIONS: Smith, S.; Jackson, P. (Eds.); A sample of publications
resulting from our work may be found in: Social Interaction and Ethnic Segregation. Academic Press, London
(in press).
Peach, C.; Robinson, V.; Smith, S. (Eds.): Ethnic Segregation in Cities. Croom Helm, London (in press).
Peach, C.; Shah, S.: The Contribution of Council House
Allocation to West Indian Desegregation in London 1961-
71, in: URBAN Studies, vol. 17, 1980, 333-41.

* * *

NO. 068   Reporting on the Integration of Migrant Workers in
           Salzburg and Munich.

INSTITUTION: Universität Salzburg, Institut für Publizistik und
                Kommunikationswissenschaft (University of Salzburg, In-
                stitute of Communication Research)
                Sigmund Haffner Gasse 18/III
                A-5020 Salzburg
                Austria
                Tel.No.: 06222/86111(ext. 388)

RESEARCHER: Segal, Michael

DISCIPLINE   Communication
AND SUBFIELD:

ABSTRACT: Reporting on migrant workers depends on the economic
               development of the host country. In case of fa-
               vourable economic development the readiness for integ-
               ration is greater than in an unfavourable one. In the
               case of primary needs readiness for integration is of
               no importance. Frequent interaction of the population
               with migrant workers leads to more unbiased reports in
               the press (Switzerland!).

GEOGR.AREA: Austria (Salzburg)/ Germany, Federal Republic (Munich)

PROCEDURE: Quantitative content analysis

LANGUAGE: German

DURATION: July 1978 - July 1979

TYPE OF   Researcher's project/ Dissertation
RESEARCH:

FUNDS: Internal sources

* * *

NO. 069   Health of Immigrants in Belgium.

INSTITUTION: Université Catholique de Louvain, Groupe d'étude des
                 migrations(Catholic University of Louvain, Research
                 Group on Migration)
                 1 b.21, place Montesquieu
                 B-1348 Louvain la Neuve
                 Belgium
                 Tel.No.: 010/418181 (ext. 4252)

RESEARCHER: Bastenier, Albert/ Dassetto, Felice

DISCIPLINE   Sociology (Sociology of Medicine/ Sociology of Migra-
AND SUBFIELD: tion)

ABSTRACT: The study comprises the following problems:
                 1. Health conditions of immigrants, particularly re-
                    garding tuberculosis, accidents at work, occupation-
                    al diseases.
                 2. Use of medical care (costs).
                 3. Socio-cultural approach to health and to the appli-
                    cation of the health system.

GEOGR.AREA: Belgium

PROCEDURE: Group discussion (Hospital);
                 Participant observation (Hospital);
                 Document analysis (1733 of 9800 bills of medical care).

LANGUAGE: French

DURATION: Jan. 1979 - Dec. 1981

TYPE OF   Sponsored research
RESEARCH:

FUNDS: External sources: Government funds

PUBLICATIONS: Bastenier, A.; Dassetto, F.: Coût de la consommation
                 des soins ordinaires par les immigrés en Belgique,
                 Feres, Louvain la Neuve 1979, offset, 91 p.
                 Bastenier, A.; Dassetto, F.: Les immigrés et l'hôpital,
                 Feres, Louvain la Neuve 1980, offset, 268 p.

* * *

NO. 070   Hospitalization of Foreign and Displaced Children (Mi-
                 grants, Refugees, Sanitary Evacuees from Overseas
                 French Departements).

INSTITUTION: Centre international de l'enfance (International Child-
                 ren's Centre)
                 Château de Longchamp, Bois de Boulogne
                 F-75016 Paris
                 France
                 Tel.No.: 1/506799 2

                 INSERM
                 44, chemin de ronde
                 F-78110 Le Vesinet
                 France
                 Tel.No.: 9763333

RESEARCHER: Pechevis, Michel/ Tursz, Anne/ Bonnal, Marie-Jo/
                 Guyot, Marie Madeleine

CONTACT: Pechevis, Michel
                 CIF-Château de Longchamp, Bois de Boulogne
                 F-75016 Paris
                 France
                 Tel.No.: 1/5067992

DISCIPLINE   Anthropology, Ethnology
AND SUBFIELD: Demography
                 Sociology (Sociology of Medicine)

ABSTRACT: Aim: to study foreign children as regards
                 - types of pathologies and motives of entering hospital
                 - mean period of those sojourns in hospital
                 - the ways of leaving hospital
                 - follow up after the stay in hospital
                 and to compare them with French children.

GEOGR.AREA: France (Paris, Ile de France, Haute Loire, Isère,
                 Moselle, Rhône, Pyrénées orientales)

PROCEDURE: Personal interview (6000 children admitted in pediatric
                 hospitals during a fortnight);
                 Questionnaire (6000 children admitted in pediatric hos-
                 pitals during a fortnight);
                 Document analysis;
                 Quantitative content analysis.

LANGUAGE: French

DURATION: Nov. 1979 - 1981

TYPE OF   Institution project
RESEARCH:

PUBLICATIONS: Rapport au XXVI congrès de l'association des pédiatres
                 de langue française, Toulouse, juillet 1980.

* * *

NO. 071   Illegal Immigrants in France and the U.S.

INSTITUTION: Université de Paris II, Laboratoire de sociologie cri-
                minelle (University of Paris II, Laboratory of Criminal
                Sociology)
                12, place du Panthéon
                F-75231 Paris Cédex 05
                France
                Tel.No.: 1/3292140

                Centre d'études sociologiques, Equipe de recherches sur
                les migrations internationales (Centre of Sociological
                Studies, Research Team on International Migrations)
                82, rue Cardinet
                F- 75017 Paris
                France
                Tel.No.: 1/2670760

RESEARCHER: Costa-Lascoux, Jacqueline/ Wenden-Didier, Catherine de/
                Kardestunger de Saint Blanquat, Emine

DISCIPLINE   Demography
AND SUBFIELD: Economics
                Law (Comparative Law)
                Political Sciences

ABSTRACT: Comparative analysis of the problem of illegal immi-
                grants in France and the U.S.
                Approaches:
                1) Institutional analysis of the situation of illegal
                   immigrants in these two countries and of the changes
                   in policy towards them
                2) Political study of the influence of illegal immi-
                   grants in social life of the country and of the at-
                   titudes of trade unions and political parties to-
                   wards them
                3) Observation of the conditions of insertion or re-
                   jection of illegal immigrants in a specific profes-
                   sional sector

GEOGR.AREA: France/ United States (New York, California)

PROCEDURE: Personal interview (30 Turkish immigrants in clothing
                industry);
                Group discussion (30 Turkish immigrants in clothing in-
                dustry);
                Participant observation (30 Turkish immigrants in
                clothing industry);
                Qualitative content analysis (American and French offi-
                cial texts).

LANGUAGE: French

DURATION: May 1981 - Oct. 1982

TYPE OF   Sponsored research/ Institution project
RESEARCH:

FUNDS: External sources: Grant of Marshall Foundation

PUBLICATIONS: Costa-Lascoux, J.: Une législation pour une nouvelle
                politique de l'immigration, in: Pluriel, n° 22, 1980,
                26 p.
                Wihtol de Wenden, C.: Les immigrés dans la cité. Paris,
                Documentation Française, 1978, 135 p.
                Wihtol de Wenden, C.: Les immigrés et l'administration.
                Paris CNRS, 1978, 266 p.
                Costa-Lascoux, J.: Rapport à la commission nationale
                informatique et libertés sur le "projet de traitement
                automatisé des titres de séjour d'étrangers". Paris,
                1980, in: GRECO 13, n° 2, 1980.

                              * * *

NO. 072   The Legal Problems of Foreign Workers as a Result of
                the Alien Policy of the Government.

INSTITUTION: Wissenschaftszentrum Berlin gGmbH, Internationales In-
                stitut für Management und Verwaltung (International
                Institute for Management and Administration)
                Platz der Luftbrücke 1-3
                D-1000 Berlin 42
                Germany, Federal Republic

RESEARCHER: Spies, Ulrich

CONTACT: Blankenburg, Erhard
                Tel.No.: 030/6913084-22

DISCIPLINE   Law (Alien Law)
AND SUBFIELD: Political Sciences (Immigration Policy)

ABSTRACT: What is the connection between the intended medium-
                and long-term integration policy and the actually prac-
                tised alien policy? Is the established (legal) advisory
                system able to contribute to the solution of (legal)
                problems of foreign workers and does it work within the
                limits of the existing law or in a different way?

GEOGR.AREA: Germany, Federal Republic (Berlin-West)

PROCEDURE: Questionnaire;
                Non-participant observation;
                Document analysis (200);
                Secondary data analysis.

LANGUAGE: German

DURATION: Aug. 1977 - Dec. 1980

TYPE OF   Dissertation
RESEARCH:

FUNDS: Internal sources

PUBLICATIONS: Spies, U.: Die Rechtsprobleme von Gastarbeitern als Er-
                gebnis staatlicher Ausländerpolitik. Internationales
                Institut für Management und Verwaltung Berlin (Wissen-
                schaftszentrum), DP 77-84, August 1977.
                Spies, U.: Rechtsverfassung und Rechtspraxis ausländi-
                scher Kinder und Jugendlicher in Berlin (West), in:
                Deutsch Lernen, Sprachverband Deutsch für ausländische
                Arbeitnehmer e.V. (Hrsg.), Heft 3/1978, S. 33 (47).
                Spies, U.: Die zweite Generation. Internationales In-
                stitut für Management und Verwaltung Berlin (Wissen-
                schaftszentrum), DP/78-78, Oktober 1978.

UNPUBLISHED   Spies, U.: Die Negativentscheidung der Ausländerbehörde.
PAPERS: Erörtert anhand der Verwaltungspraxis in Berlin, Novem-
                ber 1977, Internationales Institut für Management und
                Verwaltung.

                              * * *

NO. 073   The Question of Intercultural Contacts and That of the
                 Correct or Erroneous Interpretation of the Behavior of
                 One Cultural Group by Another.

RESEARCHER: Biskup, Manfred
                 Hofmühlgasse 7a/15
                 A-1060 Wien
                 Austria
                 Tel.No.: 0222/5668222

DISCIPLINE   Anthropology (Semantic Anthropology), Ethnology
AND SUBFIELD: Sociology

ABSTRACT: Case study of the integration of Turkish migrant wor-
                 kers including their families in a smaller Austrian pro-
                 vincial town. Descriptive account of the change in way of
                 living within the Turkish community and the types and
                 fields of interactions between Austrians and Turks.
                 Description of the cultural and communicational bounda-
                 ries, the process towards their dissolution, the effort
                 to maintain the boundary. Communal organizations working
                 towards integration, counterforces. Semantic study of
                 the rules of social perception by Turks - their projec-
                 tion of Turkish organizational patterns into the organi-
                 zation of the Austrian social environment.

GEOGR.AREA: Austria (Lower Austria)

PROCEDURE: Personal interview (130 out of 370 Turks);
                 Group discussion (5-10);
                 Expert interview (12);
                 Participant observation;
                 Non-participant observation;
                 Document analysis.

LANGUAGE: English

DURATION: May 1978 - Feb. 1979

TYPE OF   Commissioned research
RESEARCH:

FUNDS: External sources: UNESCO, Paris

UNPUBLISHED   The Question of Intercultural Contacts and That of the
PAPERS: Correct or Erroneous Interpretation of the Behavior of
                 one Cultural Group by Another. Unpublished paper at
                 UNESCO, Feb. 1979.

                         * * *

NO. 074   Italian Children in Belgium.

INSTITUTION: Université Catholique de Louvain, Groupe d'étude des
                 migrations (Catholic University of Louvain, Research
                 Group on Migration)
                 1 b 21, place Montesquieu
                 B-1348 Louvain la Neuve
                 Belgium

RESEARCHER: Bastenier, Albert/ Dassetto, Felice

DISCIPLINE   Sociology (Sociology of Migration)
AND SUBFIELD:

ABSTRACT: Studying the socialization process exercised by school
                 and family within the social and career plans of young
                 people.

GEOGR.AREA: Belgium

PROCEDURE: Questionnaire (333 out of 130,000 Italian children in
                 Belgium)

LANGUAGE: French

DURATION: Jan. 1979 - Dec. 1980

TYPE OF   Commissioned research
RESEARCH:

FUNDS: Internal sources

PUBLICATIONS: Ethique, pratique religieuse et socialisation des fils
                 d'immigrés italiens en Belgique. Social Compass, 1979/1,
                 125-144.

UNPUBLISHED   La seconde génération d'italiens en Belgique. A paraître
PAPERS: 1981.

                         * * *

NO. 075   Danish Farmers on the American Prairie.
_____   _____

INSTITUTION: University of Copenhagen, Institute of Economic History
               102 Njalsgade
               DK-2300 København S
               Denmark

RESEARCHER: Pedersen, Erik Helmer/ Jørgensen, Steffen Elmer/
               Stilling, Niels Peter

DISCIPLINE   Economics (Agriculture)
AND SUBFIELD: Sociology (Rural Sociology)
               Economic History
               Social History

ABSTRACT: Based on primary source materials in American archives,
               such as original schedules from the agricultural cen-
               suses and population census lists, we will try to grasp
               if the Danish immigrant farmers very soon adapted them-
               selves to the American agricultural practices, or on
               the contrary, strived to transplant their Danish cus-
               toms. In a wider sense we imagine that it will be pos-
               sible to make a distinction between particular (nation-
               al) and general (international) development factors as-
               sociated with the agricultural modernization process of
               the 19th century. If the Danish farmers capitulated, so
               to speak, to the American way of doing things, what mo-
               tivated them to do so, especially if we assume that
               they, in fact, were able to carry on with the moderni-
               zation process of the late 19th century?

GEOGR.AREA: USA

PROCEDURE: Secondary data analysis (Agricultural census/ Popula-
               tion census)

DURATION: May 1978 - Dec. 1983

                          * * *

NO. 076   The Swedish Immigration to Denmark 1850 - 1914.
_____   _____

INSTITUTION: University of Copenhagen, Institute of Economic History
               102 Njalsgade
               DK-2300 Københaven S
               Denmark

RESEARCHER: Willerslev, Richard

DISCIPLINE   Anthropology, Ethnology
AND SUBFIELD: Demography
               Sociology
               Social History

ABSTRACT: The Swedish immigration to Denmark of male and female
                 workers began in a small scale about 1840 but grew to a
                 mass immigration from the southern Swedish provinces
                 from 1870 to 1900. It consisted partly of seasonal wor-
                 kers, partly of workers who domiciled in Denmark. The
                 seasonal workers came from the rural districts and were
                 dominated by males who greatly contributed to the con-
                 struction works (railways, harbours, fortifications)
                 and the brickworks. The female seasonal workers made up
                 a large occupational category in the beetfields.
                 The more permanently domiciled immigrants were dominated
                 by females who mainly preferred to live in Copenhagen
                 employed as maids and industrial workers. The males -
                 many of whom were relatively skilled workers - came
                 partly from the cities in Skåne (the southernmost pro-
                 vince of Sweden) and were of great importance particu-
                 larly for the manpower in the industries of Copenhagen.
                 The main problems to be investigated are namely: How
                 great was the immigration, its structure, its correla-
                 tion with the economic expansion and business cycles in
                 Sweden and Denmark, the immigrants' occupational struc-
                 ture and social status in the course of time, the reac-
                 tion of the Danish population, and connected with this,
                 the frequency of intermarriage.

GEOGR.AREA: Denmark

DURATION: 1977-1981

TYPE OF   Sponsored research
RESEARCH:

FUNDS: External sources: The Danish Social Science Research
                 Council / The Carlsberg Foundation

                              * * *

NO. 077   Refugee Settlements in Eastern Africa. Their Develop-
                 ment and Organization.

RESEARCHER: Christensen, Hanne Steen
                 c/o United Nations Research Institute for Social Devel-
                 opment
                 Palais des Nations
                 CH-1211 Geneva 10
                 Switzerland

DISCIPLINE   Sociology (Rural Sociology)
AND SUBFIELD:

ABSTRACT: This study is undertaken to bridge a gap in African
                 refugee research by providing some previously missed
                 sociological analyses of the progress of organized ru-
                 ral settlements for refugees, which is regarded as the
                 way of integrating refugees in Africa.

The programme undertaken in some refugees' settlements in Tanzania and Zaire is analysing the development of such schemes from the establishment to the stage of so-cio-economic self-sufficiency of the settlement as such. It includes a comparative, cross-national historical account of the settlement process of the Barundi and Wanyarwanda refugee populations. It is limited to some socio-cultural determinants for this process, i.e. in particular the extent of completeness of the social networks of the refugees, the possibility of occupa-tional replacement in the settlement scheme and the ex-tent of participation in the planning and operation of the scheme.

Two empirical case-studies are undertaken in Tanzania (1980) and Zaire (1981), investigating one settlement for Barundi refugees and one for Wanyarwanda refugees. Methods applied: utilization of available documentation and semi-structured interviews of key informants in va-rious refugees' agencies and among staff members of the settlements of interest. Also focused interviewing with a sample of refugee households in the settlements se-lected at random.

GEOGR.AREA:	Eastern Africa (Tanzania, Zaire)
PROCEDURE:	Personal interview (Refugee households); Expert interview (Key informants of various refugees' agencies/ Staff members of refugees' settlements); Document analysis.
DURATION:	Sept. 1979 - Aug. 1982
TYPE OF RESEARCH:	Sponsored research
FUNDS:	External sources: The Danish Social Science Research Council

* * *

NO. 078   Migrant Labour in the Pacific - Western Samoa and New Zealand.

INSTITUTION:	Odder Museum Rosengade 84 DK-8300 Odder Denmark
RESEARCHER:	Hjarnoe, Jan Peter
DISCIPLINE AND SUBFIELD:	Anthropology, Ethnology Political Sciences Sociology Political History

ABSTRACT: The aim of this research project is to study the eco-
                nomic, social, and political effect in Western Samoa
                caused by the extensive West-Samoan labour migration to
                New Zealand. The study comprises an in-depth analysis
                of the historical relations between New Zealand and
                Western Samoa as well as results based on a series of
                surveys carried out in 1973-74.

                As part of the study the relationship between differ-
                ent ethnic groups in New Zealand is dealt with as well
                as the development in the migration policy in New Zea-
                land since the end of the 19th century.

GEOGR.AREA: Western Samoa/ New Zealand

DURATION: June 1973 - June 1983

                                * * *

NO. 079   International Migrations of North African Manpower.

INSTITUTION: Maison de la méditerrannée, Centre de recherches et
                d'études sur les sociétés méditerranéennes (Centre of
                Research and Studies on Mediterranean Societies)
                5, avenue Pasteur
                F-13100 Aix-en-Provence
                France
                Tel.No.: 42/962781

RESEARCHER: Etienne, Bruno/ Flory, Maurice/ Talha, Larbi/ Baduel,
                Pierre/ Bianquis, Marie-José

CONTACT: Talha, Larbi
                CRESM
                18, rue de l'Opéra
                F-13100 Aix-en-Provence
                France
                Tel.No.: 42/263199

DISCIPLINE   Economics (Work Economics)
AND SUBFIELD: Law (International Law)
                Sociology (Regional Sociology)
                History

ABSTRACT: Historical and economic aspects of international North
                African migrations
                1) inter North African and Interarab space: Maghreb and
                   Machrek
                2) from North Africa to Western Europe
                Publication of the Annuaire de l'Afrique du nord 1981
                on that theme.

GEOGR.AREA: North Africa/ Near East/ Europe

LANGUAGE: French

DURATION: 1981 (end)

TYPE OF   Institution project/ Researcher's project/ Academic de-
RESEARCH: gree

FUNDS: Internal sources

PUBLICATIONS: Talha, L.: Genèse et essor de l'offre de travail mi-
                 grant: le cas des maghrébins, in: Rapports de dépen-
                 dance au Maghreb, Paris CNRS,1977.
                 Baduel, P.: Société et émigration temporaire au Nef-
                 zaoua (sud tunisien), Paris, éditions du CNRS,1980.

                            * * *

NO. 080   Settlement and Permanence of the Armenian Community in
                 Southern France since 1920.

INSTITUTION: Université de Provence-Aix-Marseille I, Centre d'études
                 de la pensée politique et sociale contemporaine (Uni-
                 versity of Aix-Marseille I, Centre of Study of Contem-
                 porary Political and Social Thought)
                 29, avenue Robert Schumann
                 F-13621 Aix-en-Provence
                 France
                 Tel.No.: 42/599930

RESEARCHER: Temime, Emile/ Ayvassian, Lydie/ Janin Coste, Dominique/
                 Zarokian, Sylvie

CONTACT: Temime, Emile
                 23, rue Daumier
                 F-13008 P Marseille
                 France

DISCIPLINE   Anthropology, Ethnology
AND SUBFIELD: Demography
                 History

ABSTRACT: Study of a community whose settlement date is precisely
                 known and whose insertion can be followed upon a long
                 period. Simultaneously, there is integration into the
                 French milieu and keeping up of collective habits and
                 traditions. Quantitative study - and setting up of a
                 file based upon families - of Armenians at their arri-
                 val. Study of the numbering of 1926 in South Eastern
                 France (departements des Alpes-Maritimes, Bouches-du-
                 Rhône, Isère). Study and mapping of population move-
                 ments. Study of associations and of solidarity links in
                 different strata of the community. Study of mythology,
                 of the image of the past.

GEOGR.AREA: France (South-East region: Isère, Bouches-du-Rhône,
                 Marseille)

LANGUAGE: French

DURATION: Dec. 1979 - Dec. 1982

TYPE OF   Sponsored research/ Institution project
RESEARCH:

FUNDS: External sources: Délégation Générale à la Recherche
                 Scientifique et Technique - DGRST

* * *

NO. 081   Migrants from Maghrib: Settling, Insertion, Behavior.

INSTITUTION: Université de Provence-Aix-Marseille I, Centre d'études
                 de la pensée politique et sociale contemporaine (Univer-
                 sity of Aix-Marseille I, Centre of Study of Contempora-
                 ry Political and Social Thought)
                 29, avenue Robert Schumann
                 F-13621 Aix-en-Provence
                 France
                 Tel.No.: 42/599930

RESEARCHER: Temime, Emile/ Jollivet, Christine/ Viala, Bernard

CONTACT: Temime, Emile
                 23, rue Daumier
                 F-13008 Marseille
                 France

DISCIPLINE   Anthropology, Ethnology
AND SUBFIELD: Demography
                 History

ABSTRACT: The study combines historical, ethnological and demo-
                 graphic approaches. The aim is to study the importance
                 of migrations from North Africa, especially Algeria.
                 Problems of departure and conditions of return in the
                 region of origin (Kabylia). In the region of arrival
                 (Marseille essentially):
                 . quantitative study (1920-1940)
                 . study of socio-political and socio-economic behavior:
                   strategies of solidarity, interethnic relations
                 . study of families: lodging conditions, behavior of
                   women and children, study of the second generation

GEOGR.AREA: France (Marseille)/ Algeria (Kabylia)

PROCEDURE: Personal interview;
                 Participant observation;
                 Document analysis (Exhaustive study of archives).

LANGUAGE: French

DURATION: Jan. 1979 - Dec. 1983

TYPE OF   Sponsored research/ Institution project
RESEARCH:

FUNDS: External sources:
                 Délégation Générale à la Recherche Scientifique et
                 Technique - DGRST -
                 35, rue St. Dominique
                 F-75700 Paris
                 France

                              * * *

NO. 082   Interethnic Relations between Spanish Migrants and
                 French Populations mostly in Cities.

INSTITUTION: Université de Provence-Aix-Marseille I, Centre d'études
                 de la pensée politique et sociale contemporaine (Uni-
                 versity of Aix-Marseille I, Centre of Study of Contem-
                 porary Political and Social Thought)
                 29, avenue Robert Schumann
                 F-13621 Aix-en-Provence
                 France
                 Tel.No.: 42/599930

RESEARCHER: Temime, Emile/ Tomasi, Annie/ Tomasi, Jacques

CONTACT: Temime, Emile
                 23, rue Daumier
                 F-13008 Marseille
                 France

DISCIPLINE   Demography
AND SUBFIELD: History

ABSTRACT: Study of the settling down of Spanish migrants in France.
                 Behavior of the French population towards them. Study
                 of migrant groups of diverse origins (Aragon, Majorca,
                 etc...) of different dates of arrival (political migra-
                 tions are studied separately). Since 1976 two research-
                 es have been conducted, especially in cities
                 . Jacques Tomasi: Spaniards in Decazeville. A file has
                   been established with the help of the archives of
                   the mining company
                 . Annie Tomasi: Marseille and cities of the département
                   of Bouches-du-Rhône. Conditions of the settlement of
                   the Spaniards in this region since 1850.

GEOGR.AREA: France (Marseille, Decazeville)

LANGUAGE: French

DURATION: Jan. 1976 - Dec. 1982

TYPE OF   Institution project
RESEARCH:

FUNDS: Internal sources

* * *

NO. 083   Study of the Situation of Migrant Workers in the North
                 Region of France: Situation and Flux.

INSTITUTION: Centre de recherches économiques sociologiques et de
                 gestion (Management, Economical and Social Research
                 Centre)
                 1, rue François Baes
                 F-59046 Lille Cédex
                 France
                 Tel.No.: 20/571853

RESEARCHER: Abousada, Georges/ Tricart, Jean-Paul

CONTACT: Abousada, Georges
                 1, rue François Baes
                 F-59046 Lille Cédex
                 France
                 Tel.No.: 20/571853

DISCIPLINE   Sociology
AND SUBFIELD:

ABSTRACT: This study is preliminary to the setting-up of a per-
                 manent observatory of international migrations in this
                 region. Special attention will be paid to the sec-
                 ond generation (schooling, job insertion) and to insti-
                 tutional action towards migrants (training, social work,
                 housing..).

GEOGR.AREA: France (Northern region)

PROCEDURE: Document analysis;
                 Qualitative content analysis.

LANGUAGE: French

DURATION: Jan. 1981 - Dec. 1981

TYPE OF   Institution project
RESEARCH:

FUNDS: Internal sources

* * *

NO. 084   Algerian Immigration in France.
_____

INSTITUTION: Centre de sociologie de l'éducation et de la culture
                 (Culture and Education Sociology Centre)
                 54, boulevard Raspail
                 F-75006 Paris
                 France
                 Tel.No.: 1/5443849

RESEARCHER: Sayad, Abdelmalek

DISCIPLINE   Sociology
AND SUBFIELD:

ABSTRACT: Living conditions of immigrants or group of immigrants
                 and their distinctive, hierarchical positions within
                 the immigrant community.

GEOGR.AREA: France (Paris region - Towns: Marseille and Saint
                 Etienne)/ Algeria

PROCEDURE: Personal interview;
                 Participant observation;
                 Non-participant observation;
                 Secondary data analysis.

LANGUAGE: French

DURATION: 1975 - 1982

TYPE OF   Commissioned research/ Institution project
RESEARCH:

FUNDS: Internal sources

PUBLICATIONS: Sayad, A.: Le foyer des sans famille, in: Actes de la
                 recherche en sciences sociales, n° 32/33, avril/juin
                 1980, pp. 89-103.
                 Sayad, A.: Etude de l'immigration algérienne en France:
                 étude comparative de cas spécialement choisis en raison
                 de leur pertinence structurale. Rapport CORDES, Paris,
                 décembre 1979.

                              * * *

NO. 085   Refugees of South East Asia in Britanny.
_____

INSTITUTION: Université de Haute-Bretagne-Rennes II, Centre d'études
                 des minorités (University of Rennes II, Minorities
                 Studies Centre)
                 6, avenue Gaston Berger
                 F-35043 Rennes Cédex
                 France
                 Tel.No.: 99/592033 (ext. 451)

RESEARCHER: Robineau, Chantal/ Simon-Barouh, Ida

DISCIPLINE   Anthropology (Social Anthropology), Ethnology
AND SUBFIELD: Education and Training
                  Sociology

ABSTRACT: Study of the enforced migration of the refugees of South
                  East Asia according to the methods of social anthro-
                  pology. This enforced migration is situated within the
                  historical frame of colonial relations between France
                  and the countries of ex-French Indochina, of the Amer-
                  ican war and of the establishment of socialist regimes.
                  The study shall begin with two monographs:
                  1 - the Vietnamese , Cambodians, Laotians living in
                      Rennes
                  2 - The Hmong in the département of Ile et Vilaine

GEOGR.AREA: France (Ile et Vilaine, Rennes)

PROCEDURE: Personal interview;
                  Participant observation;
                  Document analysis;
                  Qualitative content analysis.

LANGUAGE: French

TYPE OF   Institution project
RESEARCH:

FUNDS: Internal sources

* * *

NO. 086   The Condition of Immigrant Populations in Alsace.

INSTITUTION: Université de Strasbourg II, Laboratoire de sociologie
                  régionale (University of Strasbourg II, Laboratory of
                  Regional Sociology)
                  22, rue Descartes
                  F-67000 Strasbourg
                  France
                  Tel.No.: 88/613939

RESEARCHER: Fichet, Brigitte

DISCIPLINE   Economics
AND SUBFIELD: Sociology (Regional Sociology)

ABSTRACT: 1 - Salary differences in Alsace between the French and
                      foreigners, their economic analysis
                  2 - Schooling of migrant children in Alsace
                  3 - Mobility, migrations and social classes

GEOGR.AREA: France (Alsace)

PROCEDURE: Personal interview;
                  Document analysis.

LANGUAGE: French

TYPE OF   Researcher's project
RESEARCH:

FUNDS: Internal sources

PUBLICATIONS: Fichet, B.: Immigration et discriminations salariales -
le cas d'une entreprise alsacienne, in: Revue des
sciences sociales de la France de l'est, n° 7, 1978,
pp. 38-55.

* * *

NO. 087   Population and Migrations.

INSTITUTION: Université de Lille I, Flux et organisation de l'espace
dans l'Europe du nord-ouest (University of Lille I,
Flux and Organization of Space in North-west Europe)
Bâtiment 2
F-59655 Villeneuve d'Ascq
France
Tel.No.: 20/919222 (ext. 2942)

RESEARCHER: Thumerelle, Jean Pierre/ Barre, A./ Dion, R./ Herbert,
M./ Renard, J.P.

CONTACT: Thumerelle, Jean Pierre
5, allée de la Causette
F-59650 Villeneuve d'Ascq
Tel.No.: 20/913125 or 20/919222 (exts. 2939 and 2975)

DISCIPLINE   Demography (Migrations)
AND SUBFIELD: Geography (Human Geography)
Sociology

ABSTRACT: Internal and external migrations in North-west Europe:
their relation to spatial organization and changes in
the socio-economic environment; their socio-geographic-
al and demographical consequences.
More specifically, studies of social and spatial integration of immigrant families in the region of Nord-Pas-
de-Calais and comparison with other French regions.

GEOGR.AREA: France (Nord-Pas-de-Calais)/ North-west Europe

LANGUAGE: French

DURATION: Apr. 1979 - Dec. 1982

TYPE OF   Institution Project
RESEARCH:

FUNDS: Internal sources

* * *

NO. 088   Foreigners in the Federal Republic of Germany - Present
                 Situation and Development since 1961.

INSTITUTION: Max-Planck-Institut für Bildungsforschung (Max-Planck-
                 Institute for Educational Research)
                 Lentzallee 94
                 D-1000 Berlin 33
                 Germany, Federal Republic
                 Tel.No.: 030/9285247

RESEARCHER: Köhler, Helmut/ Trommer, Luitgard

DISCIPLINE   Demography
AND SUBFIELD: Sociology (Quantitative Historical Social Research)

ABSTRACT: To collect and to comment on all official statistical
                 data available on the subject of foreigners.

GEOGR.AREA: Germany, Federal Republic

LANGUAGE: German

DURATION: Mar. 1978 - Mar. 1981

TYPE OF   Researcher's project
RESEARCH:

FUNDS: Internal sources

PUBLICATIONS: Planned

                              * * *

NO. 089   Regional Study "Social Conditions of Migrant Workers
                 and Their Families in Göttingen".

INSTITUTION: Universität Göttingen, Seminar für die Wissenschaft von
                 der Politik (University of Göttingen, Institute for Po-
                 litical Science)
                 Nikolausberger Weg 5 c
                 D-3400 Göttingen
                 Germany, Federal Republic
                 Tel.No.: 0551/397217 or 7176

RESEARCHER: Leggewie, Claus/ Stratmann, Friedrich

DISCIPLINE   Political Sciences
AND SUBFIELD: Sociology

ABSTRACT: Social conditions and problems experienced by foreigners
                 subsequent to the 1973 recruitment stop, integration
                 problems. "New phase" in the immigration policy? (local
                 vote, liberalization, etc.)

Survey of the situation of foreign families from Mediterranean countries in a medium-sized town without
a high quota of foreigners. Research areas: Firm
and trade union, social guidance, school, youth recrea-
tion, vocational training, participation, council for
foreigners.

GEOGR.AREA: Germany, Federal Republic (Southern Lower Saxony)

PROCEDURE: Expert interview (10-20 representatives of institu-
                tions dealing with foreigners);
                Document analysis (statistical data/ election campaign
                documents used during the elections for a "council for
                foreigners").

LANGUAGE: German

DURATION: Oct. 1979 - Dec. 1980

TYPE OF   Researcher's project
RESEARCH:

FUNDS: Internal sources

PUBLICATIONS: Ausländerbericht, Göttingen 1980 (to be obtained from
                the Institute).

                            * * *

NO. 090   Living Conditions of Turkish Women in the Federal Re-
                public of Germany.

INSTITUTION: Universität Marburg, Arbeitsgruppe Kultursoziologie und
                Kommunikationsforschung (University of Marburg, Working
                Group for Sociology of Culture and Communications Re-
                search)
                Landgraf-Philipp-Strasse 4
                D-3550 Marburg
                Germany, Federal Republic

RESEARCHER: Gade, Alexa

CONTACT: Gade, Alexa
                Tel.No.: 06421/26951

DISCIPLINE   Sociology
AND SUBFIELD: Women's Studies

ABSTRACT: Collection of biographic data of Turkish female workers;
                Examination of the living and working conditions of Tur-
                kish women from their point of view;
                Processing the qualitative interviews for social sci-
                ence research.

GEOGR.AREA: Germany, Federal Republic

PROCEDURE: Personal interview (8 Turkish women)

LANGUAGE: German

DURATION: Jan. 1980 - Dec. 1981

TYPE OF   Dissertation
RESEARCH:

FUNDS: Internal sources

UNPUBLISHED   4 biographies (approx. 250 pages of manuscript).
PAPERS:

* * *

NO. 091   Integration Problems of Foreign Workers in Berlin(West).

INSTITUTION: Socialdata-Institut für empirische Sozialforschung GmbH
                (Socialdata Ltd.)
                Hans-Grässel-Weg 1
                D-8000 München 70
                Germany, Federal Republic

RESEARCHER: Brög, Werner/ Iblher, Peter/ Neumann, Karl-Heinz

CONTACT: Iblher, Peter
                Tel.No.: 089/7108268

DISCIPLINE   Psychology (Social Psychology)
AND SUBFIELD: Sociology

ABSTRACT: Study of the living conditions and the integration
                chances of the most important groups of foreigners in
                Berlin (West) - Turks, Yugoslavs, Greeks - as well as
                of the German resident population's opinions, attitudes,
                and experiences concerning this problem.

GEOGR.AREA: Germany, Federal Republic (Berlin-West)

PROCEDURE: Personal interview (546 Turkish households/ 265 Yugo-
                slav households/ 202 Greek households);
                Questionnaire (3,639 German households/ 2,801 Turkish
                households/1,825 Yugoslav households/ 781 Greek house-
                holds).

LANGUAGE: German

DURATION: Jan. 1979 - Oct. 1980

TYPE OF   Commissioned research
RESEARCH:

FUNDS: External sources: Der Regierende Bürgermeister, Senats-
kanzlei, Planungsleitstelle, Berlin

PUBLICATIONS: January 1981

UNPUBLISHED   Integrationsprobleme ausländischer Arbeitnehmer in Ber-
PAPERS: lin (West) - Bericht zur Voruntersuchung - (Januar
              1979).
              Integrationsprobleme ausländischer Arbeitnehmer in Ber-
              lin (West) - Entwicklung der schriftlich/postalischen
              Erhebungsunterlagen - (August 1979) - and other papers.

* * *

NO. 092   Economic, Political and Social Aspects of German Immi-
              grants in Brazil during 1932-38; Exemplified by the
              Rolandia Settlers Led by J. Schauff and B. Koch-Weser.

INSTITUTION: Universität Würzburg, Institut für Soziologie, Lehr-
              stuhl für Soziologie I (University of Würzburg, Insti-
              tute of Sociology, Chair of Sociology I)
              Wittelsbacherplatz 1
              D-8700 Würzburg
              Germany, Federal Republic

RESEARCHER: Breunig, Bernd

CONTACT: Breunig, Bernd
              Tel.No.: 0931/705554 or 4103415

DISCIPLINE   Sociology
AND SUBFIELD: Social History
              Political History

ABSTRACT: Origin and whereabouts (integration) of emigrants
              expelled from Germany.

GEOGR.AREA: Brazil

PROCEDURE: Personal interview (30 out of approx. 300 families);
              Questionnaire (by mail) (30 out of approx.300 families).

LANGUAGE: German

DURATION: Dec. 1977 - June 1980

TYPE OF   Researcher's project/ Dissertation
RESEARCH:

FUNDS: Internal sources

* * *

NO. 093   Social and Cultural Integration Exemplified by Germans
               and German-Chileans(German Immigration) in (Southern)
               Chile.

INSTITUTION: Universität Würzburg, Institut für Soziologie, Lehr-
               stuhl für Soziologie I (University of Würzburg, Insti-
               tute of Sociology, Chair of Sociology I)
               Wittelsbacherplatz 1
               D-8700 Würzburg
               Germany, Federal Republic

RESEARCHER: Schobert, Kurt

CONTACT: Schobert, Kurt
               Tel.No.: 0931/74821

DISCIPLINE   Linguistics (Sociolinguistics)
AND SUBFIELD: Sociology (Cultural Sociology)
               Social History

ABSTRACT: Survey of German national characteristics in Chile, of
               achievements, personal relations, genealogical trees,
               social and cultural integration, influence on politics,
               social welfare and the economy of the country.
               Intermediate results:
               Integration depends on support measures from Germany,
               language habits decisive for integration, German-
               Chilean institutions are declining in number.

GEOGR.AREA: Chile

PROCEDURE: Questionnaire (3,500 out of 30,000 German-Chileans);
               Document analysis (Several thousand archives Fam. Held/
               Family archives Mrs. Schmalz de Schwarzenberg).

LANGUAGE: German

DURATION: Apr. 1979 - Apr. 1981

TYPE OF   Dissertation
RESEARCH:

FUNDS: Internal sources

                           * * *

NO. 094   Chinese in The Netherlands.

INSTITUTION: Universiteit van Amsterdam, Antropologisch-Sociologisch
               Centrum (University of Amsterdam, Anthropological So-
               ciological Centre)
               Sarphatistraat 106 a
               NL-1018 GV Amsterdam
               The Netherlands
               Tel.No.: 020/5223826

RESEARCHER: Benton, Gregor

DISCIPLINE   Sociology (Ethnic Minorities)
AND SUBFIELD:

ABSTRACT: An investigation into the diverse origins of the Chi-
                 nese in The Netherlands. Relations with other Chinese
                 communities in Western Europe and with China. Changing
                 patterns of social life and occupational structure.
                 Effects of Dutch government policy.

GEOGR.AREA: The Netherlands

PROCEDURE: Personal interview;
                 Document analysis;
                 Photographs.

LANGUAGE: English

DURATION: 1979 - 1983

TYPE OF   Institution project/ Researcher's project
RESEARCH:

FUNDS: Internal sources

                              * * *

NO. 095   Inner City Programme: Urban Institutions Project.

INSTITUTION: University of Aston in Birmingham, St. Peter's College,
                 Social Science Research Council, Research Unit on Eth-
                 nic Relations)
                 College Road, Saltley
                 GB-Birmingham B8 3TE (West Midlands)
                 United Kingdom
                 Tel.No.: 021/3270194

RESEARCHER: Cross, Malcolm/ Johnson, Mark/ Parker

CONTACT: Cross, Malcolm
                 Research Unit on Ethnic Relations, St. Peter's College
                 College Road, Saltley
                 GB-Birmingham B8 3TE
                 United Kingdom
                 Tel.No.: 021/3270194

DISCIPLINE   Geography
AND SUBFIELD: Sociology

ABSTRACT: The project attempts to evaluate access to public goods,
                 notably services in the field of primary health care,
                 housing, employment, education and the law, among eth-
                 nic minorities and other residents of the inner urban
                 areas of the West Midlands. Consideration is given to
                 a range of local authority activities to examine the

workings of the "local state". A large-scale 'consumer-survey' is to be followed by interviews with urban 'gatekeepers' (senior officials of service - providing agencies). Attention is paid to location outside the immediate inner city area and to variation between cities as well as within them. Other sources of information (such as Government Surveys) will be used as appropriate. The needs of ethnic minorities are not assumed to be homogenous, and a prime aim of the research is to investigate cumulative disadvantage.

GEOGR.AREA: United Kingdom (Wards in Birmingham, Coventry, and Wolverhampton, West Midlands)

PROCEDURE: Personal interview (100 or more local authority officers etc.);
               Questionnaire (Interview Survey/8,000 screening survey-population of 5 wards/3,000 main interviews - subset of above -);
               Document analysis (Local authority documentation);
               Secondary data analysis (National dwelling and household survey/ other data sources available).

LANGUAGE: English

DURATION: Oct. 1979 - Oct. 1982

TYPE OF   Institution project/ Researcher's project
RESEARCH:

FUNDS: Internal sources

PUBLICATIONS: Conference Papers. Cross, M.; Johnson, M.R.D.: Migration Settlement and Inner City Policy - the British Case. European Science Foundation Conference on Immigrant Workers in Metropolitan Cities,1980.
               Johnson, M.R.D.; Cross, M.; Parker, R.: Ethnic Minorities and the Inner City Institute of British Geographers Annual Conference,1981.

* * *

NO. 096   Ethnic Villages in Inner Cities.

INSTITUTION: University of Aston in Birmingham, St. Peter's College, Social Science Research Council, Research Unit on Ethnic relations
               College Road, Saltley
               GB-Birmingham B8 3TE
               United Kingdom
               Tel.No.: 021/3270194

RESEARCHER: Klimiashvilly, Ramas

DISCIPLINE   Anthropology (Cultural), Ethnology
AND SUBFIELD: Demography (Minorities)
                    Psychology (Social)
                    Sociology (Social Structure)

ABSTRACT: Survey of 500 families who are originally from Mirpur
                    district in Pakistani part of Kashmir. A similar sur-
                    vey will be conducted in East Sparkbrook, where there
                    is an even heavier density of Pakistani population. The
                    survey will try to answer a wide range of questions
                    from social structure and demography, to culture and
                    social psychology of minorities.

GEOGR.AREA: United Kingdom (Saltley, Birmingham; Sparkbrook, Birm-
                    ingham)

PROCEDURE: Personal interview;
                    Questionnaire (500 families originating from Mirpur
                    district in Kashmir-Pakistani part);
                    Non-participant observation;
                    Secondary data analysis.

LANGUAGE: English

DURATION: May 1980 - Nov. 1984

TYPE OF   Institution project
RESEARCH:

FUNDS: Internal sources

                              * * *

NO. 097   Studying Interrelations between Ethnicity and Localism,
                    around the Theme of Work - Broadly Defined, Based on
                    London Survey.

INSTITUTION: University of Aston in Birmingham, St. Peter's College,
                    Social Science Research Council, Research Unit on Eth-
                    nic Relations
                    College Road, Saltley
                    GB-Birmingham B8 3TE
                    United Kingdom

RESEARCHER: Wallman, Sandra/ Buchanan, Ian/ Clark, David/ Goldman,
                    Andra/ Khan, Verity/ Kosmin, Barry/ Webster, Ray

CONTACT: Wallman, Sandra
                    London School of Economics
                    Houghton Street
                    GB-London WC2A 2AE
                    United Kingdom
                    Tel.No.: 01/4057686

DISCIPLINE   Anthropology (Social), Ethnology
AND SUBFIELD: Demography
                    Economics (History/ Labour)
                    Political Sciences
                    Psychology (Psycho-Therapy)
                    Sociology

ABSTRACT: Orientation: Ethnicity is 'about' organization of ex-
                    perience and the organization of society. Research in-
                    to ethnicity must therefore take into account both the
                    (re)cognition of difference and 'real' differences. The
                    Ethnicity Programme was designed on the basis of a par-
                    ticular relation between anthropology and economics. It
                    has considered ethnicity as one of a number of resources
                    which may be mobilized for particular purposes in parti-
                    cular situations; which will have no relevance in the
                    pursuit of other goals and/or in other situations; and
                    which will, in still others, be ignored or denied as a
                    liability.

                    Insofar as ethnicity is conceptualised as the sense of
                    'us' in contrast or in opposition to 'them', it happens
                    at the boundary of 'us', and is a function of the sense
                    of the perception of difference.

                    While some analytical attention has been paid to parti-
                    cular markers of ethnic boundary in Britain, too little
                    has been given to the flexibility of that boundary. The
                    programme has therefore been concerned with the indices
                    or criteria of 'us', with the changing boundaries of
                    'us' from one historical or social context to another;
                    and with the circumstances in which (any of) those
                    boundaries will be maintained or fostered.

                    The Programme focussed its researches on the old London
                    Borough of Battersea and, more narrowly, on a residen-
                    tial area of 500 households within it. The collective
                    volumes now in preparation reflect the interdiscipli-
                    nary cooperation involved, and will report in detail
                    the historical and situational contexts in which eth-
                    nicity 'counts' above other principles of organization
                    or identification in one inner city area.

GEOGR.AREA: United Kingdom (Battersea, South London)

PROCEDURE: Personal interview (12 out of 500);
                    Questionnaire (500 out of 500 households- one locality);
                    Participant observation;
                    Non-participant observation;
                    Document analysis;
                    Secondary data analysis.

LANGUAGE: English

DURATION: 1975 - 1981

TYPE OF   Institution project
RESEARCH:

FUNDS: Internal sources

PUBLICATIONS: Wallman, S. (Ed.): Ethnicity at Work, Macmillan, 1979.
Khan, V.S. (Ed.): Minority Families in Britain, Mac-
millan, 1979.
Wallman, S.; Dhooge, Y.; Goldman, A.; Kosmin, B.: Eth-
nography by Proxy: Strategies for Research in the Inner
City. Ethnos, Autumn 1980.
Kosmin, B. : Archer, J.R. (1863-1932): A Pan-Africanist
in the Battersea Labour Movement, New Community, 7, 3,
430-6.
Two volumes forthcoming (1981): Wallman, S. (Ed.):
Inner City Villages (probable title).
Wallman, S. (Ed.): Options and Expectations (probable
title).

* * *

IMPACT ON THE 'IMMIGRANT' SOCIETY

NO. 098   Foreigners in Mediterranean Rural Zones.

INSTITUTION: Centre Universitaire d'Avignon, Faculté des lettres
(Avignon University Centre, Department of Philosophy)
Boulevard Raspail
F-84000 Avignon
France
Tel.No.: 90/852850

RESEARCHER: Brun, Françoise/ Bouzat, Daniel/ Grava, Yves/ Grosso,
René/ Lees, Christiane/ Moulinas, René/ Risier, Jean

CONTACT: Brun, Françoise
Centre Universitaire d'Avignon
Faculté des Lettres
Boulevard Raspail
F-84000 Avignon
France
Tel.No.: 90/852850

DISCIPLINE   Anthropology, Ethnology
AND SUBFIELD: Demography
Economics
Education and Training
Geography

ABSTRACT: Aim: to know foreigners in rural zones as well as foreigners in urban zones
Hypothesis: foreigners play a major role in a changing
agricultural system; growing importance of inhabitants
of urban origin, part time or full time (holiday residents, leisure seekers, residents working in cities)
Approach: analysis of census and statistics, surveys
amongst foreigners and in the local communities (employers, leaders, simple inhabitants of the villages)
Content: study of the different groups of workers, of
their evolution in time. Typology of urban foreigners,
quantitative and/or qualitative assessment of their

impact upon the local community in relation to this community's economic and demographic dynamism.

GEOGR.AREA: France (Provence, Côte d'Azur, Languedoc, Corsica)

PROCEDURE: Personal interview;
                 Group discussion;
                 Participant observation;
                 Non-participant observation;
                 Document analysis.

LANGUAGE: French

TYPE OF   Institution project
RESEARCH:

FUNDS: Internal sources

PUBLICATIONS: Brun, F.: La campagne provençale, espace ludique privi-
                 légié, Mélanges Dussart, Liège 1980.

                              * * *

<u>NO. 099</u>   Deviance, Marginality and Social Control. Social Groups
                 <u>with Special Status: Immigrants and Nomads.</u>

INSTITUTION: Université de Paris II, Laboratoire de sociologie cri-
                 minelle (University of Paris II, Laboratory of Criminal
                 Sociology)
                 12, place du Panthéon
                 F-75231 Paris Cédex 05
                 France
                 Tel.No.: 1/3292140

RESEARCHER: Charlemagne, Jacqueline/ Costa-Lascoux, Jacqueline

CONTACT: Lapasse, Geneviève de
                 Laboratoire de sociologie criminelle
                 12, place du Panthéon
                 F-75231 Paris Cédex 05
                 France
                 Tel.No.: 1/3292140

DISCIPLINE   Anthropology, Ethnology
AND SUBFIELD: Law
                 Psychology(Psychopathology of Acculturation)
                 Sociology (Deviancy and Social Control)

ABSTRACT: Three approaches to the immigrant and nomad minority
                 and to the attitude of French authorities towards them:
                 1 - sociological approach of representations and atti-
                     tudes towards them,
                 2 - legal approach of their special status, especially
                     in its most recent evolution,
                 3 - study of discrimination experienced by immigrants
                     and nomads and analysis of the actions of local
                     authorities and associations towards them.

GEOGR.AREA: France (Région parisienne)

PROCEDURE: Personal interview (30 immigrants);
               Questionnaire (105 - public opinion survey - Paris,
               three districts -);
               Qualitative content analysis (105 - public opinion sur-
               vey - Paris, three districts -);
               Test (30 immigrants);
               Press analysis.

LANGUAGE: French

DURATION: Jan. 1981 - Dec. 1982

TYPE OF   Institution project
RESEARCH:

FUNDS: Internal sources

PUBLICATIONS: Costa-Lascoux, J.: Une législation pour une nouvelle
              politique de l'immigration, in: Pluriel, n° 22, 1980,
              26 p.
              Costa-Lascoux, J.: A propos des immigrés de la deuxi-
              ème génération, in: Droit de l'enfance, 1979/2.
              Costa-Lascoux, J.: Les oubliés de la politique fran-
              çaise de l'immigration: Les femmes et les enfants
              d'immigrés, in: Acte du colloque international Migra-
              tions internes et externes en Europe occidentale,
              Lille 16-17 octobre 1980, CNRS, 1981.
              Charlemagne, J.: Statut juridique du tsigane, in:
              Hommes et migration, Etudes, n° 124, 1978.
              Charlemagne, J.: L'accueil des tsiganes dans les com-
              munes, in: CAF, 1980, n° 6.

UNPUBLISHED   Charlemagne, J.: Une recherche de la CEE: populations,
PAPERS: nomades et pauvreté, in: Etudes tsiganes, n° 2, 1980,
               p. 7-15.

                            * * *

NO. 100   Change of Minorities and Religious Sensibilities in
               Alsace.

INSTITUTION: Université de Strasbourg II, Laboratoire de sociologie
               régionale (University of Strasbourg II, Laboratory of
               Regional Sociology)
               22, rue Descartes
               F-67000 Strasbourg
               France
               Tel.No.: 88/613939

RESEARCHER: Raphael, Freddy

DISCIPLINE   Sociology (Regional Sociology)
AND SUBFIELD:

ABSTRACT: 1 - Consequences of the erection of a mosque in a
                        suburb of Strasbourg: interview of city authori-
                        ties,of political and religious personalities and
                        of neighbours
                    2 - Acculturation of the Jews of M'zab (Algeria) refu-
                        gees in Alsace

GEOGR.AREA: France (Alsace, suburb of Strasbourg)

LANGUAGE: French

TYPE OF   Institution project
RESEARCH:

FUNDS: Internal sources

PUBLICATIONS: Raphael, Freddy: Nostalgie de la fête chez les juifs du
                    M'zab réfugiés en Alsace, in: Revue des sciences so-
                    ciales en France de l'est, n° 8, 1979, pp. 166-184.
                    Raphael, Freddy: Les juifs du M'zab de l'est de la
                    France, in: Les relations entre juifs et musulmans en
                    Afrique du Nord, CNRS, Paris 1980, pp. 197-224.

                              * * *

NO. 101   Racism and Discrimination in French Cities.

INSTITUTION: Université de Toulouse le Mirail - Toulouse II, Centre
                    de recherches sociologiques (University of Toulouse II,
                    Sociological Research Centre)
                    109 bis, rue Vauquelin
                    F-31058 Toulouse Cédex
                    France
                    Tel.No.: 61/411105

                    Centre interdisciplinaire de recherches et d'études
                    juives (Interdisciplinary Centre of Jewish Research and
                    Studies)
                    109 bis, rue Vauquelin
                    F-31058 Toulouse Cédex
                    France

RESEARCHER: Ledrut, Raymond/ Benayoun, Chantal/ Saint Raymond,
                    Odile

CONTACT: Saint Raymond, Odile
                    Tel.No.: 61/411105 (ext. 391)

DISCIPLINE   Sociology (Urban Sociology)
AND SUBFIELD:

ABSTRACT: Analysis of the physical and symbolic decline of an an-
                    cient district inhabited by North-African immigrants.
                    Analysis of the social conditions of the perception of
                    urban space and, further, of the structure, mechanism

and components of racist thinking in itself. This study
is conducted in comparison with that of the formation
(real or imaginary) of a Jewish space within the city.

GEOGR.AREA: France (Toulouse districts)

PROCEDURE: Personal interview (10);
               Participant observation;
               Non-participant observation;
               Document analysis (Press analysis - 6 daily papers,
               6 weekly papers -);
               Qualitative content analysis;
               Experiment.

LANGUAGE: French

DURATION: Nov. 1977 - Dec. 1981

TYPE OF   Commissioned research/ Institution project
RESEARCH:

FUNDS: External sources: Commissioned research with environ-
               mental ministry

UNPUBLISHED   Saint Raymond, O.; Merghoub, A.: Rapport de Travail,
PAPERS: 1977-1978-1979, Centre de recherches sociologiques,
               Université de Toulouse, 35 et 26 p.

                         *   *   *

NO. 102   Political Effects of German Immigration to Southe..
               Brazil. The Population of German Origin and Fascist
               Tendencies in the Thirties.
               ───

INSTITUTION: Freie Universität Berlin, Fachbereich 15, Politische
               Wissenschaft (Free University Berlin, Department of
               Political Science)
               Kiebitzweg 7
               D-1000 Berlin 33
               Germany, Federal Republic

RESEARCHER: Gertz, Rene Ernaini

DISCIPLINE   Political Sciences
AND SUBFIELD: Political History
               Social History

GEOGR.AREA: Brazil (Southern part)

LANGUAGE: German

DURATION: July 1980 (end)

TYPE OF   Dissertation
RESEARCH:

FUNDS: Internal sources

* * *

NO. 103   Education and Intergroup Attitudes.

INSTITUTION: Universität Bochum, Psychologisches Institut, Arbeits-
                  einheit Sozialpsychologie (University of Bochum, Psy-
                  chological Institute)
                  Postfach 102148
                  D-4630 Bochum
                  Germany, Federal Republic

RESEARCHER: Schönbach, Peter/ Gollwitzer, Peter/ Stiepel, Gerd/
                  Wagner, Ulrich

CONTACT: Wagner, Ulrich
                  Tel.No.: 7004602

DISCIPLINE   Education and Training
AND SUBFIELD: Psychology (Social Psychology)

ABSTRACT: Connection between level of education and prejudices
                  against foreign workers (Italians, Turks). Importance
                  of cognitive factors (association flexibility, picto-
                  rial character of associations) as mediators of reject-
                  ing attitudes. Complementary and competing factors of
                  explanation.

GEOGR.AREA: Germany, Federal Republic

PROCEDURE: Questionnaire (305 pupils - at the age of about 15 -)

LANGUAGE: German

DURATION: Jan. 1975 (start)

TYPE OF   Researcher's project
RESEARCH:

FUNDS: Internal sources

PUBLICATIONS: Education and Intergroup Attitudes, Vol. 22 of the ser-
                  ies "European Monographs in Social Psychology" (Ed.
                  H. Tajfel). New York and London, Academic Press,
                  planned for 1981.

* * *

NO. 104   EC - Expansion and the Problem of Labour Migration.

INSTITUTION: Wissenschaftliche Kommission des Katholischen Arbeits-
                kreises für Entwicklung und Frieden (Scientific Commis-
                sion of the Catholic Working Group for Development and
                Peace)
                Kaiserstrasse 163
                D-5300 Bonn 1
                Germany, Federal Republic

RESEARCHER: Just, Wolf-Dieter

CONTACT: Risse, Heinz Theo
                Tel.No.: 0228/103216

DISCIPLINE   Demography
AND SUBFIELD: Political Sciences (European Policy/ International So-
                cial Policy)
                Sociology

ABSTRACT: Analysis of the economic differences between the Euro-
                pean North and South;
                Prediction of the expected migratory flows;
                Solution of the integration problems arising upon free
                movement of labour.

GEOGR.AREA: Europe (especially Southern Europe)

LANGUAGE: German

DURATION: Nov. 1980 - Dec. 1981

TYPE OF   Institution project
RESEARCH:

FUNDS: Internal sources

                          * * *

NO. 105   Attitudes and Manners of Behavior of German Pupils to-
                 wards Foreign Children and Adolescents. The Effects of
                 Two School Television Broadcasts on Prejudices, Aggres-
                 sions, and Presocial Attitudes.

INSTITUTION: Universität zu Köln, Erziehungswissenschaftliche Fakul-
                tät, Seminar für Psychologie (University of Cologne,
                School of Educational Sciences, Department of Psycholo-
                gy)
                Gronewaldstrasse 2
                D-5000 Köln 41
                Germany, Federal Republic

RESEARCHER: Six, Ulrike

CONTACT: Six, Ulrike
                Tel.No.: 0221/4002380

DISCIPLINE   Education and Training (Teaching Aid)
AND SUBFIELD: Psychology (Social Psychology/ Applied Psychology)

ABSTRACT: 1. Identification of presocial attitudes, prejudices,
                  and aggressive manners of behavior of German pupils to-
                  wards foreign children and adolescents.
                  2. Content analysis and critical evaluation of two
                  school television films.
                  3. Impact study of the effectiveness of those broad-
                  casts on various samples of pupils regarding the above
                  mentioned variables.
                  4. Development of theoretically and empirically corrob-
                  orated guiding principles for the production of new
                  television broadcasts that aim at improving the rela-
                  tionships between German and foreign children and ado-
                  lescents.

GEOGR.AREA: Germany, Federal Republic (North-Rhine Westphalia, area
                  of Cologne)

PROCEDURE: Questionnaire (500 pupils of secondary level I - Sekun-
                  darstufe I -);
                  Non-participant observation (200 pupils of secondary
                  level I - Sekundarstufe I -);
                  Qualitative content analysis (2 school television films
                  which try to reduce the prejudices against foreign
                  children);
                  Quantitative content analysis (2 school television
                  films which try to reduce the prejudices against for-
                  eign children);
                  Experiment (400 pupils of secondary level I - Sekundar-
                  stufe I -);
                  Test.

LANGUAGE: German

DURATION: Jan. 1980 - Dec. 1981

TYPE OF   Researcher's project
RESEARCH:

FUNDS: Internal sources

PUBLICATIONS: Bergler, R.; Six, U.: Psychologie des Fernsehens, Wir-
                  kungsmodelle und Wirkungseffekte unter besonderer Be-
                  rücksichtigung der Wirkungen auf Kinder und Jugend-
                  liche.

* * *

NO. 106   The Effect of Immigration on Social Structures. Part:
                 Federal Republic of Germany.

INSTITUTION: Institut für Arbeitsmarkt- und Berufsforschung der
                 Bundesanstalt für Arbeit (Institute of Employment Re-
                 search)
                 Regensburger Strasse 104
                 D-8500 Nürnberg
                 Germany, Federal Republic
                 Tel.No.: 0911/173091

RESEARCHER: Hoenekopp, Elmar/ Ullmann, Hans

DISCIPLINE   Sociology
AND SUBFIELD: Labour Market

ABSTRACT: The UNESCO project 'The Effect of Immigration on So-
                 cial Structures' deals with present developments of
                 the problems concerning foreigners. This report which
                 presents the German part of the project does not in-
                 tend to compete with the hitherto immense literature
                 concerning the research on foreigners but tries to
                 show in a brief outline, the state of the political
                 discussion, the present legal situation, the develop-
                 ments regarding the employment of foreigners, and
                 their possibilities for participation in social
                 life. This shall be done as topically and as compre-
                 hensively as possible. Therefore, for the most part,
                 only the more recent literature was referred to.

GEOGR.AREA: Germany, Federal Republic

LANGUAGE: German

DURATION: Nov. 1978 - Apr. 1979

TYPE OF   Sponsored research
RESEARCH:

PUBLICATIONS: Hoenekopp, E.; Ullmann, H.: The Effect of Immigration
                 on Social Structures, Part: Federal Republic of Ger-
                 many, type-written, Nürnberg, 5/1980 (privately print-
                 ed, will be published early in 1981).

                            * * *

NO. 107   The Role of German Emigrants in England (1933-45).

INSTITUTION: Universität Würzburg, Institut für Soziologie, Lehr-
                 stuhl für Soziologie I (University of Würzburg, Insti-
                 tute of Sociology, Chair of Sociology I)
                 Wittelsbacherplatz 1
                 D-8700 Würzburg
                 Germany, Federal Republic

RESEARCHER: Schuhladen, Franz

CONTACT: Schuhladen, Franz
                  Tel.No.: 0931/74821

DISCIPLINE   Sociology
AND SUBFIELD: Social History

ABSTRACT: To characterize the role played by German emigrants in
                  England. The study will cover various professional
                  groups and social strata and take into account the pro-
                  cess of interdependence between the emigrants' activi-
                  ties and the reaction of the English.

GEOGR.AREA: United Kingdom (England)

PROCEDURE: Personal interview;
                  Document analysis;
                  Qualitative content analysis.

LANGUAGE: German

DURATION: Oct. 1978 - Apr. 1981

TYPE OF   Researcher's project/ Dissertation
RESEARCH:

FUNDS: Internal sources

                              * * *

NO. 108   Cultural Minorities.
───

INSTITUTION: Gemeente Deventer, Sociografisch Bureau (Municipal Ad-
                  ministration of Deventer, Sociographical Office)
                  Stadhuis
                  NL-Deventer (Overijssel)
                  The Netherlands
                  Tel.No.: 05700/72121

RESEARCHER: Roelands, R.A.W.

DISCIPLINE   Sociology (Minorities)
AND SUBFIELD:

ABSTRACT: Desk research on how to manage ethnic problems in a more
                  adequate way.

GEOGR.AREA: The Netherlands (Town of Deventer)

PROCEDURE: Personal interview;
                  Group discussion;
                  Document analysis;
                  Secondary data analysis.

LANGUAGE: Dutch

DURATION: 1980

TYPE OF   Institution project
RESEARCH:

FUNDS: Internal sources

                        * * *

NO. 109   Research into the Relationship between the Police and
               Ethnic Minorities in The Netherlands.

INSTITUTION: Rijksuniversiteit Leiden, Centrum voor Onderzoek van
               Maatschappelijke Tegenstellingen (University of Leyden,
               Centre for the Study of Social Conflicts)
               Hooigracht 15
               NL-2312 KM Leiden (Zuid-Holland)
               The Netherlands
               Tel.No.: 071/148333 (ext. 6380)

RESEARCHER: Aalberts, M./ Kamminga, E./ Moll, H.

CONTACT: Aalberts, M.
               Hooigracht 15
               NL-2312 KM Leiden
               The Netherlands
               Tel.No.: 071/148333 (ext. 6380)

DISCIPLINE   Anthropology, Ethnology
AND SUBFIELD: Law (Criminology)
               Sociology

GEOGR.AREA: The Netherlands

PROCEDURE: Personal interview;
               Non-participant observation;
               Document analysis.

LANGUAGE: Dutch

DURATION: June 1980 - Dec. 1981

TYPE OF   Commissioned research
RESEARCH:

FUNDS: External sources: Government

PUBLICATIONS: Aalberts, M.; Kamminga, E.; Moll, H.: Verslag voor-
               onderzoek politie-etnische minderheden. (Report on pre-
               liminary research police-ethnic minorities).

                        * * *

NO. 110   'Pakkis and Desos'. The Norwegians' Attitudes towards
               Guest Workers Expressed in Oral Tradition.

INSTITUTION: University of Bergen, Department of Folkloristics and
               Regional Ethnology
               N-5014 Bergen
               Norway

RESEARCHER: Espeland, W.J.

DISCIPLINE   Anthropology, Ethnology
AND SUBFIELD:

ABSTRACT: The aim of the project is to reveal the attitudes to-
               wards the guestworkers expressed in genres such as
               jokes, rumours, and stories about personal experiences.
               The first part of the project consists of a theoretical
               discussion concerning possibilities and limitations by
               investigating such a problem. The second part is an
               analysis of oral tradition combined with a sociological
               attitude measurement.

GEOGR.AREA: Norway

LANGUAGE: Norwegian

DURATION: Aug. 1978 - 1982

FUNDS: External sources: Norwegian Research Council for Sci-
               ence and the Humanities

PUBLICATIONS: Espeland, W.J.(1980): Nokre tankar om grunnleggjande
               forskningsteoretiske problem i folkloristikk og etnolo-
               gi. Rapport frâ seminaret om humaniora-utgreiinga,
               Ustaoget, 1978.
               Espeland, W.J.: Om rasediskriminering i Norge, Univer-
               sitetsforlagets Vitenskapelige Pressetjeneste, UVP-
               kronikk, 1980, Thesis.

                              * * *

NO. 111   An Assessment of the Experiences of both Police and the
               Victims of Crime in Ethnic Minority Areas.

INSTITUTION: Home Office, Research Unit
               Waterloo Bridge House, Waterloo Road
               GB-London SE1 8UA
               United Kingdom
               Tel.No.: 01/2753243

RESEARCHER: Tuck, Mary

CONTACT: Tuck, Mary
                  Home Office
                  50 Queen Anne's Gate
                  GB-London SW1
                  United Kingdom
                  Tel.No.: 01/2133000

DISCIPLINE   Criminology
AND SUBFIELD:

ABSTRACT: The study analyses if there are differences in the ex-
                  periences of crime on victims, and of the police, be-
                  tween a 'black' and a 'white' population in a specific
                  inner-city area.

GEOGR.AREA: United Kingdom (part of inner Manchester)

PROCEDURE: Personal interview (Small sample of West Indians in
                  area/ 4000 for screening/ 800 full questionnaire);
                  Group discussion;
                  Expert interview (Small sample of police in area);
                  Secondary data analysis (Police statistics).

LANGUAGE: English

DURATION: 1980 - 1981

TYPE OF   Institution project
RESEARCH:

                              * * *

NO. 112   Spatial and Social Mobility of Foreign Immigrants in
                  Marseille, 1962-1975; Examination of Changing Social
                  Class Structure with Ethnic Segregation.

INSTITUTION: University of Oxford, School of Geography
                  Mansfield Road
                  GB-Oxford OX1 3TB
                  United Kingdom

RESEARCHER: Jones, A.

DISCIPLINE   Geography (Social)
AND SUBFIELD:

GEOGR.AREA: France (Marseille)

LANGUAGE: English

DURATION: 1975 - Mar. 1981

TYPE OF   Academic degree
RESEARCH:

FUNDS: External sources: Social Science Research Council

                              * * *

REPATRIATION

NO. 113   Migration and Repatriation.
_____

INSTITUTION: Ethnicon Kentron Koinonikon Erevnon - EKKE (National
                Centre of Social Research)
                1 Sofocleous
                GR-Athens
                Greece

RESEARCHER: Filias, B./ Kassimati, K./ Manganara, I./ Mousourov, L./
                Nikolinakos, M./ Paguguas, P.

DISCIPLINE   Sociology
AND SUBFIELD:

ABSTRACT: The project focuses on two main aspects; first on the
                level of the intentions, incentives, conditions and
                causes of repatriation of Greek emigrants mainly in
                Western Germany; secondly on the level of the effects
                the return of migrants has on themselves and their fam-
                ilies and on the social and economic surroundings in
                the community in which they settle upon their return.
                The research project has been designed at three levels:
                1st level: Effects of repatriation on migrants, their
                families,as well as on their social and economic envi-
                ronment in rural areas, 2nd level: Effects of repatri-
                ation on semi-urban areas, 3rd level: Research among
                Greek migrants in W.Germany on the motives, conditions,
                and causes of intentions for their repatriation.

GEOGR.AREA: Greece/ Germany, Federal Republic

DURATION: June 1981 - Dec. 1984

TYPE OF   Sponsored research
RESEARCH:

FUNDS: External sources: Stiftung Volkswagenwerk, Hannover,
               Germany, Federal Republic

                              * * *

NO. 114   Turkish Returned Migrant Workers' Re-Integration into
               Home Society and How Their Experiences in the Host So-
               ciety Affected Them after Return Home.

INSTITUTION: University of Surrey, Department of Sociology
               GB-Guildford, Surrey
               United Kingdom

RESEARCHER: Tatlidil, Ercan

DISCIPLINE   Sociology
AND SUBFIELD:

ABSTRACT: In this study the data has been chiefly collected in
               the city of Kayseri in Turkey. Migrant workers who had
               remained abroad for an average of seven years had ex-
               perience of living and working in immigrant countries.
               It proposed to: 1) - find out who these migrants were
               (looking into their background prior to departure);
               2 - How did they spend their living and working time
               abroad? (working and living surroundings, adjustment-
               or-integration into host society); 3 - Has their re-
               integration into their home society been influenced by
               their experiences abroad? (in particular has there been
               any change in the family structure, housing condition,
               working situation, approach to education, etc.).
               Preliminary results: It was found that migrant workers
               in this sample, particularly workers from rural areas
               had preferred to live amongst their ethnic community in
               the host society which caused the lack of adaption or
               integration into the host society. Their tendency to
               ammass savings in short periods abroad has meant long
               hours in the work environment for them and, therefore,
               reduced their contact with the indigenous population.

GEOGR.AREA: Turkey (City of Kayseri)/ The Netherlands

PROCEDURE: Personal interview (132 ex-migrant workers);
               Group discussion (22 ex-migrant and migrant workers);
               Expert interview (6);
               Non-participant observation (76);
               Document analysis;
               Qualitative content analysis;
               Quantitative content analysis.

LANGUAGE: English

DURATION: Oct. 1977 - Oct. 1981

TYPE OF   Ph.D.
RESEARCH:

FUNDS: External sources: Turkish Government, Ministry of Edu-
                 cation

* * *

Migrant Workers: Social Integration Measures

Public Measures

PUBLIC MEASURES: SOCIAL WORK

No. 115   Integration Aids for Children and Adolescents from
                      Foreign Workers' Families. Testing New Ways of Youth
                      Work.

INSTITUTION: Institut für Sozialarbeit und Sozialpädagogik, Projekt-
                      gruppe Bonn (Institute for Social Work and Social Edu-
                      cation - ISS)
                      Weberstrasse 33
                      D-5300 Bonn 1
                      Germany, Federal Republic

RESEARCHER: Stüwe, Gerd

CONTACT: Stüwe, Gerd
                      Tel.No.: 0228/534200-205

DISCIPLINE   Education and Training (Social Pedagogics)
AND SUBFIELD: Sociology

ABSTRACT: At present the individual measures are fragmented in-
                      stead of being coordinated in the best way, especial-
                      ly in the following four areas: 1. socio-pedagogical
                      education, meeting and support activities (centres,
                      meeting places, studies and playrooms), 2. facilities
                      for preparing vocational training, 3. counseling serv-
                      ices, 4. promotion of contacts with young Germans in
                      order to achieve conscious binationality - to which ex-
                      tent are identity and integration interrelated?

GEOGR. AREA: Germany, Federal Republic (Cologne, Duisburg, Hanover,
                      Stuttgart)

PROCEDURE: Personal interview (40-60 visitors of the institution,
                      people concerned and respective peer groups);
                      Group discussion (respective peer groups);
                      Questionnaire (all colleagues of the pilot project);
                      Participant observation;
                      Non-participant observation.

LANGUAGE: German

DURATION: Dec. 1975 - Dec. 1979

TYPE OF   Sponsored research/ Commissioned research
RESEARCH:

FUNDS: External sources: Bundesminister für Jugend, Familie
                 und Gesundheit, Bonn

PUBLICATIONS: Stüwe, G.; Lutter, W.; Vink, J.: Sozialpädagogische und
                 bildungspolitische Massnahmen für die zweite Ausländer-
                 generation - Bestandsaufnahme und Ausblick, in: Neue
                 Praxis, Heft 3/78, S. 247-249.
                 Stüwe, G.: Schon immer wollte ich in das Zuckerland,
                 in: Informationsdienst zur Ausländerarbeit, 1/79.

UNPUBLISHED   Stüwe, G.; Lutter, W.: Integrationshilfen für Kinder
PAPERS: und Jugendliche aus Familien ausländischer Arbeitneh-
                 mer; 1. Zwischenbericht; 2. modifizierte Fassung, ISS
                 Bonn 1977; 2. Zwischenbericht, ISS Bonn 1978; 3. Zwi-
                 schenbericht, ISS Bonn 1979.
                 Peters, F.; Stüwe, G.: Interaktionstheoretisches Ver-
                 fahren - eine Vermittlung von Theorie und Praxis in der
                 Jugendforschung. Klagenfurt 1979 (erscheint demnächst in
                 einem Reader).

                                    * * *

NO. 116   Second Phase of the Pilot Project 'Integration Aids for
                 Children and Adolescents from Foreign Workers' Fam-
                 ilies'.

INSTITUTION: Institut für Sozialarbeit und Sozialpädagogik, Projekt-
                 gruppe Bonn (Institute for Social Work and Social Edu-
                 cation - ISS)
                 Weberstrasse 33
                 D-5300 Bonn 1
                 Germany, Federal Republic

RESEARCHER: Schneider Wohlfahrt, Ursula/ Stüwe, Gerd

CONTACT: Stüwe, Gerd
                 Tel.No.: 0228/534200-205

DISCIPLINE   Education and Training (Social Pedagogics)
AND SUBFIELD:

ABSTRACT: Promotion of self-organized parents' groups for child-
                 ren and youth work in their respective town districts;
                 activation of open youth work in ambulatory and station-
                 ary measures taking into account the importance of peer-
                 groups and the communication between young Germans and
                 foreigners; direct influence is exerted on the social
                 infrastructure of the community in order to improve the
                 living and developmental conditions especially for

young foreigners; this is done e.g. by cooperation with the relevant bodies and by activating the public relations work in the municipal field; socio-pedagogically effective activities which correspond to an occupation orientated youth work and which guide young foreigners into the world of occupation and work. Practical projects in districts with a significant percentage of foreigners. These projects are directed especially at young foreigners who are endangered to become or who are already delinquent, at foreign girls, and at young foreigners without work.

GEOGR.AREA: Germany, Federal Republic

PROCEDURE: Personal interview;
                Participant observation;
                Non-participant observation.

LANGUAGE: German

DURATION: Jan. 1979 - Dec. 1982

TYPE OF   Sponsored research/ Commissioned research
RESEARCH:

FUNDS: External sources: Bundesminister für Jugend, Familie
                und Gesundheit, Bonn

PUBLICATIONS: Planned

UNPUBLISHED   Stüwe, G.: Konzept für eine wissenschaftliche Beglei-
PAPERS: tung, 2. Modellphase 'Integrationshilfen für Kinder und
                Jugendliche aus Familien ausländischer Arbeitnehmer'.
                ISS Bonn 1979.
                Stüwe, G.: Überlegungen zu einem Nachfolge-Projekt (In-
                tegrationshilfen für Kinder und Jugendliche aus Fami-
                lien ausländischer Arbeitnehmer). ISS Bonn 1979.

                        * * *

NO. 117   Reconstruction of the Life-World of Young Foreigners in
                Order to Construct a Qualitative Measures-Catalogue.

INSTITUTION: Institut für Sozialarbeit und Sozialpädagogik, Projekt-
                gruppe Bonn (Institute for Social Work and Social Edu-
                cation - ISS)
                Weberstrasse 33
                D-5300 Bonn 1
                Germany, Federal Republic

RESEARCHER: Stüwe, Gerd

CONTACT: Stüwe, Gerd
                Tel.No.: 0228/534200-205

DISCIPLINE   Education and Training (Social Pedagogics)
AND SUBFIELD: Sociology (Sociology of Knowledge)

ABSTRACT: This study proceeds from the stock of knowledge which
                is part of the world of everyday life of young for-
                eigners. The analysis has to pay particular attention
                to the following aspects: effects of the legal situa-
                tion on the conditions of life; effects of the family
                situation (cultural break/structural socialization con-
                flicts) on the conditions of life; effects of the edu-
                cational situation on their life; effects of the ghetto
                situation (living conditions/isolation/communication
                structure) on the conditions of life; inclusion of for-
                eign adolescents into the programmes of youth welfare
                (initiatives/independent welfare institutions/communi-
                ty); relationships between German and foreign adoles-
                cents (interaction structure/competitive behavior/pre-
                judices, etc.); action competence of foreign adoles-
                cents (orientation knowledge/degree of adaptation/in-
                teraction competence). The reconstruction of the life-
                world of foreign adolescents - viz.: how do they live
                under oppressing objective conditions, how do they think
                and act, what are their demands? - aims at establishing
                a qualitative measures-catalogue.

GEOGR.AREA: Germany, Federal Republic (Berlin-Kreuzberg)

PROCEDURE: Personal interview (10-12 interviews with
                foreign adolescents);
                Group discussion (Peer groups in the district);
                Expert interview (Opinion leaders and experts in the
                district);
                Participant observation (All social institutions and
                independent groups of the district that work with for-
                eign adolescents);
                Document analysis (Documents of the working groups and
                of the media relating to foreign adolescents in the
                district);
                Secondary data analysis (It is planned to correlate the
                available data with the qualitative measures-catalogue
                that has to be developed).

LANGUAGE: German

DURATION: Jan. 1980 - Dec. 1980

TYPE OF   Commissioned research
RESEARCH:

FUNDS: External sources: Der Senator für Familie, Jugend und
                Sport, Berlin

PUBLICATIONS: Planned

* * *

NO. 118   Extracurricular Urban Activities to Integrate Children
                     of Migrant Workers Socially and Emotionally.

INSTITUTION: Universität Bonn, Seminar für Allgemeine Pädagogik
                     (University of Bonn, Institute of General Education)
                     Römerstrasse 164
                     D-5300 Bonn 1
                     Germany, Federal Republic

RESEARCHER: Sayler, Wilhelmine/ Droste, Reinhard/ Metz, Rolf-
                     Dieter/ Moritz-Gerkens,Hiltrud/ Thomas, Christine

CONTACT: Droste, Reinhard
                     0228/550275

DISCIPLINE   Education and Training (Social Pedagogics)
AND SUBFIELD:

ABSTRACT: 1. To initiate, to support and to provide scientific
                     guidance to foster child programmes for German and
                     foreign children as well as for binational children
                     and foster parents. 2. To improve awareness of prob-
                     lems, difficulties and lack of information on the
                     part of the children and parents concerned. 3. To im-
                     prove insight into causes of conflict and tendencies
                     to avoid them. 4. To learn how to handle conflicts
                     between German and foreign children and their parents
                     and to find adequate means for overcoming them. 5. To
                     achieve overall competence and improve the social and
                     emotional integration of foreign children. 6. To de-
                     velop and test toys and learning aids as well as me-
                     thodical concepts for working with German and foreign
                     children and their parents.

GEOGR.AREA: Germany, Federal Republic (Bonn)

PROCEDURE: Experiment: Field Experiment

LANGUAGE: German

DURATION: Nov. 1980 - Nov. 1983

TYPE OF   Sponsored research
RESEARCH:

FUNDS: External sources: Deutsche Gesellschaft für Friedens-
                     und Konfliktforschung, Bonn

* * *

NO. 119   Integration of Foreign Workers.

INSTITUTION: Diakonhjemmet School of Social Work, Research Depart-
               ment
               Borgenvein 3 c
               N-Oslo 3
               Norway

RESEARCHER: Bø, B. P./ Kaasa, A.

DISCIPLINE   Sociology
AND SUBFIELD:

ABSTRACT: Topics of the project: Problems and conflicts in the
               relations between foreign workers and Norwegians in
               Oslo; the kind of conflicts, and their reasons. Re-
               sources and methods for social work facing these con-
               flicts. Social policy and integration of foreign wor-
               kers. Methods: Interviews, observation, community work.
               Mainly Pakistani immigrants are studied.

GEOGR.AREA: Norway (Oslo)

PROCEDURE: Personal interview;
               Non-participant observation;
               Community work.

DURATION: July 1980 - July 1982

FUNDS: External sources: Norwegian Research Council for Sci-
               ence and the Humanities

                              * * *

PUBLIC MEASURES: EDUCATION

NO. 120   Acculturation or Double Culture: Sociological Study on
               the Special Situation of Moslem Children in Belgium.

INSTITUTION: Centre pour l'étude des problèmes du Monde Musulman
               Contemporain (Centre of Islamic Sociology)
               44, avenue Jeanne
               B-1050 Bruxelles
               Belgium
               Tel.No.: 6488158 (ext. 3359)

RESEARCHER: Anciaux, Robert/ Dero, Anne-Claude/ Destree, Annette/
               Gilissen, Jacqueline

CONTACT: Gilissen, Jacquline
               Centre de Sociologie de l'Islam
               44, avenue Jeanne
               B-1050 Bruxelles
               Belgium
               Tel.No.: 6488158 (ext. 3359-335)

DISCIPLINE   Demography
AND SUBFIELD: Education and Training
               Sociology

ABSTRACT: Efforts to ameliorate the situation of Moslem children
               and to help them to adapt themselves to the Belgian
               educational system have been numerous but not coordi-
               nated. It seems obvious to us that nothing but coope-
               ration and comparison of facts and experiences will
               achieve results in this field.
               Our aim is to evaluate most intensely research, stud-
               ies, experiences and projects made in the field of
               educating migrant children, especially Moslem child-
               ren, in Belgium and other relevant European countries.

               It will be fruitful to analyse the given differences
               following a strict methodology - this might result in
               pragmatic proposals; the following three objectives

133

should be taken into account:
1. To allow the Moslem child to integrate sucessfully into the Belgian school system and avoid segregation.
2. To avoid that underestimation of their own culture leads to their neglecting it.
3. To enable the Moslem child to reintegrate into the school and social system of the native country.

GEOGR.AREA: Belgium (Moslem communities)

PROCEDURE: Personal interview;
               Group discussion;
               Expert interview;
               Document analysis;
               Qualitative content analysis;
               Quantitative content analysis

LANGUAGE: French

DURATION: Jan. 1981 - Dec. 1983

TYPE OF   Researcher's project
RESEARCH:

FUNDS: External sources: FRFC

                         * * *

NO. 121   Action Research Project: Information and Training of
               Teachers Instructing the Children of Migrant Workers.

INSTITUTION: Université Catholique de Louvain, Centre de Recherches
               Sociologiques (Catholic University of Louvain, Socio-
               logical Research Centre)
               1, Place Montesquieu
               B-1348 Louvain-la-Neuve
               Belgium
               Tel.No.: 010/418181 (ext. 4190, 4191)

RESEARCHER: Marques Balsa, Casimiro

DISCIPLINE   Anthropology, Ethnology
AND SUBFIELD: Education and Training
               Linguistics
               Sociology

ABSTRACT: - To investigate into the educational needs
               - To study the factors influencing school achievements
               - To develop pedagogical strategies for multicultural
                 environments and situations
               - To analyse the institution 'school' sociologically
               - To develop curricula for information and further
                 education of teachers

GEOGR.AREA: Belgium (Brussels and Liege)

PROCEDURE: Personal interview (50 members of a training group);
               Group discussion (15 groups);
               Questionnaire (150 teachers receiving training);
               Participant observation (Class);
               Qualitative content analysis (Individual interviews);
               Secondary data analysis (Ministry/ School population).

LANGUAGE: French

DURATION: Sept. 1978 - Dec. 1981

TYPE OF   Sponsored research/ Institution project
RESEARCH:

FUNDS: External sources: CEE / Ministère de l'Education Natio-
               nale et de la Culture Française

PUBLICATIONS: Les Besoins et les aspirations des familles étrangères
               établies en Belgique, 2 vols. 20/A et 20/B, Programma-
               tion de la Politique scientifique 1978.
               L'action éducative dans un environnement multiculturel
               CSRE, Louvain la Neuve 1979, pp. 14-43.
               Marques Balsa, C. (ed.): Programme de recherche action
               consacré à l'information et à la formation d'en-
               seignants accueillant des enfants étrangers.
               Doc. d'information 1/B (Avril 1980), Doc. d'information
               2/B (Mai 1980).
               Situation scolaire des enfants de travailleurs étran-
               gers, in: Recherches Sociologiques 1/2, 1979, L.L.N.,
               pp. 271-303.
               Les échecs scolaires des enfants étrangers: "une fata-
               lité?", in: Bulletin du CCCE - Liège, Nos. Juillet et
               Octobre 1980.
               Les rapports intrafamiliaux dans le cas des familles
               migrantes: l'exemple des réseaux linguistiques, in: Re-
               vue d'Action Sociale, n° 3-4, 1980, pp. 103-113.

                            * * *

NO. 122   Project Education and Culture for Immigrants (PECI).

INSTITUTION: Danish Council for Adult Education
               Løngangstraede 37 II
               DK-1468 København K
               Denmark

RESEARCHER: Andersen, Ole Stig

DISCIPLINE   Education and Training (Social Pedagogics/ Adult Educa-
AND SUBFIELD: tion)
               Psychology (Social Psychology)
               Sociology (Cultural Sociology)

ABSTRACT: During the 1960s and 1970s Denmark received a
                considerable number of immigrants from cultures quite
                different from that of Denmark. Educational and cultur-
                al activities involving immigrants take place by use of
                already existing frameworks and regulations.

                It is supposed that this situation has several short-
                comings. The purpose of the project is to collect and
                process information - quantitative as well as qualita-
                tive - on the educational and cultural institutions
                and activities concerning immigrants.

                The final report from the project will present the col-
                lected information and the findings in a format suit-
                able as a background for central and local decisions
                and initiatives within the subject in question.

GEOGR.AREA: Denmark

DURATION: Apr. 1980 - Dec. 1981

FUNDS: External sources: The Ministry of Education

                              * * *

NO. 123   Effects Caused by Intercultural School Experience
                on Sociability and Social Insertion of Migrants in a
                City District.

INSTITUTION: Groupe lyonnais de sociologie industrielle (Lyon Group
                for Industrial Sociology)
                14, rue Antoine Dumont
                F-69372 Lyon Cêdex 2
                France
                Tel.No.: 7/863223

RESEARCHER: Brachet, Olivier/ Saglio, Jean

CONTACT: Saglio, Jean
                GLYSI
                14, rue A. Dumont
                F-69372 Lyon Cêdex 2
                France
                Tel.No.: 7/863223

DISCIPLINE   Sociology (Urban Sociology/ Educational Sociology)
AND SUBFIELD:

ABSTRACT: Social insertion of migrant workers' families is modi-
                fied because of the changes that occur in the attitude
                of the school system towards migrant children.
                An analysis of those changes will be conducted by means
                of interviews and study of the local sociability sys-
                tems in the district studied.

GEOGR.AREA: France (Saint-Priest - workers' town in Lyon region)

PROCEDURE: Personal interview;
                Group discussion;
                Participant observation;
                Document analysis.

LANGUAGE: French

DURATION: Nov. 1980 – Nov. 1981

TYPE OF   Commissioned research
RESEARCH:

PUBLICATIONS: Gachet, A.; Rouge, M.; Saglio, J.: Le labyrinthe ana-
              lyse du logement des travailleurs immigrés dans l'ag-
              glomération lyonnaise. Lyon, CIMADE, 1978.

                          * * *

NO. 124   Study of the Teaching Process in School Classes with a
                High Percentage of Children of Migrants.

INSTITUTION: Freie Universität Berlin, Institut für Allg.Erziehungs-
                wissenschaft und Schulpädagogik (Free University of Ber-
                lin,Institute of General Pedagogics and School Education)
                Arnimallee 11
                D-1000 Berlin 33
                Germany, Federal Republic

RESEARCHER: Merkens, Hans/ Kodran, Raidunn/ Kosche-Nombamba,
                Gabriele/ Maiwald, Roland/ Smits, Nicolette

CONTACT: Merkens, Hans
                Tel.No.: 030/8385224

DISCIPLINE   Education and Training (Further Education/ Social Peda-
AND SUBFIELD: gogics)
                Sociology (Methodology)

ABSTRACT: The project aims at examining the experience and know-
                ledge gained by teachers instructing foreign children
                with regard to training and further educating teachers.
                Teaching will be observed in pre-school classes, pri-
                mary, second-level compulsory and vocational schools by
                participating for some time. Hence the project's aim is
                to study teaching methods adopted to meet the special
                challenge of teaching foreign children. The so-called
                soft method of 'participant observation' will at the
                same time be further developed. Methodologically the
                project follows the tradition of pedagogical factual re-
                search.

GEOGR.AREA: Germany, Federal Republic (Berlin)

PROCEDURE: Participant observation (Several classes with a high
                percentage of foreign children in pre-school classes,
                primary, second-level compulsory and vocational schools)

LANGUAGE: German

DURATION: July 1979 - July 1981

TYPE OF   Institution project
RESEARCH:

FUNDS: Internal sources

PUBLICATIONS: Maiwald, R.; Merkens, H.: Ausländer in der Berufsschule.
              Ein Bericht aus der Praxis, in: Sonderheft der Ztschr.f.
              Berufs- und Wirtschaftspädagogik,1980.

UNPUBLISHED   Merkens, H.: Die Integration von Ausländern als bil-
PAPERS: dungspolitische Aufgabe.
              Merkens, H.: Teilnehmende Beobachtung als Methode zur
              Erforschung von Erziehungswirklichkeit.
              Merkens, H.: Inhaltsanalyse.

                            * * *

NO. 125   Children of Foreign Workers in and out of School in
              Berlin (West).

INSTITUTION: Institut für Zukunftsforschung GmbH (Institute of Fu-
              ture Research)
              Giesebrechtstrasse 15
              D-1000 Berlin 12
              Germany, Federal Republic

RESEARCHER: Schröter, Ralf/ Welzel, Ute/ et alii

CONTACT: Schröter, Ralf
              Tel.No.: 030/8801222

DISCIPLINE   Education and Training
AND SUBFIELD: Political Sciences (Educational Policy)

ABSTRACT: The objective of this expert report is to develop, on
              the basis of an analysis of the school situation of for-
              eign children in Berlin (West) - with regard to models
              and problem solving approaches in other federal states
              and abroad -, proposals for measures which are apt to
              solve the specific problems of the school situation of
              foreign children in Berlin.

GEOGR.AREA: Germany, Federal Republic (Berlin-West)

PROCEDURE: Personal interview (60 school experts);
              Expert interview (30 responsible institutions and indi-
              viduals);
              Questionnaire;
              Document analysis (Statistics/ literature);
              Qualitative content analysis (Statistics/ literature);
              Quantitative content analysis (Statistics/ literature).

LANGUAGE: German

DURATION: Aug. 1979 - Aug. 1980

TYPE OF   Commissioned research
RESEARCH:

FUNDS: External sources: Der Regierende Bürgermeister, Senats-
                 kanzlei, Planungsstelle, Berlin

PUBLICATIONS: Planned for 1981

UNPUBLISHED   IFZ-Forschungsbericht Nr. 100, Berlin   1980.
PAPERS:

* * *

NO. 126   <u>Materials on Intercultural Education in Kindergartens.</u>

INSTITUTION: Institut für Sozialarbeit und Sozialpädagogik, Projekt-
                 gruppe Bonn (Institute for Social Work and Social Edu-
                 cation - ISS)
                 Weberstrasse 33
                 D-5300 Bonn 1
                 Germany, Federal Republic

RESEARCHER: Pfriem, Ruth/ Vink, Jan

CONTACT: Vink, Jan
                 Tel.No.: 0228/534200

DISCIPLINE   Education and Training (Social Pedagogics)
AND SUBFIELD:

ABSTRACT: Evaluate experiences made with intercultural education
                 of foreign and German children in kindergartens. Sit-
                 uation summary of international activities with parents.
                 Further education material for educators and counsel-
                 lors in elementary education.

GEOGR.AREA: Germany, Federal Republic

PROCEDURE: Personal interview;
                 Questionnaire.

LANGUAGE: German

DURATION: The project is completed.

TYPE OF   Commissioned research
RESEARCH:

FUNDS: External sources: Robert Bosch Stiftung, Stuttgart

PUBLICATIONS: Pfriem, R.; Vink, J.: Materialien zur interkulturellen
                Erziehung im Kindergarten, Stuttgart 1980.

* * *

NO. 127   Further Education Project "Exchange of Experiences be-
                tween Centres for Foreigners".

INSTITUTION: Institut für Sozialarbeit und Sozialpädagogik, Projekt-
                gruppe Bonn (Institute for Social Work and Social Edu-
                cation - ISS)
                Weberstrasse 33
                D-5300 Bonn 1
                Germany, Federal Republic

RESEARCHER: Vink, Jan

DISCIPLINE   Education and Training (Social Pedagogics)
AND SUBFIELD:

ABSTRACT: Further education in and exchange of experiences between
                centres for foreigners; elaborate further education ma-
                terials; counselling and guidance of personnel working
                in such centres.

GEOGR.AREA: Germany, Federal Republic (Berlin, Stuttgart, Duisburg,
                Mannheim)

LANGUAGE: German

DURATION: Apr. 1980 - Dec. 1982

TYPE OF   Commissioned research
RESEARCH:

FUNDS: External sources: Bundesverband der Arbeiterwohlfahrt,
                Bonn

PUBLICATIONS: Planned

UNPUBLISHED   Jahresbericht 1980; Fortbildungsreader.
PAPERS:

* * *

NO. 128   Further Education of Foreign Workers.

INSTITUTION: Zentrales Organisationsbüro Weiterbildung ausländischer
                Arbeitnehmer - ZOB (Central Office for the Organization
                of Further Education of Foreign Workers - ZOB)
                Kaiserstrasse 6
                D-5300 Bonn 1
                Germany, Federal Republic

RESEARCHER: Esch, Wolfgang (Duisburg)/ Fest, Johannes (Bonn)/
                Grundmann, Elisabeth (Hamburg)/ Noack, Peter Helmut
                (Mannheim)/ Rothenburg-Unz, Stephanie (Reutlingen)

CONTACT: Fest, Johannes
                Tel.No.: 0228/224076

DISCIPLINE   Education and Training (Further Education)
AND SUBFIELD: Sociology (Sociology of Education)

ABSTRACT: Whether and how an education that tries to keep in
                close contact with everyday life (orientation and so-
                cialization aids , cultural self-presentation) is able
                to improve the living conditions of foreign workers is
                tested in the cities of Hamburg, Duisburg, Mannheim,
                and Reutlingen. Content and organization of the meas-
                ures proceed from the problems, interests, and needs of
                the focal group which is in a state of apathetic integ-
                ration. Possibilities for active integration (action
                competence, communication competence) will be explored
                by offers to learn in social action fields.

GEOGR.AREA: Germany, Federal Republic (Hamburg, Duisburg, Mannheim,
                Reutlingen)

PROCEDURE: Expert interview;
                Document analysis;
                Secondary data analysis.

LANGUAGE: German

DURATION: July 1977 - Dec. 1980

TYPE OF   Sponsored research/ Commissioned research
RESEARCH:

FUNDS: External sources: Bundesminister für Bildung und Wissen-
                schaft, Bonn/ Stadt Duisburg/ Stadt Hamburg/ Stadt
                Mannheim/ Stadt Reutlingen

UNPUBLISHED   Positionspapier (Konzeptionsunterlagen und Erfahrungs-
PAPERS: bericht 1978), Bonn 1978, 1979.

* * *

NO. 129   Promotion of Foreign (Especially Turkish) Children and
                 Adolescents by Means of Pedagogical and Socio-Cultural
                 Assistance. (Activity in the Framework of the Pilot
                 Project "Regional Agencies to Promote Foreign Children
                 and Adolescents".).

INSTITUTION: Regionale Arbeitsstelle zur Förderung ausländischer
                 Kinder und Jugendlicher
                 Niederstrasse 5
                 D-4100 Duisburg 1
                 Germany, Federal Republic
                 Tel.No.: 0203/28133086

RESEARCHER: Fest, Johannes

DISCIPLINE   Education and Training
AND SUBFIELD: Social Work

ABSTRACT: Coordination and integration of hitherto isolated and,
                 therefore, inefficient measures. Great efforts are to be
                 undertaken to improve the situation of underprivileged
                 children and adolescents, especially of those of for-
                 eign workers. It will be most important to open the
                 schools towards "community education".
                 In order to achieve this, the persistent isolation of
                 the different professional groups engaged in the work
                 with children has to be overcome. Emphasis will be put
                 on the preparation of the children for schooling, on
                 the improvement of cooperation between parents and
                 schools, on the introduction of counselling and other
                 services including the non-curriculum areas, on the de-
                 velopment of supplements and alternatives to German
                 school books in the subjects of the natural sciences,
                 and on measures for job orientation and job promotion.

GEOGR.AREA: Germany, Federal Republic (Duisburg, Oberhausen, Essen,
                 Dortmund, Herne, Gelsenkirchen, Gladbeck, Hamm)

LANGUAGE: German

DURATION: Jan. 1980 - Dec. 1985

TYPE OF   Sponsored research
RESEARCH:

FUNDS: Internal sources
                 External sources: Kultusminister des Landes Nordrhein-
                 Westfalen, Düsseldorf / Stifterverband für die Deutsche
                 Wissenschaft, Essen/ Bundesminister für Bildung und
                 Wissenschaft, Bonn

* * *

NO. 130   Comparative Evaluation of Pilot Projects Concerning
School Entrance Tuition and Instruction in the Child's
Mother Tongue for Children of Migrant Workers in the
Member Countries of the European Community.

INSTITUTION: Universität Essen, Gesamthochschule, Forschungsgruppe
ALFA - Ausbildung von Lehrern für Ausländerkinder (Uni-
versity of Essen, Group ALFA - Training of Teachers for
Children of Migrant Workers)
Universitätsstrasse 2
D-4300 Essen 1
Germany, Federal Republic

RESEARCHER: Hohmann, Manfred/ Boos-Nuenning, Ursula (University of
Düsseldorf)/ Reich, Hans H. (EWH Rheinland-Pfalz,
Landau)

CONTACT: Hohmann, Manfred
Tel.No.: 0201/1832238

DISCIPLINE   Education and Training (Special Didactics)
AND SUBFIELD:

ABSTRACT: To analyse school pilot projects in Belgium, The Netherlands, Great Britain, France, with a view to the educational systems and the situation of migrant workers
in these countries. Comparison. Experiences gained by
teaching foreign children in Germany, Denmark, Luxembourg, Switzerland, and Sweden. Development of recommendations for the European Community.

GEOGR.AREA: Belgium/ The Netherlands/ Great Britain/ France/
Germany/ Denmark/ Sweden/ Switzerland/ Luxembourg

PROCEDURE: Personal interview;
Group discussion;
Expert interview;
Participant observation;
Document analysis.

LANGUAGE: German

DURATION: May 1978 - July 1980

TYPE OF   Commissioned research
RESEARCH:

FUNDS: External sources: Committee of the European Community,
Brussels

UNPUBLISHED   Progress report 1978, 79; different expertises.
PAPERS:

* * *

NO. 131   Development and Test of Courses for Young Foreign
Adults Which Enable Them to Pass the Leaving Examination of Second-Level Compulsory Schools.

INSTITUTION: Deutscher Volkshochschulverband e.V., Pädagogische Ar-
beitsstelle (Deutscher Volkshochschulverband, Pedagogi-
cal Department)
Holzhausenstrasse 21
D-6000 Frankfurt
Germany, Federal Republic

RESEARCHER: Meisel, Klaus/ Kehnen, Peter/ Pape, Christiane/
Vornoff, Hermann

CONTACT: Meisel, Klaus
Tel.No.: 0611/590988

DISCIPLINE   Education and Training (Adult Education)
AND SUBFIELD:

ABSTRACT: Introduction, conception, and evaluation of courses for
foreigners which prepare them to pass the leaving ex-
aminations of second-level compulsory schools; development of teaching and learning materials; collection,
analysis, and distribution of information regarding
adult education of foreign workers.

GEOGR.AREA: Germany, Federal Republic (Berlin-West)

PROCEDURE: Group discussion;
Expert interview;
Participant observation;
Non-participant observation;
Document analysis.

LANGUAGE: German

DURATION: May 1979 - Dec. 1982

TYPE OF   Sponsored research/ Institution project
RESEARCH:

FUNDS: External sources: Bundesminister für Bildung und Wissenschaft, Bonn

PUBLICATIONS: Informationsdienst "Bildungsarbeit mit ausländischen
Arbeitern", Pädagogische Arbeitsstelle, Deutscher Volkshochschulverband, Frankfurt am Main 1980.

* * *

NO. 132   Socialization of Children of Migrant Workers - At
               School and outside School.

INSTITUTION: Pädagogische Hochschule Freiburg, Forschungsstelle Aus-
               ländische Arbeiterkinder (Teachers' College Freiburg,
               Research Group for Children of Migrant Workers)
               Kunzenweg 21
               D-7800 Freiburg
               Germany, Federal Republic

RESEARCHER: Roth, Wolfgang/ Schmitt, Guido/ Armbruster, Thomas/
               Bartels, Siegfried/ Gehlen, Norbert/ Jung, Wolfgang/
               Kurras, Carola

CONTACT: Schmitt, Guido
               Tel.No.: 0761/682312

DISCIPLINE   Education and Training (Special Didactics/ Social Peda-
AND SUBFIELD: gogics)

ABSTRACT: Concept for teaching German in preparatory classes,
               models for leisure-time activities for children of mi-
               grant workers, school-related activities with parents
               and work with foreign adults (activities with foreign
               families and introduction of a centre for foreigners),
               problems of teacher training.

GEOGR.AREA: Germany, Federal Republic

PROCEDURE: Group discussion (30 student assistants);
               Participant observation (30-100 foreign pupils, parents
               and adults);
               Experiment (30 foreign pupils in preparatory classes).

LANGUAGE: German

DURATION: Apr. 1976 - June 1979

TYPE OF   Sponsored research
RESEARCH:

FUNDS: External sources: Stiftung Volkswagenwerk, Hannover

PUBLICATIONS: Planned

UNPUBLISHED   Schmitt, G.: Im Interesse ausländischer Arbeiterkinder,
PAPERS: Pilotstudie für das Forschungsprojekt 'Schulische und
               ausserschulische Sozialisation ausländischer Arbeiter-
               kinder', maschinenschriftliche Vervielfältigung, August
               1975, PH Freiburg.

* * *

NO. 133   Second-Class Educational Policy? Foreign Children in
                 the School System of Western Germany - from Rotation
                 via Segregation to Integration.

INSTITUTION: Hochschule der Bundeswehr Hamburg, Fachbereich Päd-
                 agogik, Professur für Politikwissenschaft insb. Bil-
                 dungspolitik (University of the Federal Armed Forces
                 Hamburg)
                 Holstenhofweg 85
                 D-2000 Hamburg 70
                 Germany, Federal Republic
                 Tel.No.: 040/65412842

RESEARCHER: Reuter, Lutz-Rainer/ Kischkewitz, Peter

DISCIPLINE   Education and Training
AND SUBFIELD: Political Sciences (Educational Policy)
                 Sociology (Sociology of Education)

ABSTRACT: Analysis of the socio-economic and legal situation of
                 foreigners in the Federal Republic of Germany; develop-
                 ment of indicators for the analysis of the educational-
                 political and educational situation of foreign children;
                 survey of the guide lines, decrees, etc. concerning the
                 schooling of foreign children/adolescents; development
                 of a pragmatic conception.

GEOGR.AREA: Germany, Federal Republic

PROCEDURE: Personal interview (200 foreign pupils/teachers/par-
                 ents in Dbg. second-level compulsory general school);
                 Expert interview;
                 Questionnaire (All ministries of education and of so-
                 cial services in the Federal Republic of Germany/ KMK -
                 Conference of the Ministers of Education - and BLK -
                 Bund-Länder-Kommission).

LANGUAGE: German

DURATION: June 1978 - Dec. 1979

TYPE OF   Researcher's project
RESEARCH:

FUNDS: Internal sources

PUBLICATIONS: Kischkewitz, P.; Reuter, L.R.: Bildungspolitik zweiter
                 Klasse? Ausländerkinder im westdeutschen Schulsystem -
                 von der Rotation über die Segregation zur Integration.
                 Verlag Rita G. Fischer, Frankfurt 1980, (Beiträge zur
                 Bildungspolitik Band 1), 250 S.

                              * * *

NO. 134   Scientific Evaluation of the School Pilot Project 'Na-
                tional Transitional Classes'.

INSTITUTION: Universität Hamburg, Psychologisches Institut 2 (Uni-
                versity of Hamburg, Department of Psychology II)
                Von-Melle-Park 5
                D-2000 Hamburg 13
                Germany, Federal Republic

RESEARCHER: Wieczerkowski, Wilhelm/ Misiak, Carlo/ Schiebel,
                Wolfgang

CONTACT: Schiebel, Wolfgang
                Tel.No.: 040/41235468

DISCIPLINE   Education and Training
AND SUBFIELD: Psychology (Child Psychology/ Psychology of Language)

ABSTRACT: Evaluation of the school pilot project. Language de-
                velopment. Bilingualism, foreign children.

GEOGR.AREA: Germany, Federal Republic (Hamburg)

PROCEDURE: Personal interview (150 pupils of 7 pilot classes);
                Participant observation (150 pupils of 7 pilot classes);
                Test (150 pupils of 7 pilot classes).

LANGUAGE: German

DURATION: Oct. 1978 - Mar. 1983

TYPE OF   Institution project
RESEARCH:

FUNDS: Internal sources

PUBLICATIONS: Planned

UNPUBLISHED   Zwischenbericht
PAPERS:

                            * * *

NO. 135   Integration of Children of Foreigners.

INSTITUTION: Pädagogische Hochschule Karlsruhe, Fachbereich 5, Sport
                und Sportwissenschaft (College for Teachers,Department:
                Sport Science and Sport Education)
                Bismarckstrasse 10
                D-7500 Karlsruhe
                Germany, Federal Republic

RESEARCHER: Rudolf, Anita/ Warwitz, Siegbert

CONTACT: Warwitz, Siegbert

DISCIPLINE   Education and Training (Special Didactics)
AND SUBFIELD:

ABSTRACT: In several primary and second-level compulsory general
                 schools with a high percentage of foreign children, at-
                 tempts are made to integrate these children on a non-
                 verbal action level (sport, arts, practical instruction)
                 and on a level of verbal understanding (theoretical
                 subjects).

GEOGR.AREA: Germany, Federal Republic (Baden-Württemberg)

PROCEDURE: Personal interview (about 300 classes of different
                 school types and levels with a high percentage of for-
                 eigners);
                 Questionnaire (about 300 classes of different school
                 types and levels with a high percentage of foreigners);
                 Participant observation (about 300 classes of different
                 school types and levels with a high percentage of for-
                 eigners);
                 Qualitative content analysis (about 300 classes of dif-
                 ferent school types and levels with a high percentage
                 of foreigners).

LANGUAGE: German

DURATION: Jan. 1978 - Dec. 1980

TYPE OF   Institution project
RESEARCH: Researcher's project

FUNDS: Internal sources

PUBLICATIONS: In: Die Deutsche Schule, 12/1980.

                            * * *

NO. 136   Types and Effects of Separate and Integrated School-
                 ing for Foreign Children in Primary, Secondary Level
                 Compulsory, and Special Schools in the School District
                 Ludwigsburg.

INSTITUTION: Pädagogische Hochschule Ludwigsburg, Fachgebiet Allg.
                 Pädagogik und Schulpädagogik (Teachers' College Lud-
                 wigsburg, Department of General and School Education)
                 Reute Allee 46
                 D-7140 Ludwigsburg
                 Germany, Federal Republic

RESEARCHER: Kehrer, Fritz/ Marschelke, Ekkehard/ Rapf, Franz

CONTACT: Rapf, Franz
                 Tel.No.: 07141/140351

DISCIPLINE   Education and Training
AND SUBFIELD:

ABSTRACT: Part 1 consists of collecting data on the <u>person</u> of
               every single child, on his or her <u>participation</u>
               in different educational offers/promotion
               courses in the current and previous school year
               as well as on entrance requirements.
               Part 2 consists of structured interviews with a sample
               of pupils and their teachers about schooling
               measures which have turned out to be successful.
               Should certain types of schooling prove to be more suc-
               cessful than others recommendations for the school or-
               ganization and curricula of Teacher Training Colleges
               (Pädagogische Hochschulen) as well as for further edu-
               cation will be made. Teachers will be offered help and
               advice for their work. Another aim is to identify groups
               with special characteristics closely connected with
               failures in the range of schooling offered.
               The results of both basic aims will be realized
               in training and further education measures by means of
               a subsequent action research project on the type of
               training necessary for teachers instructing children of
               migrant workers.

GEOGR.AREA: Germany, Federal Republic (School district Ludwigsburg)

PROCEDURE: Personal interview (Pupils/Class teachers);
               Questionnaire (8000 all foreign children in primary,
               second-level compulsory and special schools in the
               school district of Ludwigsburg);
               Document analysis (Comparison of data with official
               school statistics of previous years).

LANGUAGE: German

DURATION: July 1980 - Dec. 1981

TYPE OF   Institution project
RESEARCH:

FUNDS: Internal sources

PUBLICATIONS: Planned

                            * * *

NO. 137   Social and Socio-Pedagogical Promotion of Children from
               Foreign Workers' Families of Ludwigshafen in the Pre-
               School, School and Out-of-School Fields - in Particular
               during the Transitional Period from Pre-School to
               School, and from School to Occupation.

INSTITUTION: Fachhochschule der Pfälzischen Landeskirche für Sozial-
               arbeit und -pädagogik
               Maxstrasse 29
               D-6700 Ludwigshafen
               Germany, Federal Republic

RESEARCHER: Börsch, Ekkehard/ Hamburger, Franz (Uni Mainz)/
                 Musolino, Stefano (Ludwigshafen)

CONTACT: Börsch, Ekkehard
                 Tel.No.: 0621/518008

DISCIPLINE   Education and Training (Social Pedagogics)
AND SUBFIELD:

ABSTRACT: (A) Transition from pre-school to school: Special fur-
                 ther education of nursery-school teachers, special par-
                 ents work, special cooperation between kindergarten and
                 school - with special regard to foreign children and
                 their families. - Practice: Assistance at school en-
                 trance, cooperation between kindergarten and school be-
                 fore school entrance, intensive information of parents,
                 development of bilingual concepts.
                 (B) Transition from school to employment: Changing the
                 mode of homework assistance from supervision to possi-
                 bilities of contacts and social learning, including
                 parents, critical new conception of the so-called pre-
                 paratory classes, further education of teachers to spe-
                 cialize in the instruction of foreign children; combi-
                 nation of measures for enabling them to get the school-
                 leaving examination or for occupational integration by
                 help of youth welfare work and free time pedagogics;
                 correction of the present concepts of youth work ac-
                 cording to the needs of foreign adolescents, special
                 work with girls.
                 On the whole: Getting foreign workers into closer con-
                 tacts with democratic governing bodies on the
                 level of local authorities (new aspects for the compo-
                 sition of foreign working groups); a misunderstood
                 principle of equality leads to discrimination of for-
                 eign children in nursery-schools; opening of confession-
                 al institutions; new forms of coordinating measures of
                 various bodies on the local level.

GEOGR.AREA: Germany, Federal Republic (Ludwigshafen -Rhine)

PROCEDURE: Personal interview

LANGUAGE: German

DURATION: Feb. 1981 (end)

TYPE OF   Sponsored research/ Institution project/ Researcher's
RESEARCH: project

FUNDS: External sources: Robert Bosch Stiftung, Stuttgart/
                 Stiftung Volkswagenwerk, Hannover

PUBLICATIONS: Berichtsheft zur Einschulungshilfe; Berichtsheft Be-
                 standsaufnahme; zwei Hefte geplant; Abschlussbericht
                 Februar 1981 geplant.

* * *

NO. 138   Possible Uses of the Multi-Media System "Feature Film -
                 Adult Education" for Activities with Migrant Workers.

INSTITUTION: Adolf-Grimme-Institut
                 Eduard-Weitsch-Weg 25
                 D-4370 Marl
                 Germany, Federal Republic

RESEARCHER: Kühne-Scholand, Hildegard

DISCIPLINE   Education and Training (Adult Education)
AND SUBFIELD: Sociology (Sociology of Mass Communication)

ABSTRACT: Development, realization and evaluation of strategies
                 to integrate migrant workers by means of a multi-media
                 system combining feature film and adult education.

GEOGR.AREA: Germany, Federal Republic

PROCEDURE: Group discussion;
                 Expert interview;
                 Participant observation;
                 Document analysis.

LANGUAGE: German

DURATION: Mar. 1980 - Dec. 1983

TYPE OF   Sponsored research/ Commissioned research
RESEARCH:

FUNDS: External sources: Bundesminister für Bildung und
                 Wissenschaft, Bonn

* * *

NO. 139   Children of Migrant Workers and Television: Development
                 of Materials for Professionalizing Educators in Media
                 Pedagogics.

INSTITUTION: Deutsches Jugendinstitut e.V. (German Youth Institute)
                 Saarstrasse 7
                 D-8000 München 40
                 Germany, Federal Republic
                 Tel.No.: 089/38183 (ext. 223/221/219)

RESEARCHER: Barthelmes, Jürgen/ Herzberg, Irene/ Kloss, Gudrun/
                 Nissen, Ursula

DISCIPLINE   Education and Training
AND SUBFIELD:

ABSTRACT: Development of curriculum units and video films for
                 training and further education in the field of media
                 pedagogics or using media when working with foreign
                 children; research on the role played by television in
                 socializing foreign children as well as to give special
                 incentives for applying media pedagogics to this target
                 group; contribution to multi-cultural education; con-
                 tribution to enlarge and reformulate contents and work-
                 ing methods of teacher training and further education.

GEOGR.AREA: Germany, Federal Republic (Munich)

PROCEDURE: Personal interview;
                 Non-participant observation;
                 Action research;
                 Situation research.

LANGUAGE: German

DURATION: Jan. 1979 - Dec. 1981

TYPE OF   Commissioned research/ Researcher's project
RESEARCH:

FUNDS: External sources: Bundesminister für Bildung und
                 Wissenschaft, Bonn

PUBLICATIONS: Barthelmes, J.; Herzberg, I.: Fernsehvorschule und Kin-
                 dergarten, in: betrifft: erziehung 13/1980/2, S. 27-35.

UNPUBLISHED   Barthelmes, J.; Herzberg, I.; Nissen, U.: Zwischenbe-
PAPERS: richt II (Sept. 1979 - Sept. 1980), München, 1980.
                 Curriculum-Baustein: Wie wird Fernsehen gemacht? (un-
                 veröff. Manuskript).
                 Curriculum-Baustein: Medien für und über Ausländer (un-
                 veröff. Manuskript).

                              * * *

NO. 140   Pilot Project for Foreign Children and Adolescents.
                 Cooperative Model to Assist Foreign Adolescents at
                 School and outside School upon Leaving the Second-
                 Level Compulsory School and Beginning Work.

INSTITUTION: Deutsches Jugendinstitut e.V. (German Youth Institute)
                 Saarstrasse 7
                 D-8000 München 40
                 Germany, Federal Republic

RESEARCHER: Bendit, René/ Lopez-Blasco, Andres/ Pöschl, Angelika/
                 Steinmaier, Andrea

CONTACT: Bendit, René
                 Tel.No.: 089/38183250

DISCIPLINE   Education and Training (Social Pedagogics)
AND SUBFIELD:

ABSTRACT: Develop systematic support measures which are to assist foreign children and adolescents upon leaving the sec- ond-level compulsory school and beginning work. Support measures must include the extracurricular area and its socialization processes. The intent is not to develop general measures but to limit them to a certain part of the town, taking into consideration its characteristic features and educational opportunities. In practical application the project will also aim at coordinating the support measures of institutions and other action groups.

GEOGR.AREA: Germany, Federal Republic (Munich-Haidhausen)

PROCEDURE: Group discussion;
Expert interview;
Questionnaire;
Participant observation;
Qualitative content analysis;
Secondary data analysis.

LANGUAGE: German

DURATION: July 1977 - Dec. 1981

TYPE OF Commissioned research
RESEARCH:

FUNDS: External sources: Bundesminister für Bildung und Wissenschaft, Bonn/ Robert Bosch Stiftung, Stuttgart/ Stifterverband für die Deutsche Wissenschaft, Essen

PUBLICATIONS: Akpinar, Ü.; Lopez-Blasco, A.; Vink, J.: Pädagogische Arbeit mit ausländischen Kindern und Jugendlichen. München: Juventa Verlag,1977.
Bendit, R.; Lopez-Blasco, A.; Vink, J.: Ausländische Kinder und Jugendliche in der BRD, in: Deutsche Jugend, Heft 7/1977, S. 313-321.
Modellprogramm für ausländische Kinder und Jugendliche, u.a. Bestandsaufnahme der Ausländerarbeit in München, Verlag DJI, August 1978.
Akpinar, Ü.; Bendit, R.; Lopez-Blasco, A.; Zimmer, J.: Sozialisationshilfen für ausländische Kinder, in: b:e, H. 11/78.
Bendit, R.; Lopez-Blasco, A.: Zur Situation ausländi- scher Jugendlicher in der BRD am Beispiel des Münchner Stadtbezirks Haidhausen, in: CEDOM Selektione, H. 26, Okt. 1978.
Langeohl-Weyer, A.; Wennekes, R.; Bendit, R.; Lopez- Blasco, A.; Akpinar, Ü.; Vink, J.: Zur Integration der Ausländer im Bildungsbereich. Probleme und Lösungsver- suche. Juventa Verlag München, 1979.
Ausländerbeirat der Landeshauptstadt München/ Bayeri- scher Jugendring/ Koordinierungsgremium zu Ausländer- fragen/ Modellprogramm für ausländische Kinder und Ju- gendliche am DJI (Hrsg.): Jugendarbeit mit ausländischen Jugendlichen - Bericht einer Fachtagung - 8.-9. Februar 1979.

Bendit, R.: Zur Situation von Gastarbeiterjugendlichen
in der Berufsschule. Statistische Angaben -Beschulungs-
massnahmen und Probleme der "Ausländerklassen", in: IN-
FORMATIONEN zur Ausländerarbeit, H. 2, Nov. 1980, S.
37-54.
"Informationen zur Ausländerarbeit" - Koordinierungsgremium für Ausländerfragen in München/ Arbeitsgemein-
schaft der Fachbasis (Hrsg.), München 1980, H. 0,1,2.
Arbeitsgruppe Modellprogramm für ausländische Kinder
und Jugendliche (Hrsg.) Hans D. Walz: Zur Situation von
jungen Gastarbeitern in Familie, Freizeit, Schule und
Beruf, München 1980.

UNPUBLISHED   Koch, L.; Nowka, G.: Schulbegleitende Hilfen für aus-
PAPERS: ländische Hauptschüler in Deutschen Regelklassen zur
                  Bewältigung von Hausaufgaben, Problemen, Abschlüssen,
                  Hinführung zur Bewerbung, (unveröff. Manuskript),
                  München 1980.

                              * * *

NO. 141   Analysis of the Actual Situation: Hesse (Kindergartens
                  with a High Percentage of Foreign Children).

INSTITUTION: Deutsches Jugendinstitut e.V. (German Youth Institute)
                  Saarstrasse 7
                  D-8000 München 40
                  Germany, Federal Republic

RESEARCHER: Elschenbroich, Donata/ Krahl, Klaus-Peter/ Ledig,
                  Michael

CONTACT: Ledig, Michael
                  Tel.No.: 06452/82205

DISCIPLINE   Education and Training
AND SUBFIELD:

CONTACT: Observations and team interviews in 23 Hessian kinder-
                  gartens with a high percentage of foreigners in order
                  to document and discuss problems with foreign children
                  experienced by teachers in Hessian kindergartens.
                  Collection and discussion of statements on: basic con-
                  ditions/ funding and equipment of kindergarten work;
                  problems arising from taking care of infants up to
                  three years; early bilingualism; 'intercultural educa-
                  tion'; activities with parents; cooperation between
                  kindergarten and other institutions.

                  Development and evaluation of materials and ideas fa-
                  cilitating all activities where German and foreign
                  children can play and learn together; playing without
                  knowledge of the foreign language; learning German by
                  playing.

GEOGR.AREA: Germany, Federal Republic (Hesse)

PROCEDURE: Group discussion (23 Hessian kindergartens);
                  Expert interview (23 Hessian kindergartens);
                  Participant observation (23 Hessian kindergartens).

LANGUAGE: German

DURATION: Jan. 1979 - Dec. 1982

TYPE OF   Sponsored research/ Commissioned research
RESEARCH:

FUNDS: Internal sources
                  External sources: Land Hessen Sozialminister, Wiesbaden

UNPUBLISHED   Elschenbroich, D.; Ledig, M.; Krahl, K.P.: Bericht über
PAPERS: Hospitationen und Team-Interviews in 23 hessischen Kin-
                  dergärten mit hohem Ausländeranteil. Darmstadt/Marburg
                  1979.

                              * * *

NO. 142   "The Children of Migrant Workers" - Further Education
                  Materials for Kindergarten Teachers.

INSTITUTION: Deutsches Jugendinstitut e.V. (German Youth Institute)
                  Saarstrasse 7
                  D-8000 München 40
                  Germany, Federal Republic

RESEARCHER: Elschenbroich, Donata/ Krahl, Klaus-Peter/ Ledig,
                  Michael

CONTACT: DJI Projektgruppe "Gastarbeiterkinder"
                  Gärtnerweg 39
                  D-6000 Frankfurt 1
                  Germany, Federal Republic

DISCIPLINE   Education and Training (Further Education)
AND SUBFIELD:

ABSTRACT: The aim is to elaborate in cooperation with 11 Hessian
                  kindergartens further education materials for teachers
                  working in kindergartens with a high percentage of for-
                  eign children.
                  Emphasis is laid on:
                  - Collecting information about the countries of origin;
                    migrant workers traditionally come from (Turkey,
                    Greece, Yugoslavia, Italy, Spain);
                  - Documenting so-called key situations;
                  - Preparing media material on the subject.

GEOGR.AREA: Germany, Federal Republic (Hesse)

PROCEDURE: Action Research (11 kindergartens in Hesse/FRG)

LANGUAGE: German

DURATION: Aug. 1979 - Apr. 1983

TYPE OF   Commissioned research
RESEARCH:

PUBLICATIONS: Tertorotti, C.: Begleitheft zur italienischen Tonkas-
              sette zum Praxisfilm "Tagesablauf im deutschen Kinder-
              garten", Mai 1980.
              Elschenbroich, D.: Einwanderungsland USA, Mai 1980.
              Schweitzer, O.: Italien, September 1980.

UNPUBLISHED   Elschenbroich, D.: Die Bundesrepublik, ein Vielvölker-
PAPERS: staat? Mai 1980.
                 Ledig, M.: Gastarbeiter in der Bundesrepublik und an-
                 deren europäischen Industriestaaten, Mai 1980.
                 Ledig, M.: Ausgewählte Statistiken zur Situation von
                 Gastarbeitern in der BRD und Hessen, Mai 1980.
                 Schweitzer, O.: Die Türkei - Das Heimatland der tür-
                 kischen Gastarbeiter, Mai 1980.

                              * * *

NO. 143   Information and Counselling Agency for the Pedagogical
                 Work with Foreign Children and Their Parents.

INSTITUTION: Deutsches Jugendinstitut e.V. (German Youth Institute)
                 Saarstrasse 7
                 D-8000 München 40
                 Germany, Federal Republic

RESEARCHER: Jampert, Karin/ Lauber, Klaus/ Pöschl, Angelika/
                 Steinmayr, Andrea/ Zehnbauer, Anne

CONTACT: Hanke, Heidemarie
                 Tel.No.: 089/38183-251

DISCIPLINE   Education and Training (Social Pedagogics)
AND SUBFIELD:

ABSTRACT: Collecting and processing of information and materials on
                 the problem of migrant workers; guiding and counselling
                 foreign children in German institutions; further edu-
                 cation of kindergarten teachers. Documentation volumes
                 on various topics: DJI-series: Materials on social ac-
                 tivities with foreigners.

GEOGR.AREA: Germany, Federal Republic

PROCEDURE: Personal interview (Female teachers in kindergartens
                 and nursery-schools);
                 Questionnaire (Various experts);
                 Document analysis (Local government planning documents
                 and reports).

LANGUAGE: German

DURATION: Jan. 1980 (start)

TYPE OF   Commissioned research
RESEARCH:

FUNDS: External sources: Bundesminister für Bildung und
                 Wissenschaft, Bonn

PUBLICATIONS: Zehnbauer, A.: "Ausländerkinder in Kindergarten und
                 Tagesstätte". Eine Bestandsaufnahme zur institutionel-
                 len Betreuung von ausländischen Kindern im Vorschul-
                 alter. München, DJI Verlag, 1980.
                 Münscher, A.: "Ausländische Frauen", Annotierte Bi-
                 bliographie, München, DJI Verlag, 1980.

                          * * *

NO. 144   Development of Socialization Aids for Foreign Children
                 (Pilot Study) - A Problem-Orientated Survey of Govern-
                 ment Measures to Care for Foreign Children at a Pre-
                 School Age.

INSTITUTION: Deutsches Jugendinstitut e.V. (German Youth Institute)
                 Saarstrasse 7
                 D-8000 München 40
                 Germany, Federal Republic
                 Tel.No.: 089/38183-280

RESEARCHER: Zehnbauer, Anne

DISCIPLINE   Education and Training (Social Pedagogics)
AND SUBFIELD:

ABSTRACT: Situation regarding kindergartens and nursery-schools
                 for foreign children, measures taken for improvement;
                 pedagogical concepts for working with foreign parents;
                 concepts for teachers' further education. Data gather-
                 ed will serve as a basis for future research projects
                 and will be incorporated into future counselling and
                 information activities by the German Youth Institute.

GEOGR.AREA: Germany, Federal Republic

PROCEDURE: Personal interview (11 kindergartens and nursery-
                 schools in the city of Munich);
                 Group discussion (11 kingergartens and nursery-schools
                 in the city of Munich);
                 Expert interview (5 experts: kindergartens, research
                 groups, local representatives);
                 Questionnaire (14 Protestant kindergartens in Stutt-
                 gart/ 40 towns with a high percentage of foreigners -
                 approx. 10 percent -).

LANGUAGE: German

DURATION: Jan. 1979 - Dec. 1979

TYPE OF   Commissioned research
RESEARCH:

FUNDS: External sources: Bundesminister für Bildung und
                    Wissenschaft, Bonn

PUBLICATIONS: Zehnbauer, A.: Ausländerkinder in Kindergarten und
                    Tagesstätte. Eine Bestandsaufnahme zur institutionellen
                    Betreuung von ausländischen Kindern im Vorschulalter.
                    DJI Verlag, 1980, (überarbeiteter Abschlussbericht).

                              * * *

NO. 145   Schooling of Children of Migrant Workers in Bavaria.

INSTITUTION: Zentrum für Bildungsforschung, Staatsinstitut für Bil-
                    dungsforschung und Bildungsplanung (State Institute
                    for Educational Research and Planning)
                    Arabellastrasse 1, VI
                    D-8000 München 81
                    Germany, Federal Republic

RESEARCHER: Nowey, Waldemar

CONTACT: Nowey, Waldemar
                    Tel.No.: 089/92142560

DISCIPLINE   Education and Training
AND SUBFIELD:

ABSTRACT: Regional survey (covering the whole of Bavaria) of the
                    school organizational measures taken for foreign pu-
                    pils in elementary and second-level compulsory schools
                    for Turkish, Greek, Italian, Yugoslav, Spanish and/or
                    Portuguese pupils in small areas. School attendance in
                    bilingual (mother tongue) classes, transitional and
                    regular classes. Promotion by intensive and promotion-
                    al courses. Deficiencies in German and other advanced
                    subjects. Age grouping in the school system. School-
                    leaving examinations for foreign pupils. Reasons both
                    in and out of school: Why do foreign pupils not com-
                    plete the second-level compulsory schooling at the
                    normal school-leaving age?

GEOGR.AREA: Germany, Federal Republic (Bavaria)

PROCEDURE: Questionnaire (Approx. 60,000 pupils in about 3,000
                    elementary and second-level compulsory schools);
                    Qualitative content analysis;
                    Quantitative content analysis;
                    Secondary data analysis (School statistics of the Sta-
                    tistics Office/ Statistics on inhabitants).

LANGUAGE: German

DURATION: Jan. 1979 - Dec. 1979

TYPE OF   Institution project
RESEARCH:

FUNDS: Internal sources

PUBLICATIONS: Nowey, W.: Regionale Verteilung der ausländischen
              Schüler in Bayern. München, Hrsg.: Staatsinstitut für
              Bildungsforschung und Bildungsplanung 1979.
              Nowey, W.: Schul- und unterrichtsorganisatorische Mass-
              nahmen für ausländische Schüler in Bayern. München:
              FfB, 1980.

                            * * *

NO. 146   Pilot Project for the Promotion of German and Foreign
                Children at the Elementary Level.

INSTITUTION: Zentrum für Bildungsforschung, Staatsinstitut für Früh-
                pädagogik (State Institute of Early Childhood Educa-
                tion)
                Arabellastrasse 1
                D-8000 München 81
                Germany, Federal Republic

RESEARCHER: Fthenakis, Wassilios E./ Caesar, Sylvia-Gioia/
                Diekmeyer, Ulrich/ Merz, Hannelore/ Reidelhuber, Almut/
                Soltendieck, Monika

CONTACT: Dieckmeyer, Ulrich
                Tel.No.: 089/ 92142425 and 089/92143174

DISCIPLINE   Education and Training (Elementary Level)
AND SUBFIELD:

ABSTRACT: Development of a promotion programme for pilot groups in
                kindergartens with nationally mixed groups. The special
                objective is a bilingual and bicultural promotion by
                German and foreign teachers. In the development phase
                34 situation units as pedagogical devices were con-
                structed and handed over to the teachers in a test
                phase. Furthermore, a concept of parents' work for these
                pilot groups and a concept of further education for the
                implementation phase are developed. Starting in 1981,
                these concepts and devices will be subjected to an eval-
                uation and a revision; on the basis of experiences up
                to now an implementation phase for this mode of bi-
                lingual and bicultural promotion will be initiated at
                once. Starting with the kindergarten year 1981/82 a
                longitudinal study will be started in the framework of
                the scientific evaluation.

GEOGR.AREA: Germany, Federal Republic (Munich and other towns in
                Bavaria)

PROCEDURE: Personal interview (25-30 kindergarten teachers);
                Questionnaire (25-30 kindergarten teachers);
                Test (about 400 children in kindergartens).

LANGUAGE: German

DURATION: July 1975 - June 1983

TYPE OF   Sponsored research/ Institution project
RESEARCH:

FUNDS: Internal sources
                 External sources: Freistaat Bayern/ Bundesminister für
                 Bildung und Wissenschaft, Bonn

PUBLICATIONS: Fthenakis, W.E.: Bilingual-bikulturelle versus multi-
                 kulturelle Konzepte als Alternativen zur Förderung
                 deutscher und ausländischer Kinder in der Bundesrepu-
                 blik Deutschland. München 1979.
                 Fthenakis, W.E.: Die Förderung griechischer Kinder in
                 der Bundesrepublik Deutschland - Probleme der zweiten
                 Generation. München 1980.
                 Staatsinstitut für Frühpädagogik: Modellversuch zur
                 Förderung deutscher und ausländischer Kinder im Elemen-
                 tarbereich - Projektinformation. München 1979.

UNPUBLISHED   Deibler, Ch.; Diekmeyer, U.; Sattler, M.; Schneid, U.:
PAPERS: Situationseinheiten - Pädagogische Arbeitshilfen für
                 Erzieher in Modellgruppen. Erprobungsfassung (intern.),
                 München 1979.

                            * * *

NO. 147   Promotional Teaching for Foreign Pupils.

INSTITUTION: Pädagogische Hochschule Reutlingen, Projektgruppe För-
                 derunterricht für ausländische Schüler (Teachers' Col-
                 lege Reutlingen, Project Group Promotional Instruction
                 for Foreign Pupils)
                 Am Hohbuch, Postfach 680
                 D-7410 Reutlingen 1
                 Germany, Federal Republic
                 Tel.No.: 07121/271372

DISCIPLINE   Education and Training (Social Pedagogics/Special Didac-
AND SUBFIELD: tics)

ABSTRACT: Additional promotional teaching in small groups in the
                 classes seven to nine lasting up to four hours can be
                 introduced to those foreign pupils at second-level com-
                 pulsory schools who are in danger of not passing their
                 leaving examinations. The effectiveness of this measure
                 depends, among other things, on the organization, the
                 teaching conditions, and the teaching itself. In the
                 framework of a scientific evaluation the following is
                 planned: improvement of school success by individual
                 and differentiated teaching; special consideration of
                 the pupils' levels of performance, motivation promotion
                 and parents' work in groups of ten.

GEOGR.AREA: Germany, Federal Republic (Schools in the area of the
                 education office of Reutlingen - Baden-Wuerttemberg)

PROCEDURE: Personal interview (10 teachers concerned and pupils);
                 Group discussion (Participating teachers);
                 Expert interview;
                 Participant observation (Selected teaching units);
                 Qualitative content analysis (All curricular compo-
                 nents);
                 Experiment: Performance rating and performance examina-
                 tion;
                 Test.

LANGUAGE: German

DURATION: Sept. 1979 - Dec. 1983

TYPE OF   Sponsored research
RESEARCH:

FUNDS: External sources: Bund-Länder-Kommission für Bildungs-
                 planung und Forschungsförderung, Bonn

                            * * *

NO. 148   Scientific Evaluation of Bavarian Pilot Projects for
                 the Promotion of Foreign Children at School.

INSTITUTION: Zentrum für Bildungsforschung, Staatsinstitut für Schul-
                 pädagogik, Abt. Allgemeine Wissenschaften (State Insti-
                 tute for School Education)
                 Arabellastrasse 1
                 D-8000 München 81
                 Germany, Federal Republic

RESEARCHER: Westphalen, Klaus/ Appelt, Dieter/ Maier, Wilma

CONTACT: Alt-Stutterheim, Wolfgang von
                 Tel.No.: 0214/2598

DISCIPLINE   Education and Training (Special Didactics)
AND SUBFIELD:

ABSTRACT: This evaluation sets out to establish and to test
                 which didactic and curricular conceptions seem to be
                 suited for organizing the teaching of German as a for-
                 eign language on the one hand and the teaching of the
                 mother tongue on the other hand in such a way as to
                 enable foreign children to obtain school-leaving
                 qualifications which are offered by various types of
                 schools; which measures seem possible in order to pro-
                 mote the psycho-social integration of foreign children;
                 by which kinds of instruction (curricula) the cultural
                 values and norms of both nations can be taken into ac-
                 count or reconciled; by which curricula (including in-
                 struction planning, textbooks, etc.) qualified leaving
                 examinations of all school types of the differentiated
                 school system can be made possible; what kind of quali-

fications teachers and other professional personnel
need for the teaching and promotion of foreign children,
by which means can these qualifications be obtained.

GEOGR.AREA: Germany, Federal Republic (Bavaria)

PROCEDURE: Personal interview (20 teachers);
                 Group discussion (teachers);
                 Questionnaire (300 Turkish pupils);
                 Participant observation (80 pupils - 3 classes, 14
                 classes of the age groups 5 and 6 -);
                 Document analysis (300 Turkish pupils).

LANGUAGE: German

DURATION: Oct. 1979 - Oct. 1983

TYPE OF   Sponsored research/ Commissioned research
RESEARCH:

FUNDS: External sources: Bayerisches Staatsministerium für
                 Unterricht und Kultur, München/ Bundesminister für
                 Bildung und Wissenschaft, Bonn

PUBLICATIONS: Planned

UNPUBLISHED   Alt-Stutterheim, W. von; Maier, W.: Konzeption einer
PAPERS: Begleituntersuchung von bayerischen Modellvorhaben zur
                 schulischen Förderung ausländischer Kinder. Staatsin-
                 stitut für Schulpädagogik, München 1979.

                          * * *

NO. 149   Education and Ethnicity.

INSTITUTION: University of Aston in Birmingham, St. Peter's College,
                 Social Science Research Council, Research Unit on Eth-
                 nic Relations
                 College Road, Saltley
                 GB-Birmingham B8 3TE
                 United Kingdom
                 Tel.No.: 021/3270194

RESEARCHER: Naguib, Mohammed/ Rex, John/ Troyna, Barry/ Bhachu,
                 Parminder

CONTACT: Rex, John
                 R.U.E.R., St. Peter's College
                 College Road, Saltley
                 GB-Birmingham B8 3TE
                 United Kingdom
                 Tel.No.: 021/3270194

DISCIPLINE   Anthropology, Ethnology
AND SUBFIELD: Education and Training
                 Sociology

ABSTRACT: To study the demands made by ethnic minorities on the
                 education system and the way in which the education
                 system responds to those demands.
                 The study will include
                 (a) case studies of policy development and implementa-
                     tion in three local authorities;
                 (b) studies of Head Teachers' and Departmental Heads'
                     opinions on multi-cultural education;
                 (c) a study of school and curriculum structure in re-
                     lation to minority needs;
                 (d) a survey of parent's opinions and expectations.

GEOGR.AREA: United Kingdom (National, with most fieldwork in East
                 and West Midlands)

LANGUAGE: English

DURATION: Oct. 1980 - Oct. 1983

TYPE OF   Institution project
RESEARCH:

FUNDS: Internal sources

UNPUBLISHED   Rex, J.: The Teacher and Multi-Cultural Education - The
PAPERS: Society Context.
                 Troyna, B.: Variations on a Theme: The Educational Re-
                 sponse to Black Pupils in British Schools.

* * *

NO. 150

On-the-Job-Training and Other Measures Taken to Prepare Foreign Adolescents for Employment in the Federal Republic of Germany.

INSTITUTION:

Bundesinstitut für Berufsbildung (Federal Institute for Vocational Education)
Fehrbelliner Platz 3
D-1000 Berlin 31
Germany, Federal Republic

RESEARCHER:

Schmidt-Hackenberg, Dietrich/ Hecker, Ursula

DISCIPLINE AND SUBFIELD:

Education and Training (Vocational Training)

ABSTRACT:

To obtain data about the conditions and results of foreign adolescents' vocational training taking into special consideration status, school and the ethnic and social conditions. Quantitative and qualitative survey of current measures to prepare foreign adolescents for an occupation. Data gathered concerning difficulties and experience gained by the sponsors of these promotional courses will form the basis for developing recommendations on how to improve measures. Results envisaged: Catalogue of hypotheses to be used for a survey entitled "first vocational training". Analysis of pertinent literature and statistics about promotional measures to prepare foreign adolescents for an occupation. Tools for statistical sampling. Results of working group "Pretest". Survey of current measures to prepare foreign adolescents for an occupation. Research results (survey of vocational training for foreign adolescents). Results of an empirical survey about work experience and working conditions of sponsors. Recommendations on how to improve measures to prepare foreign adolescents for an occupation.

GEOGR.AREA:

Germany, Federal Republic

LANGUAGE: German

DURATION: Jan. 1980 - Dec. 1981

TYPE OF   Institution project
RESEARCH:

* * *

NO. 151   Case Studies on the Practice of On-the-Job-Training of
                 Foreign Adolescents in the Federal Republic of Germany.

INSTITUTION: AgaS-Arbeitsgemeinschaft für angewandte Sozialforschung
                 GmbH (AgaS-Study Group for Applied Social Research
                 Limited)
                 Blutenburgstrasse 93
                 D-8000 München 19
                 Germany, Federal Republic

                 Infratest Sozialforschung GmbH
                 Landsberger Strasse 338
                 D-8000 München 21
                 Germany, Federal Republic

RESEARCHER: Pohlmann, Günter/ Neumann, Karl-Heinz/ Schäuble,
                 Ingegerd

CONTACT: Pohlmann, Günter
                 Tel.No.: 089/132005

DISCIPLINE   Education and Training (On-the-Job-Training)
AND SUBFIELD:

ABSTRACT: Collection of exemplary cases of successful training of
                 foreign adolescents. Identification of practice orien-
                 tated and transferable experiences with provable success
                 of on-the-job-training of foreign adolescents in ap-
                 proved skilled jobs.

GEOGR.AREA: Germany, Federal Republic

PROCEDURE: Expert interview (100 company practitioners in 21 firms
                 and other experts in the regions of Berlin, Munich,
                 Stuttgart, and Cologne)

LANGUAGE: German

DURATION: June 1979 - Oct. 1979

TYPE OF   Commissioned research
RESEARCH:

FUNDS: External sources: Bundesinstitut für Berufsbildung,
                 Berlin

* * *

NO. 152   Training and Further Education of Migrant Workers.

INSTITUTION: Infratest Sozialforschung GmbH
               Landsberger Strasse 338
               D-8000 München 21
               Germany, Federal Republic

               AgaS-Arbeitsgemeinschaft für angewandte Sozialforschung
               GmbH (AgaS-Study Group for Applied Social Research Lim-
               ited)
               Blutenburgstrasse 93
               D-8000 München 19
               Germany, Federal Republic

RESEARCHER: Behringer, Friederike/ et alii

CONTACT: Behringer, Friederike
               Tel.No.: 089/5600445

DISCIPLINE   Education and Training
AND SUBFIELD: Political Sciences (Social Policy)

ABSTRACT: The project's aim is to trace firms which train and
               further educate foreigners. Such firms and the quali-
               fying measures offered to migrant workers will be de-
               scribed in 15 case studies.

GEOGR.AREA: Germany, Federal Republic

PROCEDURE: Expert interview

LANGUAGE: German

DURATION: Oct. 1980 - Jan. 1981

TYPE OF   Commissioned research
RESEARCH:

FUNDS: External sources: Bundesinstitut für Berufsbildung

                          * * *

NO. 153   The State and Black Youth in Britain: A Case Study of
               Training and Employment Programmes.

INSTITUTION: University of Aston in Birmingham, St. Peter's College
               Social Science Research Council, Research Unit on Eth-
               nic Relations
               College Road, Saltley
               GB-Birmingham B8 3TE
               United Kingdom
               Tel.No.: 021/3270194

RESEARCHER: Solomos, John

DISCIPLINE   Political Sciences
AND SUBFIELD:

ABSTRACT: This project involves a study of local and central
              state interventions in relation to the economic, social
              and political conditions of Black Youth. The research
              questions it sets out to answer are: how far, in what
              ways, for what purposes and with what consequences do
              local and central state institutions in different so-
              cio-economic milieux attempt to structure the position
              of employed, unemployed and marginalised black youth in
              specific ways? It is proposed to conduct the investi-
              gation in two areas both with identifiable inner city
              characteristics, but with different socio-political
              conditions: the Lambeth area of London and the Small
              Heath area of Birmingham. The project will examine both
              the articulation of policy alternatives, the processes
              of policy formation and the consequences. It is hoped
              by looking at two areas to elucidate the dynamics of
              interventions and non-interventions in a comparative
              manner.

GEOGR.AREA: United Kingdom (London and Birmingham)

PROCEDURE: Personal interview;
              Expert interview;
              Questionnaire;
              Participant observation;
              Document analysis;
              Secondary data analysis.

LANGUAGE: English

DURATION: May 1980 - May 1983

TYPE OF   Institution project
RESEARCH:

FUNDS: Internal sources

PUBLICATIONS: Solomos, J.: Why the Study of Employment and Race? A
              Preliminary Outline of Issues and Problems. RUER, July
              1980, 19 pages.
              Solomos, J.: Unemployment and the Marginalisation of
              Immigrant Workers in Britain: The Case of West Indian
              and Asian Youth. Paper presented at European Science
              Foundation Workshop on 'Cultural Identity and Structur-
              al Marginalisation of Migrant Workers', Bochum, Decem-
              ber 10-12, 1980.

* * *

NO. 154   The Implementation of Equal Opportunity Policy for Eth-
              nic Minorities.

INSTITUTION: Civil Service College
              11 Belgrave Road
              GB-London SW1
              United Kingdom
              Tel.No.: 01/8346644

RESEARCHER: Cohen, Gaynor/ Nixon, Jaqi

CONTACT: Cohen, Gaynor
                Civil Service College
                11 Belgrave Road
                GB-London SW1
                United Kingdom
                Tel.No.: 01/8346644

DISCIPLINE   Anthropology, Ethnology
AND SUBFIELD: Political Sciences
                Sociology
                Social Administration

ABSTRACT: The purpose of the research was to assess the interpre-
                tation and implementation of equal opportunity policy
                for ethnic minorities, following the 1976 Act at cen-
                tral and local government levels. As this is a policy
                area which requires innovation, the research was con-
                cerned with identifying processes of implementation
                which might hinder or foster innovation.

GEOGR.AREA: United Kingdom (Central Government Departments and two
                local authorities, one inner and one outer borough)

PROCEDURE: Personal interview;
                Group discussion;
                Participant observation;
                Non-participant observation;
                Document analysis;
                Secondary data analysis.

LANGUAGE: English

DURATION: Nov. 1977 - Aug. 1981

TYPE OF   Institution project/ Researcher's project
RESEARCH:

FUNDS: Internal sources

PUBLICATIONS: M. Brown and Sally Baldwin (eds.): Dimensions of Equal
                Opportunity Policy, in: Year Book of Social Policy,
                1977.

UNPUBLISHED   Cohen, G.: The Role of Educational Advisors in Imple-
PAPERS: menting Equal Opportunity Policy. Paper given at Home
                Office Research Unit Seminar, 3.2.81.

                          * * *

PUBLIC MEASURES: HOUSING

NO. 155   Availability of Housing for Foreigners and "Deagglom-
           eration" of Overcrowded Areas by Town Planning Meas-
           ures.

INSTITUTION: Freie Planungsgruppe Berlin GmbH - FPB
                Kurfürstendamm 62
                D-1000 Berlin 15
                Germany, Federal Republic

RESEARCHER: Baatz, Rainer/ Wurtinger, Hermann

DISCIPLINE   Sociology (Urban Sociology)
AND SUBFIELD: Town Planning

ABSTRACT: - Analysis of the regional distribution and housing
                  conditions experienced by foreign households
                - Determination of the foreigners' need for housing in
                  West-Berlin
                - Development of strategies and measures to improve the
                  housing conditions of foreign households in West-
                  Berlin

GEOGR.AREA: Germany, Federal Republic (Berlin-West)

PROCEDURE: Expert interview (Expert on housing conditions of for-
                eigners);
                Questionnaire (5407 households of migrant workers from
                Turkey, Yugoslavia, Greece);
                Secondary data analysis (Planning data/ Record of in-
                habitants/ Official statistics).

LANGUAGE: German

DURATION: Mar. 1979 - Sept. 1980

TYPE OF   Commissioned research
RESEARCH:

FUNDS: External sources: Der Regierende Bürgermeister, Senats-
                 kanzlei, Berlin

PUBLICATIONS: Planned

                           * * *

NO. 156   Supply of Accomodation to Foreigners and Alleviation
                 of Congested Areas by Town Planning Measures (Pilot
                 Study).

INSTITUTION: Prognos AG, Europäisches Zentrum für Angewandte Wirt-
                 schaftsforschung
                 Viaduktstrasse 65
                 CH-4011 Basel
                 Switzerland

                 Freie Planungsgruppe Berlin GmbH - FPB
                 Kurfürstendamm 62
                 D-1000 Berlin 15
                 Germany, Federal Republic

RESEARCHER: Hübschle, Jörg/ Baur, Rita

CONTACT: Hübschle, Jörg
                 Tel.No.: 004161/223200

DISCIPLINE   Political Sciences (Housing Policy)
AND SUBFIELD: Town Planning

ABSTRACT: Selection and analysis of exemplary cases (problem
                 areas and potential problem areas), classification of
                 problem areas.

GEOGR.AREA: Germany, Federal Republic (Berlin-West)

PROCEDURE: Secondary data analysis

LANGUAGE: German

DURATION: Mar. 1979 - July 1979

TYPE OF   Commissioned research
RESEARCH:

FUNDS: External sources: Der Regierende Bürgermeister, Senats-
                 kanzlei, Planungsleitstelle, Berlin

                           * * *

INITIATIVES BY MIGRANTS

NO. 157   Organization of Islam in Belgium.

INSTITUTION: Université Catholique de Louvain, Centre de Recherches
               socio-religieuses (Catholic University of Louvain, So-
               cio-Religious Research Centre)
               1 b. 21, place Montesquieu
               B-1348 Louvain la Neuve
               Belgium

RESEARCHER: Bahi, Mohamed/ Bastenier, Albert/ Dassetto, Felice

DISCIPLINE   Sociology (Sociology of Religion/ Sociology of Migra-
AND SUBFIELD: tion)

ABSTRACT: Sociographic study of adherence to the Islam among im-
               migrant communities from Turkey and Maghreb in Belgium.

GEOGR.AREA: Belgium

PROCEDURE: Recensement

LANGUAGE: French

DURATION: June 1980 - Dec. 1981

TYPE OF   Sponsored research
RESEARCH:

FUNDS: External sources: Ministère de la communauté française

                          * * *

                           173

NO. 158   The Organization Forms of Immigrant Workers in Denmark.
                 Toward Autonomy and Political Rights.

INSTITUTION: University of Copenhagen, Institute of Cultural Socio-
                 logy
                 Rosenborggade 17
                 DK-1130 København K
                 Denmark

RESEARCHER: Schwartz, Jonathan Matthew

DISCIPLINE   Political Sciences (Participation/ Social Policy)
AND SUBFIELD: Sociology (Political Sociology/ Urban Sociology)

ABSTRACT: Research has had its focus on immigrant workers' commu-
                 nities both in the sending and in the receiving socie-
                 ty. Focus is not exclusively on "integration", but
                 rather on autonomy and ethnic and class dimensions of
                 the immigrant groups. Research has been directed to-
                 wards assisting immigrants in their organization and
                 struggle for political rights in the Danish society.
                 Research project is best exemplified in the campaign
                 for re-housing of the immigrant residents of Vognmands-
                 marken, a slum section on the north-east edge of Copen-
                 hagen. My involvement with this action research project
                 started in 1974 and is currently being concluded with
                 an evaluation of the results of re-housing.

GEOGR.AREA: Denmark

PROCEDURE: Action Research

DURATION: 1974 - 1982

                              * * *

NO. 159   Conditions and Restrictions in Expanding Migrant Wor-
                 kers' Action Competence.

INSTITUTION: Freie Universität Berlin, Fachbereich 15, Politische
                 Wissenschaft, Berliner Projektverbund der Berghof-
                 Stiftung für Konfliktforschung (Free University of Ber-
                 lin, Berlin Coordination Centre of the Berghof-Founda-
                 tion for Conflict Research)
                 Winklerstrasse 4 a
                 D-1000 Berlin 33
                 Germany, Federal Republic

RESEARCHER: Decker, Frauke

CONTACT: Decker, Frauke
                 Tel.No.: 030/8928009

DISCIPLINE   Political Sciences (Conflict Research)
AND SUBFIELD: Sociology

ABSTRACT: What possibilities exist for foreigners to become in-
                volved and participate in political and social matters?
                Which of these are useful, what self-help organizations
                are available and how do they function?

GEOGR.AREA: Germany, Federal Republic (Berlin)

PROCEDURE: Action Research

LANGUAGE: German

DURATION: Aug. 1977 - Aug. 1979

TYPE OF   Researcher's project
RESEARCH:

FUNDS: Internal sources

* * *

NO. 160   Social Contacts and Participation of Migrant Workers in
                the Federal Republic of Germany.

INSTITUTION: Universität Frankfurt, FB 03, Gesellschaftswissenschaf-
                ten, Arbeitsgruppe Soziale Infrastruktur (University
                of Frankfurt, Working Group Social Infrastructure)
                Bockenheimer Landstrasse 142
                D-6000 Frankfurt
                Germany, Federal Republic
                Tel.No.: 0611/7983966

RESEARCHER: Hondrich, Karl Otto/ Koch, Claudia/ Kontos, Maria/
                Schöneberg, Ulrike

CONTACT: Schöneberg, Ulrike
                Tel.No.: 0611/7983969

DISCIPLINE   Political Sciences (Political Organizations)
AND SUBFIELD: Sociology

ABSTRACT: In addition to the question of political participation
                the project's aim is to discuss to what extent and un-
                der which conditions migrant workers have found access
                to primary and secondary groups in the Federal Repub-
                lic of Germany and how they have been influenced in
                their attitudes; furthermore, the project will examine
                which factors are responsible for changes in German
                organizations and for the establishment of national or-
                ganizations which serve the migrant workers to articu-
                late their specific and general interests and to satis-
                fy their demands.

GEOGR.AREA: Germany, Federal Republic (Hesse, large city - Frank-
                fort -, medium-sized town, probably small town)

PROCEDURE: Personal interview (550 Greeks/ 550 Italians/ 550 Turks
                 - each 18   years and above - in two or three towns of
                 various size -);
                 Expert interview (About 20-25 officials of selected
                 German and national organizations);
                 Document analysis (Qualitative analysis of the statutes
                 and annual reports of 15 organizations).

LANGUAGE: German

DURATION: June 1980 - May 1983

TYPE OF   Sponsored research
RESEARCH:

FUNDS: External sources: Stiftung Volkswagenwerk, Hannover

                            * * *

NO. 161   Foreigners as Owners of Enterprises in Nuremberg.

INSTITUTION: Universität Erlangen - Nürnberg, FB 11, Erziehungs-
                 und Kulturwissenschaften, Fach Landes- und Volkskunde
                 (University of Erlangen-Nürnberg, Institute of Ethnol-
                 ogy)
                 Regensburger Strasse 160
                 D-8500 Nürnberg
                 Germany, Federal Republic

RESEARCHER: Heller, Hartmut

CONTACT: Heller, Hartmut
                 Tel.No.: 0911/406085 or 09131/31706

DISCIPLINE   Demography
AND SUBFIELD: Sociology (Industrial Sociology)

ABSTRACT: This new collection of data aims at establishing a basis
                 for comparing them to those arrived at by an analysis
                 of the industrial card index and of interviews carried
                 out in 1974/75. Fluctuation or stability of the condi-
                 tions, changes in the proportion of the nationalities,
                 changes of location, etc. are to be studied.

GEOGR.AREA: Germany, Federal Republic (Nuremberg)

PROCEDURE: Personal interview (10 percent of foreigners who own
                 enterprises in Nuremberg);
                 Document analysis.

LANGUAGE: German

DURATION: Nov. 1974 - Dec. 1979

TYPE OF   Researcher's project
RESEARCH:

FUNDS: Internal sources

                              * * *

NO. 162   Ethnogenesis and Associational Behavior: The Political
                 Organization of Welfare in Ethnic Communities in
                 Bristol.

INSTITUTION: Bristol Polytechnic, Department of Economics and Social
                 Science
                 Coldharbour Lane
                 GB-Frenchay, Bristol BS16 1QY
                 United Kingdom
                 Tel.No.: Bristol 656261

                 University of Warwick, Department of Sociology
                 GB-Coventry CV4 7AL
                 United Kingdom

RESEARCHER: Jackson, Alun

CONTACT: Jackson, Alun
                 Department of Economics and Social Science, Bristol
                 Polytechnic
                 Coldharbour Lane
                 GB-Bristol BS16 1QY
                 United Kingdom
                 Tel.No.: Bristol 656261 (ext. 376)

DISCIPLINE   Sociology
AND SUBFIELD:

ABSTRACT: The purpose of the project is to test the utility of
                 the concept of ethnogenesis in an urban British con-
                 text. This has been done by monitoring groups behavior
                 in ethnic communities in Bristol for a four year pe-
                 riod, focussing primarily on changes in associational
                 behavior, as they reflect the degree of internal struc-
                 turing in these communities, and the nature of external
                 relations. In particular, internal and external tension
                 management processes are identified, and the role of
                 welfare provision in ethnic communities is identified
                 as a particular contribution to this process. Results
                 indicate that the concept is of only limited value, but
                 that a focus on associations is a useful approach to
                 understanding community level politics in ethnic commu-
                 nities.

GEOGR.AREA: United Kingdom (England, Bristol City area)

PROCEDURE: Personal interview (Executive and members of ethnic
                  associations);
                  Group discussion (Executive and members of ethnic asso-
                  ciations);
                  Expert interview;
                  Participant observation;
                  Non-participant observation;
                  Document analysis (Association records).

LANGUAGE: English

DURATION: 1978 - Sept. 1981

TYPE OF   Researcher's project/ Ph.D.
RESEARCH:

FUNDS: Internal sources

PUBLICATIONS: Just how relevant and accessible are Social Services
                  Departments. Social work Today, 10, 25, 1979.
                  The Fury ... the aftermath. Social work Today, 11, 32,
                  1980.
                  Social work education for multi racial practice: a
                  British example. Contemporary Social work Education,
                  3, 3, 1980.
                  A model of social work education for multi racial prac-
                  tice in Great Britain. Jnl of Education for Social
                  Work, 17 Winter, 1980.
                  Ethnocentrism and the perception of racial difference
                  by social workers. Multi Racial Social work, 1, 1981.
                  A political psychology of ethnogenesis. Human Relations
                  (forthcoming).

                              * * *

NO. 163   Retail and Service Business and the Immigrant Communi-
                  ty: A Comparative Study of Bradford, Leicester and
                  Ealing.

INSTITUTION: Liverpool Polytechnic, Department of Social Studies
                  Walton House, Tithebarn Street
                  GB-Liverpool L2 2NG (Merseyside)
                  United Kingdom
                  Tel.No.: 051/2271781

                  Edge Hill College, Department of Geography
                  GB-Ormskirk (Lancashire)
                  United Kingdom
                  Tel.No.: 0695/75171

                  Cornell University, New York State School of Industrial
                  and Labor Relations
                  P. O. Box 1000
                  Ithaca
                  US-New York 14853
                  USA
                  Tel.No.: 607 256 3048

RESEARCHER: <u>McEvoy</u>, David (Liverpool)/ <u>Cater</u>, John C. (Ormskirk)/
                 <u>Aldrich</u>, Howard E.(Ithaca)/ <u>Jones</u>, Trevor P. (Liver-
                 pool)

CONTACT: McEvoy, David
                 Department of Social Studies, Liverpool Polytechnic
                 Walton House, Tithebarn Street
                 GB-Liverpool L2 2NG (Merseyside)
                 United Kingdom
                 Tel.No.: 051/2271781

DISCIPLINE   Geography (Urban Geography/ Marketing Geography)
AND SUBFIELD: Sociology (Industrial Sociology/ Sociology of Work)
                 Business Studies (Small business sector)

ABSTRACT: Business activity of Asian immigrants in three British
                 Cities was examined in 1978 by means of:
                 i) a complete inventory of Asian and non-Asian retail
                 and service businesses in the study area;
                 ii) extensive structured interviews with approximately
                 100 Asian businesses and 100 white businesses in each
                 city;
                 iii) population data for the study areas derived from
                 name counts in electoral registers.
                 In 1980 a follow-up study ascertained survivals, re-
                 placements and disappearances for the originally inter-
                 viewed businesses. Future re-surveys are also planned.
                 Preliminary results offer support for the <u>ecological</u>
                 <u>succession concept</u> whereby residential population suc-
                 cession is parallelled by business succession. However,
                 there is some support also for the <u>middleman minority</u>
                 <u>concept</u> whereby immigrant groups occupy specific eco-
                 nomic niches by virtue of their sojourner orientation
                 towards the host society. Preliminary results do not
                 support the view that Asian businesses develop in se-
                 quence from low hierarchical order to higher hierarch-
                 ical order.

GEOGR. AREA: United Kingdom (The five wards in each of Bradford,
                 Ealing and Leicester which according to the 1971 Census
                 contained the highest proportion of immigrants from
                 India and Pakistan)

PROCEDURE: Personal interview (574 of 3,521 retail and service
                 businesses in the area studied);
                 Non-participant observation (3,521 retail and service
                 businesses in the area studied);
                 Secondary data analysis (249,405 population of area
                 examined).

LANGUAGE: English

DURATION: Apr. 1978 - Mar. 1979

TYPE OF   Sponsored research/ Institution project/ Researcher's
RESEARCH: project/ Ph.D.

FUNDS: Internal sources
                External sources: A grant for Ł 9,052 from SSRC cover-
                ed the period from April 1978 to March 1979. Continu-
                ing activity is sustained within the budgets of the
                institutions.

PUBLICATIONS: Retail and Service Business and the Immigrant Communi-
                ty: Final Report HR 5520, to Social Science Research
                Council (London), 1980, 82 pages.

UNPUBLISHED   Aldrich, H.E.; Cater, J.C.; Jones, T.P.; McEvoy, D.:
PAPERS: From Periphery to Peripheral: the South Asian Petite
                Bourgeoisie in England, forthcoming in: I.H. Simpson +
                R. Simpson (Eds.), Research in the Sociology of Work,
                Vol. 2, JAI Press, 1981 (pages not yet available).
                Aldrich H.E.; Cater, J.C.; Jones, T.P.; McEvoy, D.:
                Business Development and Self Segregation: Asian Enter-
                prise in Three British Cities, in: C. Peach (Ed.), Eth-
                nic Segregation in Cities, Croom Helm, Forthcoming.
                (A shortened version of this paper also appears in Na-
                tional Association for Asian Youth, Report of 1980 Na-
                tional Conference, Southall, 1981). Page nos. of these
                papers not yet available.

* * *

Other Ethnic Minorities

NO. 164   The Economic and Social Development of Styria, 1938 -
                 1945.

INSTITUTION: Universität Graz, Institut für Geschichte, Abt. für So-
                 zial- und Wirtschaftsgeschichte (University of Graz,
                 Institute of History, Dept. of Social and Economic His-
                 tory)
                 Heinrichstrasse 26
                 A-8010 Graz (Steiermark)
                 Austria
                 Tel.No.: 0316/32581 946

RESEARCHER: Pickl, Othmar/ Karner, Stefan

CONTACT: Karner, Stefan
                 Institut für Geschichte, Abt. für Sozial- und Wirt-
                 schaftsgeschichte, Universität Graz
                 Heinrichstrasse 26
                 A-8010 Graz
                 Austria
                 Tel.No.: 0316/32581 946

DISCIPLINE   Economics (History)
AND SUBFIELD: Sociology (History)

ABSTRACT: Political and social changes in Styria 1938-1945 (in
                 general), labour movement and social status of workers
                 1938-1945, "Volkstum" policy, desettlement of Slovenes,
                 partisan fights. Development of Styrian armament and
                 war industry (200 chronicles of firms with strong so-
                 cial emphasis). Resistance.

GEOGR.AREA: Austria (Styria)

PROCEDURE: Personal interview;
                   Questionnaire;
                   Document analysis (Archive Material/Chronicles of 200
                   firms);
                   Qualitative content analysis;
                   Quantitative content analysis;
                   Secondary data analysis.

LANGUAGE: German

DURATION: Oct. 1977 - Oct. 1980

TYPE OF   Sponsored research
RESEARCH:

FUNDS: External sources:
                   Fonds zur Förderung der Wissenschaftlichen Forschung
                   Garnisongasse 7-20
                   A-1090 Wien
                   Austria

PUBLICATIONS: Karner, S.: Der Plan einer geschlossenen Umsiedlung der
                   Grödner in die Steiermark von 1941, in: ZHUSt,1978.
                   Karner, S.: Die Aussiedlung der Slowenen in der Unter-
                   steiermark, in: OEGL, 3/78.

                              * * *

NO. 165   Genesis, Structure, and Function of the Carinthian Eth-
                   nic Minority Conflict.

INSTITUTION: Universität für Bildungswissenschaften, Institut für
                   Bildungsökonomie und Bildungssoziologie (University of
                   Educational Sciences, Institute of Educational Economy
                   and Sociology of Education)
                   Universitätsstrasse 65-67
                   A-9010 Klagenfurt (Kärnten)
                   Austria
                   Tel.No.: 04222/23730 472

RESEARCHER: Holzinger, Wolfgang

CONTACT: Steingress, Gerhard
                   Institut für Bildungsökonomie und Bildungssoziologie
                   Universität für Bildungswissenschaften Klagenfurt
                   Universitätsstrasse 65-67
                   A-9010 Klagenfurt
                   Austria
                   Tel.No.: 04222/23730 472

DISCIPLINE   Anthropology (Social Anthropology), Ethnology
AND SUBFIELD: Economics (Political Economy)
                   Linguistics (Sociolinguistics)
                   Political Sciences (International Relations)
                   Sociology (System Theory)
                   History (Social and Economic History)

ABSTRACT: A theoretical framework is to be constructed to ac-
                 count for the general situation of ethnic groupings as
                 objects of unequal societal distribution of socio-eco-
                 nomic positions and political rights. As - besides spe-
                 cific characteristics - there are primordial universal
                 characteristics to be described and explained, it is
                 the constitutional circumstances of ethnic groupings
                 and movements being relevant here. It has become more
                 and more obvious that any explanation of distinct ethnic
                 conflicts has to refer to the history and structure of
                 the contemporary capitalist world economy as the basic
                 unit of social theory and the concept of 'ethnicity'.
                 I.Wallerstein("The Modern World System I,II")proves it
                 to be a paradigm which explores the historical genesis
                 of the unity "world economy" from the standpoint of a
                 modified system theory using the "centre/periphery"-
                 model. Thus, the international world-system perspec-
                 tive figures as the main explanatory resource of any
                 contemporary societal problem in any part of the world
                 integrated into this system. This assertion also con-
                 cerns subregions of national countries, its specific
                 dependencies and problems (for instance ethnic prob-
                 lems in Carinthia).

GEOGR.AREA: Central Europe (Austrian-Hungarian Empire and Republic
                 of Austria, Carinthia)

LANGUAGE: German

DURATION: 1978 - 1983

TYPE OF   Researcher's project/ Habilitation
RESEARCH:

FUNDS: Internal sources

PUBLICATIONS: Soziale und sozialpsychische Hintergründe des Kärtner
                 Minoritätenkonflikts, in: ZEITGESCHICHTE, Nr. 9/10,
                 1976, pp. 308-318.
                 Die DDR und die Lausitzer Sorben - ein Minoritätenre-
                 port, in: MLADJE, Nr. 30, 1978, pp. 63-92, Nr. 31, 1978,
                 pp. 66-89, (with G. Steingress).
                 Die Idee der Versöhnung in ideologiekritischer Perspek-
                 tive, in: F. Dotter, et. al. (ed.), Christliche Markie-
                 rungen, Europa Verlag, Wien 1979, pp. 43-64.
                 Konstitutionsprobleme des europäischen Gesellschafts-
                 und Staatensystems, in: Zehn Jahre Universität Klagen-
                 furt, Band "Forschungsperspektiven '80", Klagenfurt
                 1980, pp. 75-92.

                         * * *

NO. 166   'Dolomiten' and 'Alto Adige'. A Comparison in Form and
                   Content of the Newspapers for the German and Italian
                   Speaking Ethnic Groups in South Tyrol from 1945 to 1972.

INSTITUTION: Universität Salzburg, Institut für Publizistik und Kom-
                   munikationswissenschaft (University of Salzburg, Insti-
                   tute of Communication Research)
                   Sigmund Haffner Gasse 18/III
                   A-5020 Salzburg
                   Austria
                   Tel.No.: 0622/86111 388

RESEARCHER: Ramminger, Helmut K.

CONTACT: Ramminger, Helmut K.
                   Faberstrasse 28/6/12
                   A-5020 Salzburg
                   Austria
                   Tel.No.: 06222/779224

DISCIPLINE   Communication
AND SUBFIELD:

ABSTRACT: Comparative study of content and form by means of con-
                   tent analysis. Hypothesis: the two newspapers represent
                   their ethnic group and serve as an instrument of propa-
                   ganda for their specific political aims. They facilitate
                   easier identification of the group members with the
                   group and its aims. Additional question: is the news-
                   paper 'Dolomiten' in a language ghetto? Preliminary re-
                   sults: Frequency and length of politically relevant con-
                   tributions correlate with political activity. The trans-
                   mitter function of the newspapers is confirmed by fre-
                   quency of appearing categories.

GEOGR.AREA: Italy (South Tyrol)

PROCEDURE: Quantitative content analysis (532 out of 17,000 newspapers)

LANGUAGE: German

DURATION: Mar. 1980 (end)

TYPE OF   Dissertation
RESEARCH:

                                  * * *

NO. 167   The Carinthian Slovenes in the Austrian Daily Press -
                   Minorities in Mass Media Reporting.

INSTITUTION: Universität Salzburg, Institut für Publizistik und Kom-
                   munikationswissenschaft (University of Salzburg, Insti-
                   tute of Communication Research)
                   Sigmund Haffner Gasse 18/III
                   A-5020 Salzburg
                   Austria
                   Tel.No.: 0622/86111 388

RESEARCHER: Strobl, Rudolf Ludwig

CONTACT: Strobl, Rudolf Ludwig
                 Tel.No.: 06274/78143

DISCIPLINE   Communication
AND SUBFIELD:

ABSTRACT: The analysis focusses on the kind of information that
                 is being spread by the Austrian daily newspapers
                 (written for the majority of the population) about the
                 situation and the problems of the Slovenian minority.
                 The question how the 'majority media' handle the infor-
                 mation about the minority and how the minority is being
                 presented by the press shall be answered by means of an
                 analysis of the commentary newspaper articles.
                 Questions: 1. What is the position of the Austrian dai-
                 ly newspapers regarding the problems of minorities?
                 1.1. How do the newspapers describe the laws concerning
                 minorities? 1.2. What is the opinion of the daily news-
                 papers regarding the minority-supporting (democracy-
                 supporting) postulates?

GEOGR.AREA: Austria

PROCEDURE: Quantitative content analysis (19 Austrian newspapers -
                 published from June 23 to July 27, 1976 and during No-
                 vember 1976 - analysis of the commentary articles -)

LANGUAGE: German

DURATION: Sept. 1976 - June 1979

TYPE OF   Dissertation
RESEARCH:

* * *

NO. 168   The Role of a Minority (Bukarim) in the Process of In-
                 dustrialization in Japan - Exemplified by the Textile
                 Industry.

INSTITUTION: Universität Wien, Institut für Japanologie (University
                 of Vienna, Institute for Japanese Studies)
                 Universitätsstrasse 7
                 A-1010 Wien
                 Austria
                 Tel.No.: 0222/4300 2556

RESEARCHER: Kaneko, Martin

DISCIPLINE   Social History
AND SUBFIELD:

ABSTRACT: Since official history almost completely ignores the
history of the minorities there is little knowledge
about the role of the Bukarim, the biggest minority
within Japan, in the Japanese industrialization process.
In his dissertation the author could compile some material on the connection of Bukarim and coal mining and
matches' productions. About the role of the Bukarim in
the textile industry, the very branch which furthered
the growth of the Japanese economy, little research has
been done now in Japan. Written documents are hardly
available since informants are mostly illiterate. The
number of the informants is constantly reduced due to
their age. By interviewing Bukarim who have worked in
the textile industry, it is planned to secure material
which proves the exploitation of the Bukarim as low
cost employees in the Japanese industrialization process. The present work will constitute part of a
planned social history of the Bukarim.

GEOGR.AREA: Japan

PROCEDURE: Personal interview;
                   Group discussion.

LANGUAGE: German

DURATION: Jan. 1979 - July 1979

TYPE OF   Researcher's project
RESEARCH:

FUNDS: Internal sources

                              * * *

NO. 169   The Role of a Discriminated Minority (Bukarim) in the
                   Japanese Textile Industry before World War II.

INSTITUTION: Universität Wien, Institut für Japanologie (University
                   of Vienna, Institute for Japanese Studies)
                   Universitätsstrasse 7
                   A-1010 Wien
                   Austria
                   Tel.No.: 0222/4300 2556

RESEARCHER: Kaneko, Martin

DISCIPLINE   Social and Economic History
AND SUBFIELD:

ABSTRACT: The Bukarim, Japan's biggest minority, have been partially excluded from access to modern branches of industry
through discrimination. This fact has been somewhat gen-
eralized by Japanese researchers. The researcher tries
to show that the Bukarim, too, depending on the situation of the labour market, have been recruited to work
in the textile industry. Interviews showed that in some

parts of the country, e.g. South Osaka, the Bukarim
have been employed in great numbers in spinning mills.
In the enterprises where the Bukarim worked the wage
level was especially low. Furthermore, in these enterprises a great number of Korean workers have been employed, these people also being a discriminated minority. It seems that there were enterprises which employed neither Bukarim nor Koreans to avoid conflicts
among the workers. On the other hand there were enterprises which to a great extent recruited their manpower
from socially discriminated groups (Bukarim, Koreans,
people from Okinava) to keep an especially low wage
level.

GEOGR.AREA:	Japan
PROCEDURE:	Personal interview (30 Bukarim); Document analysis.
LANGUAGE:	German
DURATION:	Feb. 1979 - Feb. 1981
TYPE OF RESEARCH:	Sponsored research
FUNDS:	External sources: Fonds zur Förderung der Wissenschaftlichen Forschung Garnisongasse 7-20 A-1090 Wien Austria

* * *

NO. 170   The Role of Assimilation Organizations within the Assimilation Policy towards the Korean Minority in Japan
1910 - 1945 - with Special Consideration to the Prefec-
ture Osaka.

INSTITUTION:	Universität Wien, Institut für Japanologie (University of Vienna, Institute for Japanese Studies) Universitätsstrasse 7 A-1010 Wien Austria Tel.No.: 0222/4300 2556
RESEARCHER:	Ringhofer, Manfred
DISCIPLINE AND SUBFIELD:	Social and Economic History

ABSTRACT: Aims and type of the assimilation policy towards Koreans
in comparison to the colonial policy in Korea; the role
of the assimilation organizations in assimilation policy, especially the role of Osaka. The question of the
existence of continuity of assimilation organizations
before the foundation of a national assimilation orga-

nization 1935 /36 . Description of the activities of assimilation organizations and evaluation of the "success"; the understanding of the situation before 1945
is a precondition for the understanding of the present
situation of the Korean minority, especially with re-
gard to Osaka, where the largest percentage of Coreans
live and only limited research has been done due to
very scarce and scattered sources of information. Nu-
merous contradictions between goals and reality, some
"success" in the fields of culture and education, which
also continued after 1945, no "success" in eliminating
the discrimination practiced by the Japanese; no essen-
tial differences in the assimilation policy before and
after 1945.

GEOGR.AREA: Japan

PROCEDURE: Personal interview (15 Koreans/ 5 Japanese);
               Group discussion (15-20 Japanese and Koreans);
               Expert interview (25-30 Japanese and Koreans);
               Document analysis;
               Qualitative content analysis;
               Quantitative content analysis.

LANGUAGE: German

DURATION: Apr. 1977 - Jan. 1980

TYPE OF   Dissertation
RESEARCH:

FUNDS: External sources: Japanese Ministry for Culture

                              * * *

NO. 171   Slovenes in Carinthia. Conditions for Language Sociali-
               zation.

INSTITUTION: Universität Wien, Institut für Slawistik (University of
               Vienna, Institute of Slavistic Studies)
               Liebiggasse 5
               A-1010 Wien
               Austria
               Tel.No.: 0222/435149

RESEARCHER: Fischer, Gero

DISCIPLINE   Linguistics (Sociolinguistics)
AND SUBFIELD:

ABSTRACT: History; social, economic and political conditions
               causing a language conflict. Survey on cultural history,
               development of literature and standard language. Legal
               regulations concerning languages incl. education. Types
               of documents (legal texts etc.). Political articulation
               of conflict on the linguistic and social level.

GEOGR.AREA: Austria (Carinthia)

PROCEDURE: Document analysis

LANGUAGE: German

DURATION: Feb. 1977 - Jan. 1979

TYPE OF   Researcher's project
RESEARCH:

PUBLICATIONS: Fischer, G.: Zum Sprachenkonflikt in Südkärnten, in:
                Osnabrücker Beiträge zur Sprachtheorie, 5, 1977, S. 29-
                59.
                Fischer, G.: Das Slowenische in Kärnten. Bedingungen
                der sprachlichen Sozialisation, Wien 1979.

* * *

NO. 172   The Slovaks in Lower Austria.

INSTITUTION: Universität Wien, Institut für Slawistik (University of
                Vienna, Institute of Slavistic Studies)
                Liebiggasse 5
                A-1010 Wien
                Austria
                Tel.No.: 0222/435149

RESEARCHER: Fischer, Gero

DISCIPLINE   Linguistics (Socio linguistics)
AND SUBFIELD:

ABSTRACT: Immigration; language behavior, social structure, prob-
                lems of acculturation. Documents (Chronicles).

GEOGR.AREA: Austria (Lower Austria)

PROCEDURE: Document analysis

LANGUAGE: German

DURATION: Oct. 1978 - Aug. 1979

TYPE OF   Sponsored research
RESEARCH:

FUNDS: External sources:
                Federal Ministry of Science and Research
                Minoritenplatz 5
                A-1014 Wien
                Austria

PUBLICATIONS: Fielhauer, H.: Das Ende einer Minderheit, in: Rhein.
                Jahrbuch für Volkskunde, 22, 1978, S. 95-151.

* * *

NO. 173   Language Socialization of the Croats in Burgenland.

INSTITUTION: Universität Wien, Institut für Slawistik (University of
                Vienna, Institute for Slavistic Studies)
                Liebiggasse 5
                A-1010 Wien
                Austria
                Tel.No.: 0222/435149

RESEARCHER: Fischer, Gero

DISCIPLINE   Linguistics (Sociolinguistics)
AND SUBFIELD:

ABSTRACT: Characteristics of the settlement region; historical,
                social and economic factors ; cultural-political sit-
                uation; legal regulations; language behavior. Documen-
                tations.

GEOGR.AREA: Austria

PROCEDURE: Document analysis

LANGUAGE: German

DURATION: Mar. 1979 - June 1980

TYPE OF   Researcher's project
RESEARCH:

PUBLICATIONS: Fischer, G.: Bemerkungen zum Sprachtod, in: Sprache und
                Herrschaft, 1, 1978, S. 7-26.

                            * * *

NO. 174   Politics and Language Policies in Austria-Hungary: Oc-
                cupational Structure, Ideologies and Language Conflicts.

INSTITUTION: Universität Wien, Institut für Zeitgeschichte (Univer-
                sity of Vienna, Institute of Contemporary History)
                Rotenhausgasse 6
                A-1090 Wien
                Austria

                Universität Wien, Institut für Soziologie (University
                of Vienna, Institute of Sociology)
                Neutorgasse 12/9
                A-1010 Wien
                Austria
                Tel.No.: 632878

RESEARCHER: Simon, Walter/ Brix, Emil/ Diethart, Johannes/ Enderle,
                Peter/ Forst-Battaglia, Jakob/ Lichtenberg-Fenz,
                Brigitte/ O'Grady, Paul/ Radzyner, Joanna

CONTACT: Simon, Walter B.
                 Inst. f. Soziologie
                 Neutorgasse 12/9
                 A-1010 Wien
                 Austria
                 Tel.No.: 632878

DISCIPLINE   Sociology (Political Sociology)
AND SUBFIELD:

ABSTRACT: Thesis to be tested:
                 Multilingualism becomes a source of conflict only as a
                 consequence of changes in the occupational structure
                 so that language competence affects career chances.
                 We find no language conflicts in pre-industrial or agra-
                 rian societies, or where dialects are spoken or where
                 language groups accept established language usage.
                 Language conflicts are especially difficult to resolve
                 because
                 a) there is no infinite divisibility of the stakes as
                    in economic conflicts;
                 b) tolerance is ineffective here because the interests
                    involved are too basic;
                 c) those most strongly affected by language policies
                    are students who are well able to impede compromise
                    solutions;
                 d) because of the above, language conflicts tend to re-
                    main latent until they become explosive.

                 Language conflicts develop in the wake of industriali-
                 zation and urbanization. Especially in language con-
                 flicts we may observe the relationships between "peace-
                 ful moderates" and "militant extremists" within antag-
                 onistic camps.

GEOGR.AREA: The Austro-Hungarian Monarchy before 1918

PROCEDURE: Document analysis (Historical research);
                 Secondary data analysis (Census data and election re-
                 sults).

LANGUAGE: German

DURATION: Jan. 1975 - Dec. 1981

TYPE OF   Sponsored research/ Researcher's project
RESEARCH:

FUNDS: External sources: Jubiläumsfondprojekt der Österreichi-
                 schen Nationalbank Nr. 779

PUBLICATIONS: Simon, Walter B.: A Comparative Study of the Problem of
                 Multilingualism, Mens en Maatschappij, Amsterdam,
                 spring of 1967.
                 Alle Menschen werden Nachbarn - nicht Brüder, Europä-
                 ische Rundschau, Wien   1974/2.
                 A Sociological Analysis of Multilingualism, Languages
                 and Cultures in Multi-Ethnic Society, (edited by Paul
                 Migus), Peter Martin Ass., Toronto 1975.

Occupational Structure, Multilingualism, and Social
Change, in: Multilingual Political Systems, editors
Savard & Vigneault, Laval University Press, Quebec
Univ., 1975.
Brix, E.: Die Erhebungen der Umgangssprache im zis-
leithanischen Österreich (1880 - 1910), in: Mitteilun-
gen des Instituts für österreichische Geschichtsfor-
schung, Verlag Böhlau, Wien-Köln-Graz 1979.
Kultureller Pluralismus, by W. Simon, published by
Inst. f. Soziologie, 1979.

UNPUBLISHED   Radzyner, J.: Der ruthenische Nationswerdungsprozeß in
PAPERS: Galizien.
                   Löw, R.: Sprachen - und Nationalitätenkonflikte in der
                   österreichischen Sozialdemokratie 1889 - 1914.
                   Lichtenberg-Fenz, B.: Die italienische Universitäts-
                   frage in Österreich (1861 - 1918).
                   Diethart, Johannes M.: Der Fall des slowenischen Gym-
                   nasiums in Cilli.
                   Approaching completion: Forst-Battaglia, J.: Die
                   Sprachanfrage an den Universitäten und Mittelschulen
                   Galiziens (1772 - 1918).
                   Of special interest: Paul O'Grady is preparing a card
                   catalogue with references to language conflicts as they
                   appear in Reichsratsdebates and are recorded in the
                   Protokoll des Reichsrats.

                              * * *

NO. 175   Social Psychological and Socio-Economic Aspects of the
                   Ethnic Structure in Carinthia.

RESEARCHER: Bichlbauer , Dieter/ Flaschberger, Ludwig/ Haas, Hans/
                   Reiterer, Alfred/ Stuhlpfarrer, Karl

CONTACT: Bichlbauer, Dieter
                   Weinlechnerg. 8/13
                   A-1030 Wien
                   Austria
                   Tel.No.: 0222/531495 (Office); 0222/.7367885 (private)

DISCIPLINE   Anthropology, Ethnology
AND SUBFIELD: Linguistics
                   Political Sciences
                   Psychology (Social Psychology)
                   Sociology

ABSTRACT: Purpose: - Historical analysis of the educational poli-
                              cy of the Austrian Government with regard to
                              the Slovenian minority
                            - Social and economic conditions in Southern
                              Carinthia
                            - Empirical research on language behavior and
                              ethnic prejudices
                            - Theoretical and conceptual research on the
                              concepts of State, Nation, Nationality and
                              Minority

Some results: There are strong prejudices in the population of Carinthia against the Slovenian
minority. These negative attitudes are
the reason why daily life is quite difficult for the minority.
The Slovenian language is spoken in family, neighbourhood and in the church but
not in public and at work.
The Slovenian language is becoming ex-
tinct because most parents do not speak
with their children in their own language.
A high percentage of Slovenes have an in-
feriority complex against German speaking
people which has a historical basis.

GEOGR.AREA: Austria (Southern Carinthia)

PROCEDURE: Personal interview (400 people of Völkermarkt, Carin-
thia);
Document analysis;
Secondary data analysis.

LANGUAGE: German

DURATION: May 1975 - Sept. 1979

TYPE OF
RESEARCH: Sponsored research

FUNDS: External sources: Ministry for Science and Research

PUBLICATIONS: The Daily Defence (Der tägliche Abwehrkampf), Verlag
Wilhelm Braumüller, Universitäts-Verlagsbuchhandlung
GmbH, Vienna 1980.

* * *

NO. 176 The Ethnic Pattern of the Flemish Population in
Brussels.

INSTITUTION: Vrije Universiteit Brussel, Centrum voor Sociologie
(University of Brussels, Centre of Sociology)
Pleinlaan 2
B-Brussel
Belgium
Tel.No.: 6481102

RESEARCHER: Louckx, Fred

DISCIPLINE
AND SUBFIELD: Sociology (Sociology of Language)

ABSTRACT: Language behavior and language attitudes of the Flemish
people in Brussels.

GEOGR.AREA: Belgium (Brussels)

PROCEDURE: Personal interview;
                  Document analysis;
                  Secondary data analysis.

LANGUAGE: Dutch

DURATION: Nov. 1977 - Nov. 1980

TYPE OF   Institution project
RESEARCH:

FUNDS: Internal sources

                              * * *

NO. 177   Problems Arising in Connection with the Involvement of
                  Local People in Development of Local Communities Exem-
                  plified by Greenland and Western Samoa.

INSTITUTION: Aalborg Universitetscenter, Institut for Samfundsfag og
                  Plan laegning
                  Fibigerstraede 11
                  DK-9100 Aalborg
                  Denmark

RESEARCHER: Gullestrup, Hans/ et alii

DISCIPLINE   Political Sciences
AND SUBFIELD:

ABSTRACT: The aims of two larger studies, "The Community Develop-
                  ment in Western Samoa" and "The Community Study of
                  Greenland" have been to analyse the Samoan and the
                  Greenlandic populations' own possibilities of influ-
                  encing the development of their respective countries.
                  This has been done as field work based on some analytic
                  models developed for this purpose. For the moment more
                  basic theoretical work is being done in order to set up
                  more general models about development problems for eth-
                  nic minorities and people in local areas.

GEOGR.AREA: Greenland/ Western Samoa

DURATION: The project has been running for a long time

                              * * *

NO. 178   Integration of Ethnic Groups in Uganda.

INSTITUTION: University of Copenhagen, Institute of Political Stud-
                 ies
                 Rosenborggade 15
                 DK-1130 København K
                 Denmark

RESEARCHER: Hansen, Holger Bernt

DISCIPLINE   Anthropology, Ethnology
AND SUBFIELD: Political Sciences (Methodology)
                 Sociology (Political Sociology)

ABSTRACT: One first aim has been to make the concept of ethnici-
                 ty manageable and operational in a concrete political
                 analysis. For that purpose a particular definition of
                 ethnicity is suggested and a scheme of analysis estab-
                 lished, inspired by Fr. Barth. The political saliency
                 of ethnic groups for the development in Uganda is then
                 examined. The degree of integration is especially meas-
                 ured by a comparison between ethnic groups and reli-
                 gious divisions in society and by the significance
                 which can be ascribed to ethnic groups within an insti-
                 tution like the army.

GEOGR.AREA: Uganda

DURATION: 1974 (start)

                          * * *

NO. 179   Corsicans in Southern France: Marseille, Toulon, Nice.

INSTITUTION: Université de Provence-Aix-Marseille I, Centre d'études
                 de la pensée politique et sociale contemporaine (Uni-
                 versity of Aix-Marseille I, Centre of Study of Contem-
                 porary Political and Social Thought)
                 29, avenue Robert Schumann
                 F-13621 Aix-en-Provence
                 France
                 Tel.No.: 42/599930

RESEARCHER: Pomponi, Francis/ Temime, Emile/ Kolodny, Emile/
                 Maraninchi, Marie Françoise

CONTACT: Pomponi, Francis
                 5, avenue des Belges
                 F-13000 Aix-en-Provence
                 France
                 Tel.No.: 42/264183

DISCIPLINE   Anthropology, Ethnology
AND SUBFIELD: Demography
                 History

ABSTRACT: Emigration and settlement of Corsicans on the continent
                   (especially Marseille) since 1900.
                   Usual research methods: analysis of census, oral surveys,
                   analysis of Marseilles' Corsican press, have been used
                   in the preliminary phase.
                   Statistical data, percentage , maps, chronology, inter-
                   pretations, are being prepared.
                   A parallel study will be conducted by the Institute of
                   Corsican Studies upon departure regions.

GEOGR.AREA: France (Corsica, Marseille, Toulon, Nice)

LANGUAGE: French

DURATION: June 1979 - Dec. 1982

TYPE OF   Institution project
RESEARCH:

FUNDS: External sources: Délégation Générale à la Recherche
                   Scientifique et Technique - DGRST

                            * * *

NO. 180   Language and Culture in Regional Identity and Develop-
                   ment.

INSTITUTION: Commission nationale pour les études et les recherches
                   interethniques (Interethnical Research and Study Na-
                   tional Commission)
                   54, boulevard Raspail
                   F-75006 Paris
                   France
                   Tel.No.: 5443849

RESEARCHER: Giordan, Henri

DISCIPLINE   Anthropology, Ethnology
AND SUBFIELD: Geography
                   Linguistics
                   Political Sciences
                   Sociology
                   History

ABSTRACT: Image of the minority concept in recent literary and
                   social sciences publications. Regions studied are:
                   Britanny, Occitany, Corsica, Catalogna (North), Alsace.

GEOGR.AREA: France (Britanny, Occitanny, Corsica, Catalogna (North),
                   Alsace)

PROCEDURE: Non-participant observation;
                   Document analysis.

LANGUAGE: French

DURATION: 1977 - 1981

TYPE OF   Institution project
RESEARCH:

FUNDS: External sources: Délégation à l'Aménagement du Terri-
                 toire et à l'Action Régionale - DATAR

                              * * *

NO. 181   Cultural Communities and National Identities: the Im-
                 portance of Foreigners in National and Social Move-
                 ments.

INSTITUTION: Université de Haute-Bretagne-Rennes II, Centre d'études
                 des minorités (University of Rennes II, Minorities
                 Studies Centre)
                 6, avenue Gaston Berger
                 F-35000 Rennes
                 France
                 Tel.No.: 99/592033

                 Maison des sciences de l'homme, Groupe d'études sur
                 l'autogestion (Study Group on Self-Management)
                 54, boulevard Raspail
                 F-75006 Paris
                 France
                 Tel.No.: 1/5443849

RESEARCHER: Bourdet, Yvon/ Couper, Kristin/ Weill, Claudie/ Cuche,
                 Denys/ Galissot, René/ Marienstras, Elise/ Marienstras,
                 Richard/ Simon-Barouh, Ida

CONTACT: Simon, Pierre Jean
                 20, rue de Paris
                 F-35000 Rennes
                 France
                 Tel.No.: 99/301675

DISCIPLINE   Political Sciences
AND SUBFIELD: Sociology
                 Social History

ABSTRACT: Cultural communities and national identities: the im-
                 portance of foreigners in national and social move-
                 ments.
                 Study of the function of a reference to self-management
                 in minorities'movements
                 Comparative socio-historical studies
                 - problems of integration of immigrants in 1850-1900
                   (USA)
                 - problems of minorities and Austrian-Marxist solutions
                   (empire of Austria-Hungary)
                 - projects upon national problems different from the
                   Bolchevik model (USSR)
                 - attitudes of the international workers movement to-
                   ward migrations (IInd and IIIrd International).

GEOGR.AREA: USA/ USSR/ Austria-Hungary

LANGUAGE: French

TYPE OF   Commissioned research
RESEARCH:

FUNDS: External sources: CNRS eventuality

PUBLICATIONS: Bourdet, Y.: Autogestion et minorités nationales, in:
               Pour, n° 71, Paris, mars 1980, p. 24-28.
               Weill, C.: Le débat sur les migrations ouvrières dans
               la IIe Internationale, in: Pluriel, n° 13, Paris 1978,
               p. 55-73.
               Marienstras, E.: Mythe et ambiguités de l'identité eth-
               nique aux Etats-Unis, in: Identités collectives et
               changements sociaux, Privat, Toulouse 1980.

                              * * *

NO. 182   Regional Identities and Problems of Minorities in In-
               dustrial Countries: the Case of Britanny.

INSTITUTION: Université de Haute-Bretagne - Rennes II, Centre
               d'études des minorités (University of Rennes II, Minor-
               ities Studies Centre)
               6, avenue Gaston Berger
               F-35043 Rennes Cédex
               France
               Tel.No.: 99/592033 (ext. 451)

RESEARCHER: Simon, Pierre-Jean/ Elegoet, Franck/ Quere, Louis/
               Simon-Barouh, Ida

CONTACT: Simon, Pierre-Jean
               20, rue de Paris
               F-35000 Rennes
               France
               Tel.No.: 99/301675

DISCIPLINE   Anthropology (Cultural Anthropology), Ethnology
AND SUBFIELD: Linguistics (Sociolinguistics)
               Sociology
               History

ABSTRACT: Analysis of Breton identity, combining the approaches
               of social anthropology, sociology and history:
               - Study of contemporary linguistic behavior and analy-
                 sis of the Breton linguistic problem since 1900
               - Study of contemporary processes of the non-communica-
                 tion of cultural traits in Britanny: women and child-
                 ren or adolescents
               - Analysis of Breton ethnicity: its negative minority
                 aspect, Breton neo-ethnicity, importance of the Bre-
                 ton movement
               - Analysis of Breton identity in social movements in
                 Britanny

GEOGR.AREA: France (Britanny)

PROCEDURE: Personal interview;
                 Participant observation;
                 Document analysis;
                 Qualitative content analysis.

LANGUAGE: French

TYPE OF   Institution project
RESEARCH:

FUNDS: Internal sources

PUBLICATIONS: Elegoet, F.: Prêtres, nobles et paysans en Léon au dé-
                 but du 20e siècle: Feiz ha Breiz, 1900-1914, in: Plu-
                 riel, n° 18, 1979, pp. 31-90.
                 Quere, L.: Les revendications nationalitaires dans les
                 transformations sociales, in: Economie et Humanisme,
                 mai-juin 1979.
                 Simon, P.-J.: Le mouvement breton, expression ou créa-
                 teur de la question bretonne?, in: Pluriel, n° 15,
                 1978, pp. 27-45.
                 Simon, P.-J.: Aspects de l'ethnicité bretonne, in: Plu-
                 riel, n° 19, 1979, pp. 23-43.

                              * * *

NO. 183   Regional Identities and Problems of Minorities in In-
                 dustrial Countries: the Case of Aquitaine.

INSTITUTION: Université de Haute-Bretagne - Rennes II, Centre
                 d'études des minorités (University of Rennes II, Minor-
                 ities Studies Centre)
                 6, avenue Gaston Berger
                 F-35043 Rennes Cédex
                 France
                 Tel.No.: 99/592033 (ext. 451)

RESEARCHER: Coulon, Christian/ Simon, Jean-Pierre/ Ritaine, Evelyne/
                 Viaut, Alain

CONTACT: Coulon, Christian
                 28, rue Socrate
                 F-33600 Pessac
                 France
                 Tel.No.: 56/458105

DISCIPLINE   Political Sciences
AND SUBFIELD: Sociology
                 History

ABSTRACT: Regional dimensions of contemporary problems in Aqui-
                 taine
                 1 - Historical and sociological approach of the expres-
                     sions of regional consciousness in the region of
                     Bordeaux

                    2 - Duality of regional thematic
                        - Process of fetishization and institutionalization
                        - Process of conflict and perception of the region
                          as a base for political solidarity

GEOGR.AREA: France (Aquitaine)

PROCEDURE: Personal interview;
                Group discussion;
                Participant observation;
                Qualitative content analysis.

LANGUAGE: French

PUBLICATIONS: Coulon, Ch.: La revendication occitane: repères biblio-
                graphiques, in: Pluriel, n° 16, 1978.

UNPUBLISHED   Ritaine, E.: Les actions culturelles en Aquitaine,
PAPERS: Bordeaux 1976.
                Viaut, A.: Le texte occitan du Médoc: inventaire bi-
                bliographique, Talence 1977, 133 p.

                            * * *

NO. 184   Research upon Occitan Identity.

INSTITUTION: Université de Toulouse le Mirail - Toulouse II, Centre
                de recherches sociologiques (University of Toulouse II,
                Sociological Research Centre)
                109 bis, rue Vauquelin
                F-31081 Toulouse Cédex
                France
                Tel.No.: 61/411105

RESEARCHER: Morin, Françoise/ Viguier, Marie-Françoise/ Granie,
                A.-M./ Pouget, G.

CONTACT: Morin, Françoise
                Université de Toulouse le Mirail, Institut de sciences
                sociales
                109 bis, rue Vauquelin
                F-31058 Toulouse Cédex
                Tel.No.: 61/411105

DISCIPLINE   Anthropology, Ethnology
AND SUBFIELD: Linguistics
                Sociology

ABSTRACT: Research upon identity:
                - analysis of Occitan discourse (the notion of the im-
                  age of Occitan amongst school-attendants, amongst Oc-
                  citans, in songs)
                - the notion of Occitan ethnic identity: ethnicity con-
                  ceived as a dynamic phenomenon, the language as em-
                  blem, the written works (press, songs), the frontiers

  - the experience of negative identity in a peasant pop-
    ulation (Lomagne)
  - the notion of "pays" (region, home) in Occitan cul-
    tural identity

GEOGR.AREA: France (Languedoc, Gascogne)

PROCEDURE: Personal interview;
               Group discussion;
               Participant observation;
               Document analysis;
               Qualitative content analysis;
               Quantitative content analysis.

LANGUAGE: French

DURATION: 1976 - 1982

TYPE OF   Institution project
RESEARCH:

FUNDS: Internal sources

PUBLICATIONS: Viguier, M. C.: Occitans sens o saber?, Vent Terral,
               1979, 190 p.
               Pour une sociologie occitane, in: Pluriel, n° 15, 1978.
               L'occitanie à la recherche de son eime, n° spécial
               Aica e ara, 1980.
               Morin, F.: Langue et identité ethnique: le cas occitan,
               in: Pluriel, n° 15, 1978, p. 9-27.
               Production et affirmation de l'identité, Privat, 1980.
               Pratiques anthropologiques et histoire de vie, in:
               Cahiers internationaux de sociologie, 1980.
               Morin, F.; Rivals, C.; Pouget, G.; Granie, A.M.: Iden-
               tité, différence et idéologie, in: Société, n° spécial,
               Tome XV, 1979.

                            * * *

NO. 185   Object Construction on the Basis of National Basque
               Myth.

INSTITUTION: Université de Toulouse le Mirail - Toulouse II, Centre
               de recherches sociologiques (University of Toulouse II,
               Sociological Research Centre)
               109 bis, rue Vauquelin
               F-31081 Toulouse Cédex
               France
               Tel.No.: 61/411105

RESEARCHER: Forne, José

DISCIPLINE   Sociology
AND SUBFIELD:

ABSTRACT: Articulation of the processes of collective identity to
                   reach national consciousness; these processes create
                   or re-create Basque identity.

GEOGR.AREA: Spain and France (Basque region)

PROCEDURE: Personal interview;
                   Document analysis (Regional press);
                   Qualitative content analysis.

LANGUAGE: French

DURATION: Nov. 1980 - July 1981

FUNDS: Internal sources

UNPUBLISHED   Bortoli, D.; Forne, J.: Impact social de la formation
PAPERS: sur une population de migrants, Pau et Toulouse,octobre
                   1977 - mai 1978, 250 p.

                              * * *

NO. 186   German Speaking Population in East Belgium. Change of
                   Social Structure and Political Consciousness.

INSTITUTION: Technische Hochschule Aachen, Seminar für Soziologie
                   (Technical University of Aachen, Sociological Seminar)
                   Ahornstrasse 55
                   D-5100 Aachen
                   Germany, Federal Republic
                   Tel.No.: 0241/803614

RESEARCHER: Rosensträter, Heinrich

DISCIPLINE   Political Sciences (Regionalism)
AND SUBFIELD: Sociology

ABSTRACT: Change of the economic structure; cultural and social
                   continuity; political activities and a new political
                   goal: more autonomy in order to preserve one's own language
                   and culture, independence from the Walloon region as a
                   goal. Specific problem of a minority: assimilation or
                   conservation?

GEOGR.AREA: Belgium (German speaking region - Eupen, Malmedy,
                   St. Vith)

PROCEDURE: Personal interview (150 inhabitants of 25 communities -
                   altogether 63,000 inhabitants -);
                   Group discussion;
                   Expert interview (23/63,000 inhabitants - mainly in two
                   small towns -);
                   Non-participant observation (25 observation groups in
                   25 communities);
                   Document analysis.

LANGUAGE: German

DURATION: July 1978 - July 1981

TYPE OF   Researcher's project
RESEARCH:

FUNDS: Internal sources

PUBLICATIONS: Planned

                         * * *

NO. 187   The German Minority in North Schleswig.

INSTITUTION: Universität Bonn, Institut für Gesellschafts- und Wirt-
                 schaftswissenschaften, Gesellschaftswissenschaftliche
                 Abteilung (University of Bonn, Institute of Social Sci-
                 ences)
                 Adenauerallee 24-42
                 D-5300 Bonn 1
                 Germany, Federal Republic
                 Tel.No.: 0228/739194

RESEARCHER: Zeh, Jürgen

DISCIPLINE   Linguistics (Sociolinguistics)
AND SUBFIELD: Political Sciences (Political Organizations/ Electoral
                 Behavior)
                 Sociology

ABSTRACT: Subjects of this study are the social relations between
                 the minority, society of origin, and host society, the
                 formation of these relationships and their changes in
                 the course of time. Among others are analysed: the use
                 of language and of media, the attitudes towards their
                 original and their host society, the political atti-
                 tudes, the electoral behavior, the degree of organiza-
                 tion, and the question of the minority's chances of
                 survival.

GEOGR.AREA: Denmark (North Schleswig)

PROCEDURE: Questionnaire (244 of the German minority in North-
                 Schleswig - above the age of sixteen -)

LANGUAGE: German

DURATION: Apr. 1977 - Sept. 1980

TYPE OF   Sponsored research/ Researcher's project
RESEARCH:

FUNDS: Internal sources
                External sources: Deutsche Forschungsgemeinschaft, Bonn

PUBLICATIONS: In preparation for 1981

UNPUBLISHED   Zeh, J.: Nordschleswig 1978 - Ergebnisse einer empiri-
PAPERS: schen Untersuchung der deutschsprachigen Bevölkerung
               in Nordschleswig.

                            * * *

NO. 188   Regionalism or Ethnicity? On the Territorialization of
                Social and Sectional Conflicts in France.

INSTITUTION: Universität Heidelberg, Institut für Politische Wissen-
                schaft (University of Heidelberg, Institute for Polit-
                ical Science)
                Marstallstrasse 6
                D-6900 Heidelberg
                Germany, Federal Republic
                Tel.No.: 06221/542860

RESEARCHER: Gerdes, Dirk

DISCIPLINE   Political Sciences (Regional Policy/ Regionalism)
AND SUBFIELD: Sociology (Social Conflict)

ABSTRACT: Investigation of the conflict behavior and conflict po-
                tential of regionalistic movements in Corsica, Southern
                France, and Britanny, on the background of state
                regional policy and tendencies towards a polarization
                of the economic structure. Ethnic nationalism as an
                ideological expression of a structurally conditioned
                territorialization of social and sectional conflicts
                in France.

GEOGR.AREA: France (Britanny, Corsica, Southern France)

PROCEDURE: Personal interview (Elite groups of regionalistic or-
                ganizations);
                Group discussion (French political scientists);
                Questionnaire (Regionalistic 'militants');
                Participant observation (Annual meeting of regional-
                istic organizations);
                Document analysis (Statistics/ Reports/ Dossiers);
                Qualitative content analysis (Programmatic literature
                etc.).

LANGUAGE: German

DURATION: Jan. 1978 (start)

TYPE OF   Habilitation
RESEARCH:

FUNDS: Internal sources

PUBLICATIONS: Gerdes, D.: Frankreich - 'Vielvölkerstaat' vor dem Zer-
                fall, in: Aus Politik und Zeitgeschichte, März 1980.
                Gerdes, D. (ed.): Aufstand der Provinz. Regionalismus
                in Westeuropa, Frankfurt-New York, Campus, 1980.
                Gerdes, D.: Minderheitenschutz - eine internationale
                Rechtsnorm auf der Suche nach ihrem Gegenstand, in:
                Vereinte Nationen, 4/80, August 1980.

UNPUBLISHED   Papers, manuscripts.
PAPERS:

                            * * *

NO. 189   The Sorbian Ethnic Group in Lusatia (Lausitz) 1949 -
                1977. A Documentary Report.

INSTITUTION: Johann-Gottfried-Herder-Institut
                Gisonenweg 7
                D-3550 Marburg 1
                Germany, Federal Republic

RESEARCHER: Urban, Rudolf

CONTACT: Urban, Rudolf
                Jenaer Weg 5
                D-3550 Marburg
                Germany, Federal Republic

DISCIPLINE   Political Sciences (Cultural Policy/ Political History
AND SUBFIELD: since 1945)
                Sociology

ABSTRACT: Description of the development of the Sorbian ethnici-
                ty in the German Democratic Republic.

GEOGR.AREA: Germany, Democratic Republic (Upper and Lower Lusatia
                - Lausitz -)

LANGUAGE: German

DURATION: The project is completed.

TYPE OF   Sponsored research
RESEARCH:

PUBLICATIONS: Urban, R.: Die sorbische Volksgruppe in der Lausitz
                1949 - 1977. Ein dokumentarischer Bericht, Marburg
                (Lahn), Verlag J.G. Herder-Institut, 1980, ISBN
                3-87969-151-7.

                            * * *

NO. 190   Judging the Personalities of Dutch and Frisian Speaking
                 Social Workers.

INSTITUTION: Rijksuniversiteit Groningen, Sociaal Hoger Onderwijs
                Friesland (University of Groningen, School of Social
                Studies)
                Haniasteeg 7
                NL-8911 BX Leeuwarden (Friesland)
                The Netherlands
                Tel.No.: 05100/51015

RESEARCHER: Plank, Pieter van der

DISCIPLINE   Psychology (Language/ Social Psychology)
AND SUBFIELD:

ABSTRACT: Frisian and Dutch ss. had to determine personality
                traits of Dutch and Frisian social workers (therapists)
                from their voices (textual fragments were recorded and
                evaluated by the SS.) in order to provoke their stereo-
                typed reactions towards Dutch and Frisian speaking
                people.

GEOGR.AREA: The Netherlands (the province of Friesland)

PROCEDURE: Test

LANGUAGE: Dutch and Frisian

DURATION: Jan. 1979 - Feb. 1979

TYPE OF   Institution project
RESEARCH: Researcher's project

FUNDS: Internal sources

PUBLICATIONS: Tussen Welzijn en Wolwêze, onderzoeksverslag, in:
                Redsumens, n° 3, 1980.

* * *

NO. 191   Research Project on Language Behavior and Language At-
                titude in Friesland, The Netherlands.

INSTITUTION: Nederlandse Organisatie voor Zuiver-Wetenschappelijk
                Onderzoek - Z.W.O. (Netherlands Organization for the
                Advancement of Pure Research)
                P.O.Box 93138
                NL-2509 AC 's-Gravenhage
                The Netherlands
                Tel.No.: 070/839100

                Fryske Akademy (Frisian Academy)
                Doelestrjitte 8
                NL-8911 DX Leeuwarden (Friesland)
                The Netherlands
                Tel.No.: 05100/31414

Rijksuniversiteit Groningen, Sociaal Hoger Onderwijs
Friesland (University of Groningen, School of Social
Studies)
Haniasteeg 7
NL-8911 BX Leeuwarden (Friesland)
The Netherlands
Tel.No.: 05100/51015

RESEARCHER: Gorter, Durk/ Jelsma, Gjalt/ Plank, Pieter van der

CONTACT: Plank, Pieter van der
                Haniasteeg 7
                NL-8911 BX Leeuwarden
                The Netherlands
                Tel.No.: 05100/51015

DISCIPLINE   Sociology (Sociology of Language)
AND SUBFIELD:

ABSTRACT: Detailed description of the domains of language use in
                Friesland, especially those where use of Frisian lan-
                guage has been retained and those where there has been
                a change.
                Description and analysis of the relationships between
                language use, linguistic competence, retention and
                change and socio-economical status, educational level,
                degree of urbanization.
                Further development of the theoretical concept "ethnici-
                ty".

GEOGR.AREA: The Netherlands (the province of Friesland)

PROCEDURE: Personal interview;
                Group discussion.

LANGUAGE: Dutch/ Frisian/ English

DURATION: Mar. 1979 - Mar. 1982

TYPE OF   Researcher's project
RESEARCH:

FUNDS: External sources: Z.W.O. - Nederlandse Stichting voor
                Zuiver-Wetenschappelijk Onderzoek

UNPUBLISHED   Plank, P. van der; et al.: Etniciteit in Friesland, al-
PAPERS: so in English: Ethnicity and language in Friesland,
                July 1980.
                Taalbeheersing in Friesland, (Linguistic competence in
                Friesland), April 1980.
                Taalsocialisatie in Friesland, (Linguistic socializa-
                tion of Frisian; Dialect and Dutch in Friesland), March
                1980.
                Taal in Burgum en Stiens, (Language in Burgum and
                Stiens), September 1980 (date of publication).

* * *

NO. 192   The Lappish Minority.
_____

INSTITUTION: University of Tromsø, Department of Social Science
                Postboks 1040
                N-9001 Tromsø
                Norway

RESEARCHER: Mathiesen, Per/ Thuen, Trond

DISCIPLINE   Anthropology, Ethnology
AND SUBFIELD: Economics
                Sociology

ABSTRACT: The Department of Social Science, University of Tromsø,
                has a comprehensive research programme on the Lappish
                situation in Norway and neighbouring countries. The
                team is interdisciplinary.

GEOGR.AREA: Norway and neighbouring countries

LANGUAGE: Norwegian

PUBLICATIONS: Thuen, Trond (ed.): Samene-Urbefolkning og minoritet
                (The Lapps - indigenous people and minority), Universi-
                tetetsforlaget, 1980, with bibliography.

                              * * *

NO. 193   Direction and Tendencies of Socio-Cultural Development
                of Peoples of the USSR; Interaction of National Cul-
                tures.
_____

INSTITUTION: Academy of Sciences of USSR, Institute of Ethnography
                Dm. Uljanova, 19
                SU-Moscow
                USSR
                Tel.No.: 1269425; 1239036

RESEARCHER: Arutjunjan, Jury/ Drobisheva, Leokadia/ Guboglo,
                Mikael/ Kondratiev, Valeri/ Pankratova, Maja/
                Ostapenko, Ljuba/ Savoskul, Alex/ Shamshurov, Valeri

CONTACT: Arutjunjan, Jury
                Institute of Ethnography
                Dm. Iljanova 19
                SU-Moscow
                USSR
                Tel.No.: 1269425

DISCIPLINE   Sociology (Ethno-Sociology/ Rural Sociology)
AND SUBFIELD:

ABSTRACT:

The study makes it possible to analyse the cultural interaction of the nations of the Soviet Union, establishment of the common and specific features of the cultural make-up of different peoples. The sample includes approximately 4,000 people. Several research methods involve the combination of descriptive materials concerning individuals obtained through polling, along with objective data describing the environment. Research has already been completed in some republics. The material obtained so far suggests that a single cultural structure exists through the USSR. The superstructure is based on the uniformity of the USSR populations, where every nation is comprised of similar groups. The objective basis for this singular culture common to the entire Soviet society has been created by industrialization and urbanization.

GEOGR.AREA: USSR (Modavia, Georgia, Estonia, Uzbekistan, Russian Federation)

PROCEDURE: Personal interview (40,000 members of a population of Soviet Republics, Russian Federation, Moldavia, Georgia, Uzbekistan);
Document analysis (Documents of central and local organizations);
Qualitative content analysis (Newspapers - 6 titles -);
Panel investigation (10,000 members of a population of capitals of Republics).

LANGUAGE: Russian

DURATION: 1970 - 1985

TYPE OF   Institution project
RESEARCH:

FUNDS: External sources: The Institute of Ethnography of the Academy of Sciences of the USSR

PUBLICATIONS: Arutjunjan, J.; Kachk, J. (eds.): Sociological investigation of Soviet Estonia, Tallin 1979, 150 p.
Arutjunjan, J. (ed.): Experience of ethno-sociological investigation of mode of life, Moscow 1980, 270 p.
Arutjunjan, J.: The Cultural Convergence of the Soviet Peoples. Data of a sociological survey, in: Social Theory and Practice, n° 7, 1979.
Arutjunjan, J.: The continuity, interaction and mutual influence of national cultures in the USSR, Reports, IX World Congress of Sociology, Moscow 1979, 12 p.
Arutjunjan, J.: Quality of Life of Rural Population in the USSR: General Characteristics and Specific Features of National Regions, Report for V. Congress of Rural Sociology, 1980, 16 p.

* * *

NO. 194   Jewish Identity and Politics.

INSTITUTION: Université de Toulouse le Mirail - Toulouse II, Centre
              de recherches sociologiques (University of Toulouse II,
              Sociological Research Centre)
              109 bis, rue Vauquelin
              F-31081 Toulouse Cêdex
              France
              Tel.No.: 61/411105

RESEARCHER: Benayoun, Chantal/ Zerbib, Alain

CONTACT: Benayoun, Chantal
              15, rue Bernard Palissy
              F-31200 Toulouse
              Tel.No.: 61/473906

DISCIPLINE   Anthropology, Ethnology
AND SUBFIELD: Political Sciences (Voting Behavior)
              Sociology (Political Sociology)
              History

ABSTRACT: Study of the relationship between the Jewish minority
              and the socio-political French environment (image of
              the other one, social distance, racism) and its politi-
              cal attitudes (vote). The diversity of the sociological
              composition (profession, origins, cultures, etc...) of
              the Jewish community forbids to think that the politi-
              cal attitudes and the voting behavior might be homoge-
              nous within it. The first results - from a survey real-
              ized in March 1978 - seem to confirm this hypothesis.
              Also in progress: study of political commitment in
              Jewish circles, antisemitic racism through the national
              press, stories of the lives of militants.

GEOGR.AREA: France and south-west of France

PROCEDURE: Personal interview (30 political militants);
                  Questionnaire (140 Jews from Toulouse);
                  Document analysis (National press);
                  Qualitative content analysis;
                  Quantitative content analysis.

LANGUAGE: French

DURATION: Jan. 1979 - Dec. 1984

TYPE OF   Commissioned research/ Institution project/ Doctorat de
RESEARCH: 3° cycle

FUNDS: Internal sources
                  External sources: Conseil scientifique de l'université
                  Toulouse II

PUBLICATIONS: Benayoun, Ch.: Judicité et politique, in: Société, n° 4,
                  Toulouse 1979.
                  Benayoun, Ch.: Comportement électoral et attitudes po-
                  litiques en milieu juif, Rapport de recherche UTM,
                  CNRS, 1979.
                  Benayoun Ch.; Rojman, P.J.: Les juifs en Occitanie, in:
                  Aici e ara, n° 7, mai 1980.

                            * * *

NO. 195   Jews and their Relationship with the Environment in the
                  South of France.

INSTITUTION: Université de Toulouse le Mirail - Toulouse II, Centre
                  interdisciplinaire de recherches et d'études juives
                  (University of Toulouse II, Jewish Studies and Research
                  Interdisciplinary Centre)
                  109 bis, rue Vauquelin
                  F-31081 Toulouse Cédex
                  France
                  Tel.No.: 61/411105

RESEARCHER: Anatole, Christian/ Benayoun, Chantal/ Rojtman, Pierre
                  Jacques/ Fijalkow, Jacques/ Levy, Jean Paul/
                  Morgenstzern, Isy/ Sempere, Henri/ Sztulman, Henri/
                  Viguier, Marie-Claire

CONTACT: Rojtman, Pierre Jacques
                  34, rue de Languedoc
                  F-31000 Toulouse
                  France
                  Tel.No.: 61/ 539988

DISCIPLINE   Anthropology, Ethnology
AND SUBFIELD: Geography
                  Psychology
                  Sociology

ABSTRACT: - Socio-economic and spatial structures in their rela-
                   tion to social representations: study of Saint Rome
                   district in Toulouse
                   - Contemporary testimonies concerning the Jews and es-
                   pecially internment of Jews during the 1939-45 war in
                   camps in the region of Toulouse and the south of France
                   (Noe, Recebedou, Gors...)
                   - Jewish insertion in Occitan cultural space: study of
                   literary and iconographic production of Jews and
                   about Jews

GEOGR.AREA: France (Toulouse and south of France)

PROCEDURE: Personal interview;
                   Questionnaire;
                   Non-participant observation;
                   Document analysis;
                   Qualitative content analysis;
                   Quantitative content analysis.

LANGUAGE: French

DURATION: Jan. 1980 - Dec. 1985

TYPE OF   Researcher's project
RESEARCH:

FUNDS: Internal sources

PUBLICATIONS: Benayoun, Ch.; Rojman, P.J.: Les juifs en Occitanie, in:
                   AICE E ARE, n° spécial, juillet 1980.

                            * * *

NO. 196   Study on the Social and Economic History of the Jews in
                   the Area of Hamburg in the Seventeenth and Eighteenth
                   Century.

INSTITUTION: Institut für Geschichte der deutschen Juden (Institute
                   for the History of the German Jews)
                   Rothenbaumchaussee 7
                   D-2000 Hamburg 13
                   Germany, Federal Republic

RESEARCHER: Freimark, Peter

CONTACT: Freimark, Peter
                   Tel.No.: 040/41232618

DISCIPLINE   Social History
AND SUBFIELD: Economic History

ABSTRACT: Interpretation of epitaphs, death card-indices, tax-
                   books, and documents of the Jewish communities in Alto-
                   na, Hamburg, and Wandsbek.

GEOGR.AREA: Germany (Area of Hamburg)

LANGUAGE: German

DURATION: Dec. 1985 (end)

TYPE OF   Institution project
RESEARCH:

FUNDS: Internal sources

* * *

NO. 197   History of the Jews in Cologne at the Beginning of the
                 Nineteenth Century.

INSTITUTION: Universität zu Köln, Historisches Seminar, Forschungs-
                 abteilung (University of Cologne, Historical Institute)
                 Weyertal 80
                 D-5000 Köln-Lindenthal
                 Germany, Federal Republic

RESEARCHER: Müller, Alwin

CONTACT: Müller, Alwin
                 Mauenheimer Strasse 60
                 D-5000 Köln 60
                 Germany, Federal Republic
                 Tel.No.: 0221/7603499

DISCIPLINE   Law
AND SUBFIELD: Sociology (Sociology of Religion)
                 Social History
                 Legal History

ABSTRACT: Historical development of the legal side of the emanci-
                 pation as a primary precondition for the Jews to achieve
                 equal rights with the Christians; process of the cultur-
                 al, social, economic, political, and psychological in-
                 tegration into the middle class ('Bürgerturm'); devel-
                 opment of the collective public opinion towards the
                 emancipation of the Jews; antisemitism ('Hep-Hep-move-
                 ment'); social structure of the Jewish community; study
                 of the residential quarters of the Jews (ghetto forma-
                 tion?); penetration of the Jews into corporations and
                 associations; alphabetization.

GEOGR.AREA: Germany (Cologne, Rhineland)

PROCEDURE: Document analysis (up to 1,000 people)

LANGUAGE: German

DURATION: July 1979 - July 1981

TYPE OF   Researcher's project/ Dissertation
RESEARCH:

FUNDS: Internal sources
                 External sources: Fellowship

* * *

NO. 198   Demographic and Social History of the Jewish Community
                 of Niedenstein (1653 - 1866). Description and Documents.

INSTITUTION: Kommission für die Geschichte der Juden in Hessen
                 (Commission for the History of the German Jews)
                 Mainzer Strasse 80
                 D-6200 Wiesbaden
                 Germany, Federal Republic

RESEARCHER: Demandt, Karl E.

DISCIPLINE   Demography
AND SUBFIELD: Sociology
                 Social History

ABSTRACT: History of the Jewish population and links between in-
                 dividual families. Documents on social history (proper-
                 ty, gainful employment, social position).

GEOGR.AREA: Germany (Kurhessen)

PROCEDURE: Document analysis

LANGUAGE: German

DURATION: Jan. 1975 - Dec. 1980

TYPE OF   Institution project/ Researcher's project
RESEARCH:

FUNDS: Internal sources

* * *

NO. 199   The Jewish Population of Lower Franconia 1817 - 1875.

INSTITUTION: Universität Würzburg, Institut für Geschichte, Lehr-
                 stuhl für Geschichte, insb. Mittelalterliche Sozial-
                 und Wirtschaftsgeschichte (University of Würzburg, In-
                 stitute for History)
                 Am Hubland
                 D-8700 Würzburg
                 Germany, Federal Republic

RESEARCHER: Löffler, Karl-Ludwig

DISCIPLINE   Demography
AND SUBFIELD: Sociology (Sociology of Religion)
                Social History

ABSTRACT: The demographic, social, economic, religious, and eman-
                cipatory changes of a Jewish minority in a regionally
                limited area since the introduction of the Bavarian
                Jews-edict of 1813 are demonstrated.

GEOGR.AREA: Germany (Lower Franconia)

PROCEDURE: Document analysis (about 1,500 records regarding Jews)

LANGUAGE: German

DURATION: Dec. 1979 (end)

TYPE OF   Researcher's project/ Dissertation
RESEARCH:

* * *

GYPSIES

NO. 200   Nomads and Sedentary People, Reciprocal Images.
                 _____

INSTITUTION: Université René Descartes - Paris V, Centre de recher-
                 ches tsiganes (University of Paris V, Gypsy Research
                 Centre)
                 106, quai de Clichy
                 F-92110 Clichy
                 France
                 Tel.No.: 1/2707040

RESEARCHER: Degrance, Michel/ Liegeois, Jean-Pierre/ Michon, Jean-
                 Claude/ Cauli, Rita/ Duteuil, Jean Pierre

CONTACT: Liegeois, Jean-Pierre
                 Centre de recherches tsiganes
                 106, quai de Clichy
                 F-92110 Clichy
                 Tel.No.: 1/2707040

DISCIPLINE   Anthropology, Ethnology
AND SUBFIELD: Psychology (Social Psychology/ Social Representation)
                 Sociology

ABSTRACT: Within a research upon the analysis of poverty situa-
                 tions, study of the image: - that sedentary people and
                 institutions have of nomads and gypsies
                 - that nomads and gipsies have of those who surround
                 them
                 Our hypothesis: when gypsies are poor, their poverty is
                 a consequence of their rejection by society (this re-
                 jection being caused by prejudices and stereotypes) but
                 not of a job inadequacy.

GEOGR.AREA: France

PROCEDURE: Personal interview (84);
                 Questionnaire (2,000 French people);
                 Participant observation (Gypsy families - France -);
                 Qualitative content analysis.

LANGUAGE: French

DURATION: Oct. 1978 - Nov. 1980

TYPE OF   Commissioned research
RESEARCH:

FUNDS: External sources: Commission of European Community
                (Bruxelles)

PUBLICATIONS: Liegeois, J.-P.: Nomades et sédentaires, images réci-
                proques, Centre de recherches tsiganes, Paris 1980,
                250 p.

                            * * *

NO. 201   Political Racism in Germany - Exemplified by the Gypsies'
                Persecutions.

INSTITUTION: Universität Gießen, Institut für Politikwissenschaft
                (University of Giessen, Institute of Political Science)
                Karl-Glöckner-Strasse 21
                D-6300 Giessen
                Germany, Federal Republic

RESEARCHER: Hohmann, Joachim S.

CONTACT: Hohmann, Joachim S.
                Tel.No.: 06652/2991

DISCIPLINE   Political Sciences (Ideology)
AND SUBFIELD: Psychology (Social Psychology)
                Sociology
                Political History
                Social History

ABSTRACT: This project analyses the political and historical
                causes of gypsies' persecutions since the appearance of
                gypsy ethnic groups at the end of the 14th century in
                Europe, particularly in Germany. "Political racism"
                means the discrimination and persecution for "socio-
                political" reasons. It can also mean discrimination for
                political reasons with underlying religious motives as
                happened in the 15th and 16th centuries.
                Emphasis will be placed on the development of "modern"
                racist ideologies starting with the second half of the
                19th century as a basis for the emergence of the "Third
                Reich" and its inheritance (reparation laws, etc.).
                The question is: What relationships are there between
                the organization of a state/a society and its "minority
                politics"? What "images" are there of the discriminated
                minority, the gypsies? Which political processes follow
                non-political processes (e.g. anxiety and horror syn-
                dromes?).

GEOGR.AREA: Germany (in its varying historical dimensions)

PROCEDURE: Document analysis (Manuscripts/ Records/ Literary and
                scientific testimonials - 16th century until present -)

LANGUAGE: German

DURATION: May 1979 - Nov. 1980

TYPE OF   Researcher's project/ Dissertation
RESEARCH:

FUNDS: Internal sources

PUBLICATIONS: Hohmann, J.S.: Zigeunerverfolgung in Deutschland. (Ar-
                beitstitel), Frankfurt, Campus-Verlag, 1981.
                Hohmann, J.S.:Zigeuner und Zigeunerwissenschaft. Ein
                Beitrag zur Grundlagenforschung des Völkermordes im
                "Dritten Reich",Marburg, Guttandin & Hoppe, 1980.

                          * * *

NO. 202   Cultural Alternatives and Integration. The Example of
                the Gypsies.

INSTITUTION: Universität Giessen, Institut für Soziologie (Universi-
                ty of Giessen, Institute of Sociology)
                Karl-Glöckner-Strasse 21, Haus E
                D-6300 Giessen
                Germany, Federal Republic

RESEARCHER: Münzel, Mark (Museum für Völkerkunde, Frankfurt)/
                Streck, Bernhard (Institut für Ethnologie, FU Berlin)/
                Gerth, Edith/ Gronemeyer, Reimer/ Rakelmann, Georgia

CONTACT: Streck, Bernhard
                Tel.No.: 030/3962762

DISCIPLINE   Political Sciences (Cultural Policy/ Social Policy)
AND SUBFIELD: Sociology

ABSTRACT: Chances of an autocentred development in a peripheral
                subculture; cooperation between science and public ad-
                ministration in the field of minority politics; Euro-
                pean comparison; case studies in Hesse, Palatinate,
                Switzerland, and Hungary.

GEOGR.AREA: Europe, with emphasis on Central Europe

PROCEDURE: Personal interview (People concerned in 'problem housing
                estates'/ gypsy-'functionaries');
                Expert interview (Gypsy research workers/ Social wor-
                kers/ Missionaries/ Gypsy welfare officials abroad);
                Questionnaire (Social services departments/ Gypsy mis-
                sions/ Local authorities);
                Participant observation (Gypsy pilgrimages/ Gypsy meet-
                ings/ Inhabitant assemblies/ Legal and illegal camp
                sites);

Document analysis (Documents with respect to former integration efforts - emphasis is placed on the time
since 1870 and 1933-45 -);
Action Research (Gypsy music festival).

LANGUAGE: German

DURATION: Jan. 1978 - Dec. 1979

TYPE OF   Sponsored research
RESEARCH:

FUNDS: External sources: Deutsche Gesellschaft für Frieden-
                 und Konfliktforschung e.V., Bonn

PUBLICATIONS: Streck, B.: Zigeuner - III. Welt vor unserer Tür. Dritte
                 Welt Information EPD, Frankfurt   1978.
                 Streck, B.: Die 'Bekämpfung des Zigeunerunwesens'. Ein
                 Stück moderner Rechtsgeschichte, in: Zuelch, I. (ed.):
                 In Auschwitz vergast, bis heute verfolgt, Reinbek,
                 Rowolth, 1979. Projektgruppe Tsiganologie und Arbeits-
                 stelle für Erwachsenenbildung der ev. Kirche.
                 Hessen/Nassau (Eds.): Musikfest der Zigeuner, Programm-
                 heft, Darmstadt   1979.
                 Gerth, E.; Gronemeyer, R.; Henkes, F.: So wurde vorge-
                 schlagen, das Lager mit Stacheldraht zu umzäunen. Zi-
                 geuner in einer deutschen Kleinstadt, in: Zuelch a.a.O.

UNPUBLISHED   Gerth, E.; Gronemeyer, R.; Münzel, M.; Streck, B.:
PAPERS: Kulturelle Alternativen und Integration. Zigeuner und
                 andere marginale Gruppen. Projektentwurf. Justus Liebig
                 Universität, FB Gesellschaftswissenschaften, Inst. f.
                 Soziologie, Diskussionspapier Nr. 3, Dezember 1977.
                 Gerth, E.: Projekt Tsiganologie. Erste Zwischenbilanz.
                 Justus Liebig Universität, a.a.O., Dez. 1978.
                 Gronemeyer, R.: Zigeuner in Ungarn. Marginalität in
                 einem sozialistischen Land. Justus Liebig Universität,
                 a.a.O., Juli 1979.
                 Streck, B.: Zigeuner in Auschwitz. Chronik des Lagers
                 B IIe, Frankfurt, März 1979.

                                   * * *

NO. 203   Project to Improve the Situation of a Group of Gypsies
                 in Düsseldorf-Eller.

INSTITUTION: Katholische Fachhochschule NRW, Zentralverwaltung (Ca-
                 tholic College of NRW, Central Administration)
                 Alfred-Schütte-Allee 10
                 D-5000 Köln 21
                 Germany, Federal Republic
                 Tel.No.: 0221/232770

RESEARCHER: Baltes, Joachim/ Boskamp, Peter/ Scheuß

DISCIPLINE   Social Work
AND SUBFIELD:

ABSTRACT: The project on the improvement of the situation of the
                 gypsies is being carried out by a group of students and
                 two professors of the Catholic College as well as by
                 members of the parish of St. Gertrud in Düsseldorf-
                 Eller and parson Scheuß.
                 The gypsies, with a total of 106 persons, consisting of
                 22 families within 5 clans, are at present living on a
                 paved site in Düsseldorf-Eller. This site is too small
                 for the 106 persons, the caravans - some of them in a
                 very bad condition - are located too close together.
                 At the site only one public lavatory - very dirty - and
                 one water tap are available for the whole group. The
                 housing and living conditions are, therefore, unbear-
                 able. For this reason an improvement of the housing
                 conditions should be achieved within the first project
                 phase. Negotiations between the parish and the town
                 administration have been in process for the last six
                 months. Through these negotiations will be tried to
                 provide the gypsies with plots of approximately 300
                 square meters for each family. Every plot should have
                 its own connexion for water and electricity. On the
                 site there should be a brick building containing a
                 wash house and lavatory for each family. The plots must
                 have paved roads to enable the moving   of the caravans.
                 Several families will need a better caravan before the
                 beginning of next winter. Negotiations with the town
                 administration are already in progress. Furthermore, it
                 is planned to build a community centre on the new site.
                 Besides the planning and negotiations the students or-
                 ganize play afternoons with the smaller children and
                 arrange tutoring for the school children. Further
                 phases within the project will try to improve educa-
                 tional opportunities for the adults, their economic
                 conditions and their relations with the social environ-
                 ment in this part of town.

GEOGR.AREA: Germany, Federal Republic (Düsseldorf-Eller, Am Hacken-
                 bruch)

LANGUAGE: German

DURATION: Jan. 1979 (start)

TYPE OF   Researcher's project
PROJECT:

FUNDS: Internal sources

PUBLICATIONS: Katholische Fachhochschule NW (ed.): Dokumentation über
                 die Zigeunersiedlung "Am Hackenbruch" in Düsseldorf-
                 Eller, 1961/62 - 1980, Diözesan-Caritasverband, Köln
                 1980.

* * *

NO. 204   Integration Measures for Gypsies and Other Non-Sedenta-
                 ry People in the Federal Republic of Germany.

INSTITUTION: Universität Erlangen-Nürnberg, Sozialwissenschaftliches
                 Forschungszentrum (University of Erlangen-Nürnberg, So-
                 cial Science Research Centre)
                 Findelgasse 7-9
                 D-8500 Nürnberg
                 Germany, Federal Republic

RESEARCHER: Wurzbacher, Gerhard/ Freese, Christoph/ Murko, Matthias

CONTACT: Wurzbacher, Gerhard

DISCIPLINE   Political Sciences (Social Policy)
AND SUBFIELD: Sociology

ABSTRACT: The aim of this project is a survey of all the measures
                 that have been taken up to now in order to integrate
                 gypsies and other non-sedentary people according to
                 paragraph 72 BSHG (Bundessozialhilfegesetz), an evalu-
                 ation of the success of these measures, and the concep-
                 tion of a model of comprehensive assistance according
                 to paragraph   72 BSHG.

GEOGR.AREA: Germany, Federal Republic

PROCEDURE: Personal interview;
                 Group discussion (150 social workers, social peda-
                 gogues);
                 Expert interview (60 social workers, social pedagogues,
                 town council);
                 Questionnaire (all social services departments of towns
                 and counties/ 30 social welfare bodies - concerned
                 with work for gypsies and non-sedentary people -);
                 Qualitative content analysis (4 towns where complex
                 measures have been implemented).

LANGUAGE: German

DURATION: Dec. 1976 - Dec. 1979

TYPE OF   Commissioned research/ Dissertation
RESEARCH:

FUNDS: External sources: Bundesminister für Jugend, Familie
                 und Gesundheit, Bonn

PUBLICATIONS: Freese, C.; Murko, M.; Wurzbacher, G.: Hilfen für Zi-
                 geuner und Landfahrer, Bd. 86 der Schriftenreihe des
                 Bundesministers für Jugend, Familie, Gesundheit, Bonn-
                 Bad Godesberg 1980 and Verlag Kohlhammer.

UNPUBLISHED   Wurzbacher, G.; Freese, C.; Murko, M.: Hilfen für Zi-
PAPERS: geuner und Landfahrer. Zwischenbericht I, IIa und IIb.
                 (Several papers for conferences at the University of
                 Erlangen-Nürnberg 1978 and 1979).

* * *

NO. 205   Gypsies. Contributions to the Culture of a Minority.

INSTITUTION: Universität Würzburg, Institut für Deutsche Philologie,
               Lehrstuhl Deutsche Philologie und Volkskunde (Univer-
               sity of Würzburg, Institute for German Philology)
               Am Hubland
               D-8700 Würzburg
               Germany, Federal Republic

RESEARCHER: Daxelmüller, Christoph

CONTACT: Daxelmüller, Christoph
               Tel.No.: 0931/888608

DISCIPLINE   Anthropology, Ethnology
AND SUBFIELD: Sociology (Cultural Sociology)
               Social History

ABSTRACT: Cultural development possibilities of the Sinte as a
               marginal group within their present social situation.

GEOGR.AREA: Germany, Federal Republic (Northern Bavaria)

PROCEDURE: Personal interview;
               Participant observation;
               Document analysis.

LANGUAGE: German

DURATION: Jan. 1980 - July 1981

TYPE OF   Researcher's project
RESEARCH:

FUNDS: Internal sources

                              * * *

NO. 206   Prejudices against Gypsies and other Non-Sedentary
               People of High School Pupils at the Age of 12 to 14.

RESEARCHER: Hohmann, J. S.
               Bachstrasse 15, Postfach 29
               D-6418 Huenfeld 1
               Germany, Federal Republic
               Tel.No.: 06652/2991

DISCIPLINE   Education and Training
AND SUBFIELD: Psychology (Social Psychology)

ABSTRACT: Which attitudes do 12 to 14 year - old pupils of secon-
               dary schools have towards alternative, generally under-
               privileged ways of life and towards those who lead such
               a life? Are there any connections between prejudices
               against non-sedentary people, against an 'independent' life
               without regular work, etc., and middle-class and per-

formance-orientated pupils? What kind of ideas of a
'vagrant life' exist in the interviewed group? Of which
kind are the prejudices, stereotypes, and myth-cathect-
ed images of the 'vagrant life'? Are there connections
between a 'romantic phase' (puberty) of the inter-
viewees and a largely positive attitude towards 'vagrant life'? In what do the attitudes of the interviewed pupils and the stereotypes of gypsies differ from
those we find in the specialist literature?

GEOGR.AREA: Germany, Federal Republic

PROCEDURE: Group discussion (150 pupils - boys and girls at the
               age of 12-14 -);
               Questionnaire (80 pupils - boys and girls at the age of
               12-14 -);
               Document analysis (Literature on Gypsies since 1900).

LANGUAGE: German

DURATION: July 1978 - July 1979

TYPE OF   Researcher's project
RESEARCH:

FUNDS: Internal sources

PUBLICATIONS: Hohmann, J.S.: Zigeunermythos- und Vorurteil, in:
               Hohmann, J.S.; Schopf, R. (Hrsg.): Zigeunerleben. Zur
               Sozialgeschichte einer Verfolgung, ms-Edition, Darm-
               stadt 1979.
               Hohmann, J.S.: "Geh' mir ja nicht zu diesen Zigeunern."
               2. Auflage, 1980.
               Hohmann, J.S.: Zigeuner und Zigeunerwissenschaft. Ein
               Beitrag zur Grundlagenforschung und Dokumentation des
               Völkermords im "Dritten Reich", Verlag Guttandin und
               Hoppe, Reihe Metro, Marburg 1980.

* * *

Name Index

Here the leaders of and the workers on the
research projects are listed. The numbers
following the names refer to the current
number of the research projects that have
been documented. It is possible that because
of non-uniform details in the questionnaires some persons are listed several times
(e.g. with and without their first names).

Subject Index

The titles and contents of the research
projects were made accessible by the
controlled distribution of key-words.
When looking for projects dealing with
particular topics it is recommended to
consult related, more general or more
specific key-words as well as the division of contents (table of contents).
The figures following the key-words
refer to the relevant current numbers
of the research projects documented
in this book.

Institution Index

Here the research institutions are listed alphabetically according to countries as well as within the countries themselves. The figures following the institutions refer to the relevant current numbers of the research projects documented in this book.

INSTITUTION INDEX

AUSTRIA

Europäisches Zentrum für Ausbildung und Forschung auf dem Gebiet der sozialen Wohlfahrt (European Centre for Social Welfare Training and Research)   029, 045

Universität für Bildungswissenschaften, Institut für Bildungsökonomie und Bildungssoziologie (University of Educational Sciences, Institute of Educational Economy and Sociology of Education)   165

Universität Graz, Institut für Geschichte, Abt. für Sozial- und Wirtschaftsgeschichte (University of Graz, Institute of History, Dept. of Social and Economic History)   164

Universität Innsbruck, Institut für Soziologie (University of Innsbruck, Institute of Sociology)   044

Universität Salzburg, Institut für Publizistik und Kommunikationswissenschaft (University of Salzburg, Institute of Communication Research)   068, 166, 167

Universität Wien, Institut für Japanologie (University of Vienna, Institute for Japanese Studies)   168, 169, 170

Universität Wien, Institut für Slawistik (University of Vienna, Institute of Slavistik Studies)   171, 172, 173

Universität Wien, Institut für Soziologie (University of Vienna, Institute of Sociology)   174

Universität Wien, Institut für Zeitgeschichte (University of Vienna, Institute of Contemporary History)   174, 175

INSTITUTION INDEX

Appendix

E C S S I D   Working Group 2 - Documentation of on-going
Research
Pilot Project

Questionnaire

Research Projects in Progress in the Field of Social Integration
of Ethnic Minorities including Migrant Workers

In answering this questionnaire please consult the attached
explanatory notes.

1. Title of project

_____

_____

_____

_____

XXXXXXXXXXXXXXXXXXXXXXXXXXXXXXXXXXXXXXXXXXXXXXXXXXXXXXXXXXXXXXX

2. Working language

_____

XXXXXXXXXXXXXXXXXXXXXXXXXXXXXXXXXXXXXXXXXXXXXXXXXXXXXXXXXXXXXXX

3. Research institution

Name (Original) _____

_____

_____

Name (English translation) _____

_____

_____

Address
Street/Place/Box _____
Town/City _____
County/Province/State _____
Country _____
Telephone number _____

....

Research institution
Name (Original) _____
_____
_____
Name (English translation) _____
_____
_____
Address
Street/Place/Box _____
Town/City _____
County/Province/State _____
Country _____
Telephone number _____
....
Research institution
Name (Original) _____
_____
_____
Name (English translation) _____
_____
_____
Address
Street/Place/Box _____
Town/City _____
County/Province/State _____
Country _____
Telephone number _____

XXXXXXXXXXXXXXXXXXXXXXXXXXXXXXXXXXXXXXXXXXXXXXXXXXXXXXXXXXXXXXXXXX

4. Principal researcher(s)

Surname _____
First name _____
....
Surname _____
First name _____
....
Surname _____
First name _____

XXXXXXXXXXXXXXXXXXXXXXXXXXXXXXXXXXXXXXXXXXXXXXXXXXXXXXXXXXXXXXXXXX

5. Researcher(s)

   Surname _____

   First name _____
   ....

   Surname _____

   First name _____
   ....

   Surname _____

   First name _____
   ....

   Surname _____

   First name _____
   ....

   Surname _____

   First name _____
   ....

   Surname _____

   First name _____
   XXXXXXXXXXXXXXXXXXXXXXXXXXXXXXXXXXXXXXXXXXXXXXXXXXXXXXXXXXX

6. Person to be contacted for further information

   Surname _____

   First name _____

   Address _____

   _____

   Telephone number _____
   XXXXXXXXXXXXXXXXXXXXXXXXXXXXXXXXXXXXXXXXXXXXXXXXXXXXXXXXXXX

7. Duration of the project

   Starting date _____
                                     (year, month)

   End of the project (estimated) _____
                                     (year, month)
   XXXXXXXXXXXXXXXXXXXXXXXXXXXXXXXXXXXXXXXXXXXXXXXXXXXXXXXXXXX

8. Type of research

   ☐ sponsored research

   ☐ commissioned research (including consultancy work)

   ☐ institution project

   ☐ researcher's project

   ☐ work done for an academic degree,
     please specify (in original language) _____

   _____

   _____

☐ other, please specify _____

_____

XXXXXXXXXXXXXXXXXXXXXXXXXXXXXXXXXXXXXXXXXXXXXXXXXXXXXXXXXXXX

9. Sources of Funds

Who finances the research?

☐ internal sources
☐ external sources, specify _____

_____

_____

XXXXXXXXXXXXXXXXXXXXXXXXXXXXXXXXXXXXXXXXXXXXXXXXXXXXXXXXXXXX

10. Abstract (purpose, approach, contents, preliminary results)

_____

_____

_____

_____

_____

_____

_____

_____

_____

_____

_____

_____

_____

_____

_____

_____

_____

XXXXXXXXXXXXXXXXXXXXXXXXXXXXXXXXXXXXXXXXXXXXXXX XXXXXXXXXXXXXXX

11. Geographical area covered by the research project

_____

_____

_____

XXXXXXXXXXXXXXXXXXXXXXXXXXXXXXXXXXXXXXXXXXXXXXXXXXXXXXXXXXXX

12. Discipline and Subfield

      Discipline   Subfield

☐ Anthropology ....   _____
   (Social and Cultural)
   Ethnology

☐ Demography   ....   _____

☐ Economics   ....   _____

☐ Education and Training .....   _____

☐ Geography   ....   _____
   (Human, Economic and Social)

☐ Law   ....   _____

☐ Linguistics ....   _____

☐ Management   ....   _____

☐ Political Sciences ....   _____

☐ Psychology ....   _____

☐ Sociology   ....   _____

☐ Other, please
   specify: _____

XXXXXXXXXXXXXXXXXXXXXXXXXXXXXXXXXXXXXXXXXXXXXXXXXXXXXXXXXXXXXXXXX

13. Keywords

_____

_____

_____

_____

_____

_____

Source of Keywords

☐ researcher
☐ in house system
☐ controlled list, please specify: _____

_____

_____

XXXXXXXXXXXXXXXXXXXXXXXXXXXXXXXXXXXXXXXXXXXXXXXXXXXXXXXXXXXXXXXXX

14. Project products

☐ Publication(s)

☐ unpublished paper(s), manuscript(s)

Publication(s): _____

_____

_____

_____

_____

_____

_____

_____

_____

_____

. . . .

Unpublished paper(s): _____

_____

_____

_____

_____

_____

_____

_____

_____

_____

_____

_____

_____

XXXXXXXXXXXXXXXXXXXXXXXXXXXXXXXXXXXXXXXXXXXXXXXXXXXXXXXXXXXXXX

15. Procedure for gathering information

PROCEDURE:		Size of Sample	Universe
1. Questioning, oral			
personal interview	☐		
group discussion	☐		
expert interview	☐		
2. Questioning, written			
Questionnaire	☐		
3. Observation			
participant observation	☐		
non-participant observation	☐		
4. Document analysis	☐		
5. Content analysis			
qualitative content analysis	☐		
quantitative content analysis	☐		
6. Secondary data analysis	☐		
7. Experiment	☐		
8. Test	☐		
9. Other procedures	☐		

Thank you for your cooperation !